IDEAS
INTO ACTION

University of Miami Publications in
English and American Literature
Number III   November, 1958

IDEAS
INTO ACTION

A Study of Pound's Cantos

By CLARK EMERY

UNIVERSITY OF MIAMI PRESS
Coral Gables, Florida

Copyright © 1958
Clark Emery

Second Printing, 1969
Library of Congress Catalog Card Number 58-14060
SBN 87024-005-6

Quotations from the works of Ezra Pound are re-
published here by permission of New Directions,
Norfolk, Connecticut

Manufactured in the United States of America

Foreword

"The task of education," Henry Adams wrote, is "from cradle to grave this problem of running order through chaos, direction through space, discipline through freedom, unity through multiplicity, as it is the moral of religion, philosophy, science, art, politics, economy." Ezra Pound, facing the dislocations of the modern world as Adams did, has been saying the same sort of thing in the *Cantos,* and accepting the moral challenge in all fields. The brave comprehensiveness of the *Cantos,* as well as its redefinition of the Sublime, make it the most ambitious poem of our century as it is also one of the most influential.

To discuss, as Clark Emery does, a work of art which is still in progress is a tricky matter. Ultimate form depends upon the final canto. Yet already in the *Cantos* we can follow the soul in its passage through time and conditions, a journey latently of an Odysseus or a Dante as they proceed towards Penelope and Paradise. The poem begins and re-begins the journey, through repetition and metamorphosis, in flashes of men and moments ruled purely by the emotions; then passes through the Purgatorio of man's efforts to search for government and order: efforts which at least in vision will result in the cornerstone and walls of "the city of Dioce whose terraces are the colour of stars."

Already, too, this intimation of an ideal City of Man begins to take form in the *Cantos* from the carved blocks of history and personal experience which recall both chaos and repose. "Past time is present feeling" in the Jamesian sense. In choosing his instances from the welter, Pound has, as Mr. Emery points out, worked much as a meticulous scientist might when among the slides of his data he picks the illustrations to focus on disease and health. The literary method, to quote Mr. Emery, is one of "abbreviated images, each having what is necessary for Pound's general statement, juxtaposed to produce that statement (or ideogram). It is a method altogether of a piece with Pound's general thinking, his predisposition for the hard, the definite, the precise; the observed specific object; the image as primary pigment; the individual's own experience, in religion; in ethics, the individual's gaze into his heart." Pound echoes the answer which Louis Agassiz gave when asked what he regarded as his greatest accomplishment: "I have taught men to observe."

What Mr. Emery does is to supply for Pound's *Cantos* the sort of introduction and glossing which we take for granted in reference to literary works of the past. Nor is it too much to say that a vast modern audience is led to its knowledge of history, mythology, and philosophy through the means of established works of art which embody precisely these keys. The average reader of a contemporary classic, however, feels most helpless, most belligerently defensive, when the unaided challenge of a fresh *paideuma* faces him. Still, once the footnotes have been produced he can begin to settle back familiarly, as he now does with *The Waste Land* after the scholars have charted it. Increasingly the *Cantos* are becoming an education. What is striven for is, as Pound would put it, "Respect for the intelligence working in nature, needing no dogma to maintain it." Pound's resolution is not theological but religious, and the gods still "float in the azure air."

Norman Holmes Pearson

Yale University.
13 April 1958

Preface

Taking a hint from Mr. Pound's *ABC of Reading* and *ABC of Economics*, I might have called this collection of essays *An ABC of Ezra Pound's Cantos*. For it pretends to be no more. Literary critics have written excellent studies of the poem—for other critics; scholars have made original contributions to the knowledge of other scholars. It appears to be time to offer the lay-reader who stands in bemusement before the epic's variegated bulk something in the way of aid and comfort.

That the need exists is evidenced by the interesting case of the junior executives who, a few years ago, were sent to the University of Pennsylvania to acquire a liberal education. While there, they were compelled to read literary works from various ages and cultures and on various levels of difficulty—from, for example, the *Odyssey* of Homer to the *Ulysses* of Joyce. Of all the works they read, the one which most successfully defied their efforts toward comprehension was Pound's *Cantos*. This despite the fact that commentary was supplied by one of the nation's leading Pound scholars.

I propose, in this present study, to approach the poem indirectly, through Pound's prose, bringing to attention the ideas which he has expressed with remarkable consistency (and even more remarkable vigor) over the forty-year period which has seen the growth of his major work. Having done this, I shall try to show what means he has employed to incorporate these ideas in the poem, and what means have served to form the ninety-seven cantos (as the poem stands; more are to follow) into a unified whole.

But no really informative book about the *Cantos*, however carefully organized to afford a gradual approach, can succeed in being an *ABC*. The poem's scope is so vast, on the one hand, each page so closely packed with allusive (and elusive) materials, on the other, that even the most glittering generalities must ultimately fail to illuminate. There are, therefore, many pages in this book which can be of no possible value to the reader who does not have his copy of the *Cantos* at hand and, if he is a truly serious student, John Edwards's excellent *Annotated Index to the Cantos of Ezra Pound*. Still, if what is presented here is not an *ABC*, I hope that it will prove sufficiently elucidative to ensure that, when the next group of businessmen collect at Pennsylvania, they will be able to read the poem as a poem, not decipher it as a puzzle.

Some of the material of the first chapter derives from an unpublished thesis written by Miss Barbara Charlesworth. I need to thank her for this and other signal aids, as I need to thank Margaret and Laurence Donovan for various services, and above all, my wife, who has functioned as activator and critic.

This book represents a drastic compression of an original manuscript which included explications of some forty cantos. Both Mr. and Mrs. Pound read this earlier version and often set me right when I was dead wrong in fact or theory. Norman Holmes Pearson and John Edwards also read the original manuscript. I am grateful to both of them for advice and encouragement. None of these are in any way responsible for my errors of omission or commission.

Acknowledgement must be made to the following publishing houses for permission to quote from their publications.

Columbia University Press, New York, for *Motive and Methods in the Cantos of Ezra Pound;*

Harcourt, Brace and Company, Inc., New York, for Lincoln Steffens's *The Autobiography of Lincoln Steffens;*

Harvard University Press, Cambridge, Mass., for T. S. Eliot's *The Use of Poetry and the Use of Criticism;*

Indiana University Press, Bloomington, Indiana, for Rolfe Humphries' translation of Ovid's *Metamorphoses;*

Little, Brown & Company, Boston, for Alfred North Whitehead's *Dialogues,* as recorded by Lucien Price;

The Nation, New York, for David Rattray's *Weekend with Ezra Pound;*

The New Yorker Magazine, New York, for Albert Hubbell's review of Ezra Pound's *Guide to Kulchur;*

Penguin Books, Ltd., Harmondsworth, Middlesex, England, for E. F. Watling's translation of Sophocles' *Elektra and Other Plays;*

The University of Pennsylvania Press, Philadelphia, for Sona Raiziss' *The Metaphysical Passion;*

Poetry Magazine, Chicago, for Hugh Kenner's *Homage to Musonius;*

Peter Russell, Fairwarp, Sussex, England, for the six Money Pamphlets by Pound *(Introduction to the Economic History of the United States; Gold and Work; What is Money For?; A Visiting Card; Social Credit, an Impact;* and *America, Roosevelt, and the Causes of the Present War);*

Charles Scribner's Sons, New York, for George Santayana's *The Life of Reason;*

The Sewanee Review, Sewanee, Tenn., for Forrest Read's *The Pattern of the Pisan Cantos.*

CONTENTS

Chapter 1

It is in its literal sense of "lover of wisdom" that the word "philosopher" has its broadest meaning; and it is only in this sense that Ezra Pound can be reckoned a philosopher. He has never codified his beliefs to produce a dogmatic structure and would, indeed, consider it an act of treason against himself and his beliefs to do so. Nevertheless, he holds firm views on many subjects of interest to philosophers and theologians; and, if he has not articulated them as dogma, he has not failed to utter them dogmatically, though disparately.

Pound visualizes himself as a pathfinder, a guide to culture; assuming 20th century man to be lost and beleaguered by the three beasts as Dante was, Pound offers his Vergilian services. The goal to be won is a civilization in place of present squalor. The prime means to the end is the study of history. For, as he says:

> The capitalist imperialist state must be judged not only in comparison with unrealized utopias, but with past forms of the state; if it will not bear comparison with the feudal order; with the small city states both republican and despotic; either as to its 'social justice' *or* as to its permanent products, art, science, literature, the onus of proof goes against it. (*The Exile*, no. 1, p. 88.)

Pound therefore looks to the past and compels his reader to do likewise. This, though it seems easy enough, is not done without difficulty, for those who profit by maintaining the status quo have effective means of blocking the historical view.

> The power of putrefaction aims at the obfuscation of history; it seeks to destroy not one but every religion, by destroying the symbols, by leading off into theoretical argument. Theological disputes take the place of contemplation. Disputation destroys faith, and interest in theology eventually goes out of fashion . . . .
> Suspect anyone who destroys an image, or wants to suppress a page of history. (*Visiting Card*, p. 18.)

The difficulties are great since the forces of obfuscation are powerful. But the effort must be made. Pound has made the effort; the succeeding pages are a resumé of what he has found.

One basic discovery he has made is this: that a civilization cannot exist or endure without a vital faith in the divine. "The worship of the supreme intelligence of the universe," he has written, "is neither an inhuman nor bigoted action." And again: "Without gods no culture. Without gods,

1

something is lacking." *(Guide to Kulchur*, pp. 189 and 126.) But the faith must be vital, must "go into effect repeatedly in the persons of the participants." If, as so often happens, man's attention and activity are diverted from the worship of the supreme intelligence to the support of a dogma relating to that intelligence, the religious spirit diminishes and civilization wanes. Pound has described the process:

> Our only measure of truth is . . . our own perception of truth. The undeniable tradition of metamorphoses teaches us that things do not remain always the same. They become other things by swift and unanalysable process. It was only when men began to mistrust the myths and to tell nasty lies about the Gods for a moral purpose that these matters became hopelessly confused. Then some unpleasing Semite or Parsee or Syrian began to use myths for social propaganda, when the myth was degraded into an allegory or a fable, and that was the beginning of the end. Gods no longer walked in men's gardens. The first myths arose when a man walked sheer into "nonsense," that is to say, when some very vivid and undeniable adventure befell him, and he told someone else who called him a liar. Thereupon, after bitter experience, perceiving that no one could understand what he meant when he said that he "turned into a tree," he made a myth—a work of art that is—an impersonal or objective story woven out of his own emotion, as the nearest equation that he was capable of putting into words. The story, perhaps, then gave rise to a weaker copy of his emotion in others, until there arose a cult, a company of people who could understand each other's nonsense about the gods.
>
> These things were afterward incorporated for the condemnable "good of the State," and what was once a species of truth became only lies and propaganda. And they told horrid tales to little boys in order to make them be good, or to the ignorant populace in order to preserve the empire; and religion came to an end and civic science began to be studied. Plato said that artists ought to be kept out of the ideal republic, and the artists swore by their gods that nothing would drag them into it. That is the history of "civilization," or philology, or Kultur. *(Pavannes and Divisions,* pp. 143-4.)

William Blake, in *The Marriage of Heaven and Hell,* has said much the same thing:

> The ancient Poets animated all sensible objects with Gods or Geniuses, calling them by the names and adorning them with the properties of woods, rivers, mountains, lakes, cities, nations, and whatever their enlarged and numerous senses could perceive.
>
> And particularly they studied the genius of each city and country, placing it under its mental deity;
> Till a system was formed, which some took advantage of & enslav'd the vulgar by attempting to realize or abstract the mental deities from their objects: thus began Priesthood;
>
> Choosing forms of worship from poetic tales.
>
> And at length they pronounc'd that the Gods had order'd such things.

Thus men forgot that All deities reside in the human breast.

In his search for a faith which would satisfy him, Pound has observed—and found wanting—Judaism, Catholicism, Protestantism, Hinduism, and Mohammedanism. The Old Testament he conceives to be "the record of a barbarian tribe full of evil"; and of Old Testament Jewish organization he has said:

> There was a law but not an ethical system. This law was a set of finicking prohibitions and there was little distinction between the transgressions. What there was, related mostly to the main purpose of that law; namely, to provide fines, payable to a gang or tribe of allegedly religious superiors, who seem to have had no particular ethical status. Irresponsible taxation; taxation to and for the benefit of a gang of exploiters.
>
> I ask why was Christ crucified! . . . . He was crucified for trying to bust a racket . . . . What stirred up the big men in the country? Will you note that there is in the Christian gospel no provision for taxing the public. There is no institution of a central governing authority authorized to tax the people for infringement of un-understandable infractions of a finicking code of laws.
>
> (Broadcast, 4 May 1943. The transcript of the broadcasts contains many errors; I have silently corrected the more obvious of them, here and in later quotations.)

In Christ he recognizes a figure of very great stature but nevertheless one possessing deficiencies. Pound describes him as being

> . . . a most profound philosophic genius . . . an intuitive, inexperienced man dying before middle age. The things unthought of in his philosophy are precisely the things that would be unthought of in the philosophy of a provincial genius, a man of a subject nation. The whole sense of social order is absent. *(The New Age,* 21 (1917), p. 268.)

The Catholic Church, combining Christ's philosophy with such sense of social order as had been inherited from the Roman Empire, built a religious faith and initiated a civilization which had its glories. Indeed, Pound thinks that it comes close to satisfying the needs of 20th century man, as these quotations from varying parts of *The Guide to Kulchur* indicate:

> Christianity has been cursed by sectarian snobism. It escaped in the saints. As it escaped, pari passu, it gave order to Europe, it gave peace in one time or place or another, it built the cathedrals. (P. 30.)
>
> The Catholic Church rises and sinks with civilization circumvolving it. Again I repeat: I cd. be quite a "good catholic" IF they wd. let me pick my own saints and theologians. (P. 189.)
>
> I repeat: the Catholic Church went out of business when its hierarchy ceased to believe its own dogma. Leo X didn't take Luther's thought as a serious matter. He didn't expect others to do so.

Scotus Erigena held that: Authority comes from right reason. I suppose he thought himself a good catholic.

This page can stand in lieu of an Agony Column. I still invite correspondence as to the trial of Erigena and his condemnation centuries after his death.

I can still see a Catholic renaissance or the Church "taken seriously once again" if Rome chose to dig up the records, if Rome chose to say the trial was a mistrial, if Rome chose to say that Scotus was heretical because of some pother about the segments of the trinity but that on "Authority" he was sound, a son faithful, etc. (P. 75.)

This much I believe. Given Erigena, given St. Ambrose and St. Antonino, plus time, patience and genius you cd. erect inside the fabric [of the Catholic Church] something modern man cd. believe . . . . This much I believe to be also true: there is more civilization lying around unused in the crannies, zenanas, interstices of that dusty and baroque fabric than in all other institutions of the occident. (Pp. 76-7.)

But the Church has not chosen to say that Scotus Erigena's trial was a mistrial, nor is it willing to permit Pound to pick his own saints and theologians. Consequently, though he seems to be hovering about the periphery of the soul of the Church, he has not been assimilated into its body.

Such sympathy as Pound reveals toward Catholicism he denies to Protestantism, primarily because its effect has been "semitically to obliterate values, to efface grades and graduations." (Guide, p. 185.) Luther and Calvin did not rise without antecedent causes, of course: the Church had, prior to their appearance, undergone a decline as a social and intellectual force in proportion as the "hierarchy ceased to believe their own dogmas." (Guide, p. 27.) As a significant example, the Church had at an early date established the concept of the "just price"; that is, it had stood firmly against usury. But the time came when, though the concept remained, only lip-service was paid it. Pound has said in one of his recent cantos (96), "The temple is holy, because it is not for sale." When, in effect, it came to be for sale, it was inevitable that the Church should split and Protestantism, in Pound's estimation an apologia for usury, take form.

Perhaps Pound's gravest charge against Protestantism is that it inculcates the monotheistic temperament, which, in turn, promotes intolerance. His own personal experience has provided evidence for this belief.

In 1907, Pound left the graduate school of the University of Pennsylvania to embark upon a career as a college teacher. His career, however, was aborted by the administrators of Wabash College, who were distressed by the intrusion of a "Latin Quarter" type into their small-town Indianian Kultur. This event had somewhat greater impact upon Pound's thinking than it has usually been given credit for. The college officials revealed themselves to be prudish, provincial, and snoopy. And Pound has erected into an important part of his philosophy his reaction to all such people and to all ethical systems which produce such people. One of the tensions over the 90-odd cantos of his great epic poem is the effort to bring together the Eleusinian (or Dionysian) concept of natural fecundity and the Confucian concept of human ordering. Prudery, of course, is an enemy of the former drive, distorting and making it shameful. It is false and petty "ordering," no less anti-Confucian than anti-Eleusinian in its assumption of the privilege of "messing in other people's business." On the one hand it completely falsifies and commercializes the concept of love (as on the economic level the concept of natural abundance is negated); on the other, it betrays the idea of individual liberty as the right to do anything that does not injure others, producing Volsteads, Comstocks, and Calvins, bureaucracies and passport requirements, censorship and inquisition.

These ideas (and their ramifications) did not have their genesis in Pound's dismissal. But this compelling personal experience certainly confirmed a belief, which he has never abandoned, that the major problem of our time is that of the relation of the individual to the state—the classic problem of Antigone. "In politics *the* problem of our time is to find the border between public and private affairs." *(ABC of Economics,* p. 40.) He finds the problem in microcosm in the universities where, as he quotes Felix Schelling as having said, there is no place for the unusual man. (The man in question was Carl Sandburg.) His own experience had verified the statement. And he determines that this way of thinking transcends the state and is part and parcel of international Christianity. He labels the attitude which produces the problem "provincialism," which he defines as

(a) An ignorance of the manners, customs and nature of people living outside one's own village, parish, or nation.

(b) A desire to coerce others into uniformity. *(The New Age,* 21 (1917), p. 244.)

As has been said, Pound discovered that attitude in Christ himself. But he finds it to an infinitely greater degree in contemporary churchmen, "an organized set of men using a set of arbitrary, unprovable statements about the unknown to further their own designs" *(The New Age,* 21 (1917), p. 245), who combine the teaching of the New Testament with the far more egregiously provincial teachings of the Old Testament. For, he says:

Christ can very well stand as an heroic figure. The hero need not be of wisdom all compounded. Also he is not wholly to blame for the religion that's been foisted on to him . . . . Christianity as practiced resumes itself into one commandment dear to all officials, American Y. M. C. A., Burocrats, etc., 'Thou shalt attend to thy neighbor's business before attending to thine own.' *(Letters,* p. 183.)

Even so, to combat "the curse of our time," the provincial or monotheistic temperament — that of the vendor of taboos, the bigot who
demands the right to interfere, the practitioner of sacerdotal mono-
polies—Pound evolved his creed of Anti-Christmonopoly: "Intellectual
Honesty, the Abolition of Violence, the Fraternal Deference of Confucius,
and Internationalism." *(The New Age*, 22 (1917-18), p. 69.) Of Confucian
fraternal deference he says that it would "if introduced, finish off
Christianity."

Thus, if Christianity were to be preached at all, it would have to be on
pragmatic grounds, and it would have to be renovated, as he suggested
in a letter to Henry Swabey:

> Xtianity a poor substitute for the truth, but the best canned goods
> that can be put on the market immediately in sufficient quantity for
> general pubk.? ? ? I admit the problem is difficult. Mebbe best line is
> to get rid of worst and rottenest phases first, i.e., the old testy-munk,
> barbarous blood sac, etc., and gradually detach Dantescan light (peel-
> ing off the Middle Ages bit by bit, that bloody swine St. Clement, etc.)
> Omnia quae sunt, lumina sunt. *(Letters*, p. 345.)

In place of "the old testy-munk" Pound would supply Ovid's *Metamorphoses*—"a sacred book." There are several reasons for his preference.

In the first place, Pound prefers the Hellenistic spirit to the Hebraic.
And he does so, in part, because the former is pro-art, the latter anti-art;
that is, Judaism's Jehovah requires that there be no graven images
whereas, to the contrary, where the pagan spirit dominates, "the grove
demands the goddess." Pound is emphatic upon this point:

> To replace the marble goddess on her pedestal at Terracina is worth
> more than any metaphysical argument. And the mosaics in Santa
> Maria in Trastevere recall a wisdom lost by scholasticism, an under-
> standing denied to Aquinas. *(A Visiting Card*, p. 21.)

> Of religion it will be enough for me to say . . . . "every self-respecting
> Ravennese is procreated, or at least receives spirit or breath of life,
> in the Mausoleum of Galla Placidia." . . . . Tradition inheres . . .
> in the images of the gods and gets lost in dogmatic definitions.
> History is recorded in monuments, and *that* is why they get destroyed.
> *(Ibid.*, pp. 23-4.)

The creation of an art-object glorifying the gods is an act of faith on the
part of the creator producing a revitalized faith (a sense of the gods'
immediacy) in the observer; it is an act of affirmation without taint (for
creator or observer) of pejorative tabu. To have found in the stone a god
represents for the creator an active participation in the gods' most characteristic function—that of making quick the dead; for the observer, the

art-object is a testament verifying his faith emotionally and intellectually.
Here he has before him clear evidence of the substantiality of the gods
(and therefore of the soul) whereas dogma renders the lively feeling dead
in abstract words, "wafts us out in mere nomenclatures." And, it might
be added, the translation of the spiritual (still maintaining its spirituality)
into the material is as much an act of metamorphosis as the translation,
in Ovid, of the human into bestial or vegetable.

Men are aware by intuition that mysteries lie behind the phenomenal
world. The great virtue of the artist is that he can give that intuition a
certitude. "Art," Pound notes, "is, religiously, an emphasis, a segregation
of some component of that intelligence [the supreme intelligence of the
universe], for the sake of making it more perceptible." *(Guide,* p. 189.)
In so doing the mythopoeic artist refrains from generalizing his intuition
as if, instead of a flash of perception, he had been granted a revelation of a
total, closely-meshed truth. This latter is the sin of prose philosophers.
Aquinas articulates a system; Ovid expresses an intuition "without dent-
ing the edges or shaving off the nose and ears of a verity." *(Guide,* p. 127.)
He "knows where to stop . . . he don't try to level out all differences and
state what he doesn't know." *(Guide,* p. 128.)

The philosopher with a system, a Truth, is inexorably monotheistic.
Having shaved off the nose and ears of a verity to make it fit his scheme,
he will not hesitate to do as much to human beings to compel them to
adopt it. And in so doing he produces a society in which "the snot of
pejoracy, sans bonhomie and good humour" wield the Flail of Jehovah
against tolerance:

> It is because the inspectors in the port of New York are told that they
> represent justice that they behave like gorillas. Strong in the might of
> the Lord, burning with righteousness, etc., crusading ever in the name
> of one Highest. *(The Exile,* no. 4, p. 13.)

> The drear horror of American life can be traced to two damnable
> roots, or perhaps it is only one root: 1. The loss of *all* distinction
> between public and private affairs. 2. The tendency to mess into
> other people's affairs before establishing order in one's own affairs
> and in one's thought. To which one might add the lack in America
> of any habit of connecting or correlating *any* act or thought to *any*
> main principle whatsoever: the ineffable rudderlessness of that peo-
> ple. The principle of good is enunciated by Confucius; it consists in
> establishing order within oneself. This order or harmony spreads by a
> sort of contagion without specific effort. The principle of evil consists
> in messing into other people's affairs. Against this principle of evil no
> adequate precaution is taken by Christianity, Moslemism, Judaism,
> nor. so far as I know, by *any* monotheistic religion. Many 'mystics'
> do not even aim at the principle of good; they seek merely establish-
> ment of a parasitic relationship with the unknown. *(The Exile,* no. 2,
> p. 35.)

Santayana held much the same opinion. In *The Life of Reason*, for example, he contrasted the "puerile scholasticism and rabid intolerance" of Jewish thought with the "enlightened and ingenuous" philosophy of the Greeks and complained of the "heated and fanatical atmosphere" in which the Hebrew tradition had enveloped religious discussion.

Clearly, Pound's religious position is not far removed from that of the humanists of the Italian Renaissance. He is against a monopoly of faith and the imposition by monopolists of their faith. He is for tolerance of variants and for personal apprehension of the bases of faith. A characteristic anecdote illuminates the former desideratum. He was making one of his visits to the Tempio Malatestiano, the famous structure erected by Sigismondo Malatesta. A country priest, he says, was not the least disturbed that he should be making his obeisance to certain stone elephants rather than to the "altar furniture." And he had "still further sign of enlightenment from old nun in hospital: E.P. not catholic. No, thank heaven! NOT protestant, not jew, but accepted greek deities. To which the nun replied wisely and tolerantly, 'Ze tutta un religione'—Oh well, it's all a religion." *(Guide,* p. 301.) Thus was restored to him the idea that there could be a clean and beneficent Christianity.

And as for the requirement that one experience the mysteries in person, it is stated as clearly as ever Pound has stated it in a little mock-catechism called *Religio, or the Child's Guide to Knowledge:*

What is a god?
A god is an eternal state of mind.
What is a faun?
A faun is an elemental creature.
What is a nymph?
A nymph is an elemental creature.
When is a god manifest?
When the state of mind takes form.
When does a man become a god?
When he enters one of these states of mind.
What is the nature of the forms whereby a god is manifest?
They are variable, but retain certain distinguishing characteristics.
Are all eternal states of mind gods?
We consider them so to be.
Are all durable states of mind gods?
They are not.
By what characteristics may we know the divine forms?
By beauty . . . .
What are the kinds of knowledge?
There are immediate knowledge and hearsay.
Is hearsay of any value?
Of some.
What is the greatest hearsay?
The greatest hearsay is the tradition of the gods.
Of what use is this tradition?

It tells us to be ready to look.
In what manner do gods appear?
Formed and formlessly.
To what do they appear when formed?
To the sense of vision.
And when formless?
To the sense of knowledge . . . .
What are the gods of this rite?
Apollo, and in some sense Helios, Diana in some of her phases,
also the Cytherean goddess.
To what other gods is it fitting, in harmony or in adjunction
with these rites, to give incense?
To Koré and to Demeter, also to lares and to oreiads and to
certain elemental creatures . . . .
Are these things so in the East?
This rite is made for the West.
(Pavannes and Divisions, p. 115.)

Some of Pound's opinions in this matter are quite similar to those of Thaddeus Zielinski, author of a little-known book called *La Sibylle.* Zielinski's major effort in this book—and Pound thinks it criminal that the work has not been widely disseminated in this country—is to prove that true Catholicism derives, not from Judaism but from paganism, not from the barren wastes of Asia Minor but from the Mediterranean basin; that, specifically, the advent of Catholicism was psychologically prepared for by the cult of Eleusis, the cult of the Great Goddesses, the cult of Apollo, and the cult of Isis. That is to say, the true Old Testament was pagan teaching rather than Mosaic. The implication of this proposition is, of course, that when Christian theologians turned from pagan teaching to Judaic, from Ovid and Hesiod to Moses and David, they falsified the true faith. It was Zielinski's hope to open his readers' eyes to that falsification.

It is equally Pound's.

He will, therefore, substitute for the Moses of the Old Testament the Ovid of the *Metamorphoses,* with his recognition of the vivifying personal immediacy of supernatural forces and the constant penetration of the supernatural into the natural, producing change; his good sense in maintaining a separateness of the empirically knowable from the experienced unknowable and in accepting the fact of the unknowable instead of speculating upon, generalizing from, and dogmatizing in terms of it; and his polytheistic tolerance so sharply to be discriminated from the dictatorial nay-saying which Pound finds characteristic of the Jewish scripture.

On a higher level (from a professional philosopher's point of view) is the next of the significant influences upon Pound's thinking about the man-God relationship—namely, neo-Platonism. Among the great names in neo-Platonism are those of Plotinus, Porphyry, Iamblichus, and Proclus, all of whom are mentioned in the *Cantos*. Their effort was to establish a philosophy or religion which would be, unlike Christianity, Hellenic, and, unlike Stoicism and Epicureanism, idealistic. In Plotinus, the true source of reality is the One which, being totally free of matter, is totally light, and which, being good, diffuses its goodness like light.

In the *Guide*, Pound speaks of those who have become "suddenly conscious of the reality of the *nous*, of mind, apart from any man's individual mind, of the crystalline and enduring, of the bright as it were molten glass that envelops us, full of light." (P. 44.) And, that Light ("the tensile light," "the undivided light") has become one of the most significant themes in the *Cantos* is indicated by such brief assertions as "let the light pour"; "To build light, said Ocellus"; "Lux in diafana, creatrix, oro"; "The light there almost solid"; "Omnia quae sunt, lumina sunt"; and so on; by extended passages in which "the bright as it were molten glass" envelops Pound or other figures in the *Cantos* "full of light"; and by expository comments such as the following:

> Above prana, the light,
>   past light, the crystal.
> Above crystal, the jade!
> The clover enduring,
>   basalt crumbled with time.
>   *(Rock-Drill*, p. 94.)

Thus Pound has accepted the basic idea of Plotinus, that of the image of light as the source of goodness, beauty, and creativity through the universe. According to the neo-Platonists, for those who have acquired the capability of contemplating the Intellectual-Principle (the veritable, abiding, and non-fluctuant), "all is transparent, nothing dark, nothing resistant; every being is lucid to every other, in breadth and depth; light runs through light." That Pound had achieved that capability in the dark days immediately following World War I is revealed in Canto 15 where, with the assistance of Plotinus, he is led out of London's hellishness:

> (Helios ah Helios)
>   blind with the sunlight
> Swollen-eyed, rested,
>   lids sinking, darkness unconscious.*

The neo-Platonists have borne witness that men can achieve a state in which clarity of intellect and harmony of soul obtain. But Pound is emphatic (in the *Guide*, p. 223) in dissociating this state, "the ecstatic-beneficent-and-benevolent," from another species of mystical state: "the bestial, namely the fanatical, the man on fire with God anxious . . . to reprove his neighbor for having a set of tropisms different from that of the fanatics . . . . the second set of mystic states is manifest in scarcity

*All quotations from the *Cantos* are from the New Directions edition.

economists, in repressors, etc." Here he is saying in other terms very much what he had said in the earlier book *Make It New* (p. 17) where he argues that "the opposing systems of European morality go back to the opposed temperaments of those who thought copulation was good for the crops, and the opposed faction who thought it was bad for the crops (the scarcity economists of pre-history.) " That is, in each case he is taking his stand with the Yea-sayer against the Nay-sayer, and therefore specifically with the humanists of the Platonic Academy, who, "messing up Christian and Pagan mysticism, allegory, occultism, demonology, Trismegistus, Psellus, Porphyry, into a most eloquent and exciting and exhilarating botch-patch . . . 'did for' the mediaeval fear of the *dies irae* and for human abasement generally." *(The New Age,* 11 Feb., 1915, p. 409.)

The tradition of the undivided light is to be found in the writings of the 9th century philosopher Johannes Scotus Erigena, whose statement "Omnia quae sunt lumina sunt" appears in various places and in various forms in the *Cantos.* In Erigena, as in the neo-Platonists, we find an expression of belief in a permanent, unchangeable force within and beyond all the seeming change and impermanence of the universe, with the image of light as the symbol of that permanence. And Pound speaks often and affirmatively of the later, Renaissance figure, Gemisto Plethon, who "brought a brand of Platonism into Italy and is supposed to have set off a renaissance." *(Guide,* p. 45.)

Both Erigena and Gemisto are "serious characters," members of the "conspiracy of intelligence" who have managed in various times and places to sustain civilization against the nefarious efforts of the obfuscators. The Roman Empire and the Church of the Middle Ages supplied some of these members. Among them were such men as these: Antoninus Pius, who brought the abstract concept of justice down to earth in his differentiation between maritime usury and agrarian usury; St. Ambrose, who imagizes "a transition from self-centered lust after eternal salvation into a sense of public order"; Augustine, who countered the Judaic strain in Catholicism with his neo-Platonism; Richard St. Victor, with his idea of the three modes of thought—cogitation, meditation, and contemplation—in the first of which "the mind flits aimlessly about the object, in the second it circles about it in a methodical manner, in the third it is unified with the object," an idea which, unlike the syllogism, does not lose its grip on reality; Scotus Erigena again, with his argument that authority comes from right reason; Grosseteste and Albertus Magnus, who worked in ideas with the rigorous precision demanded now of a scientist in a laboratory.

It is noticeable that such thinkers as these (and more recent ones, like Remy de Gourmont, Leo Frobenius, and Professor Agassiz) found favor with Pound particularly because they kept their feet on the ground, avoided the aridities of futile metaphysics, and concerned themselves with making philosophical thought useful to men in their communities. Such concern as they had with the man-God relation did not stop there but carried over into the relations between man and nature, man and man, and man and self.

Above all these "serious characters" in teaching men how to maintain the four relations effectively was Kung. Of him and his disciple Mencius, Pound wrote:

> Kung and Mencius do not satisfy all the real belief of Europe. But all valid Christian ethics is in accord with them. In fact, only Kung can guide a man, so far as I know, through the jungle of propaganda and fads that has overgrown Xtian theology. The mysteries are *not* revealed and no guide book to them has been or will be written. *(Letters,* p. 327.)

No mystery attaches to Pound's reverence for Kung nor for his belief that Kung's teaching could educe an ordered civilization from America's confused strivings. Kung himself had lived when a dynasty was decaying, when China was divided into inimical feudal states over which the Emperor was unable to exert control.

Kung learned from his study of history that China had been well governed in the past; his effort was to acquire from that study a set of principles which had worked in the past and which could be applied to bring order out of present chaos. He taught his students (many of them sons of noble families) these principles and tried to persuade the feudal lords to adopt them. In the latter attempt he failed. But, ironically, after his death his teachings were so esteemed that they became required reading for all aspirants to administrative positions. According to Pound:

> His analysis of why the earlier emperors had been able to govern greatly was so sound that every durable dynasty, since his time, has risen on a Confucian design and been initiated by a group of Confucians. China was tranquil when her rulers understood these few pages of *The Great Digest.* When the principles here defined were neglected, dynasties waned and chaos ensued. The proponents of a world order will neglect at their peril the study of the only process that has repeatedly proved its efficiency as social coordinate. *(Confucius,* p. 19.)

For Kung, government was of men, not of laws. He devoted his life to teaching his followers to be total men and therefore equitable governors. A right society would follow inevitably, he believed, from government by such men. The following excerpts from his teachings (translated by Pound) will suggest the tenor of his ethic-polity:

> What heaven has disposed and sealed is called the inborn nature. The realization of this nature is called the process. The clarification of this process . . . is called education. *(Confucius,* p. 99.)

He who defines his words with precision will perfect himself and the process of this perfecting is in the process (that is ... the total process of nature). *(Ibid.,* p. 177.)

The great learning ... takes root in clarifying the way wherein the intelligence increases through the process of looking straight into one's heart and acting on the results; it is rooted in watching with affection the way people grow; it is rooted in coming to rest, being at ease in perfect equity. *(Ibid.,* p. 27.)

You improve the old homestead by material riches and irrigation; you enrich and irrigate the character by the process of looking straight into the heart and then acting on the results ... it is for this reason that the great gentleman must find the precise verbal expression for his inarticulate thoughts. *(Ibid.,* p. 51.)

Tze-Lu said: The Lord of Wei is waiting for you to form a government, what are you going to do first?

He (Kung) said: Settle the names (determine a precise terminology ....) If words (terminology) are not (is not) precise, they cannot be followed out, or completed in action according to specifications. When the services (actions) are not brought to true focus, the ceremonies and music will not prosper; where rites and music do not flourish punishments will be misapplied, not make bullseye, and the people won't know how to move hand or foot .... Therefore, the proper man must have terms that can be spoken, and when uttered be carried into effect; the proper man's words must cohere to things, correspond to them (exactly) and no more fuss about it. *(Analects,* Bk. 13, III.)

The proper man gives substance ... to his acts by equity .... He proceeds according to the rites, puts them forth modestly, and makes them perfect by sticking to his word. That's the proper man (in whom's the voice of his forebears). *(Ibid.,* Bk. 15, XVII.)

Tze-kung asked if there were a single verb that you could practice thru life up to the end. He said: Sympathy ... what you don't want (done to) yourself, don't inflict on another. *(Ibid.,* Bk. 15, XXIII.) There are five activities of high importance under heaven, and they are practiced with three virtues. I mean there are the obligations between prince and minister; between father and son; between husband and wife; between elder and younger brothers; and between friends. Those are the five obligations that have greater effects under heaven. The three efficient virtues are: Knowledge, humanity, and energy; and they are to be united in practice, do not attempt to split them apart one from the other. *(Confucius,* p. 151.)

He who knows these three (virtues) knows the means to self-discipline, he who can rule himself can govern others, he who can govern others can rule the kingdoms and families of the Empire. *(Ibid.,* p. 155.)

All who have families and kingdoms to govern have nine rules to follow, to wit: to control themselves, to honor men of honest talent, to treat their relatives with affection, to respect the great ministers, to maintain the *esprit de corps* of the rest of the officers and officials, to treat the people as children. to attract the artisans of the hundred trades to the country. to show courtesy to those who come from afar, and to show tact in dealing with the princes and great feudal chiefs of the states. *(Ibid.,* pp. 155-6.)

Discriminate, illuminate; use abundantly all things available; do not drive toward anything that is contrary to the rites, these are the modes of self-discipline, the instruments of self-discipline. Keep calumny afar off, get rid of viscid show, hold material riches in low esteem and in high esteem that conduct which comes from the straight gaze into the heart, from the inner clarity. . . . *(Ibid.,* p. 159.)

Here, capsulized, is the ethic propounded in the *Cantos.* Kung's primary task was to instruct potential rulers, but his ethic holds for subject as well as administrator: " 'The art,' says my venerable colleague, once Vorticist W. Lewis, 'of being ruled!' The art of not being exploited begins with 'Ch'ing Ming' " *(Guide,* p. 244). And Kung taught how to live rather than how to die. His ethic was not distorted or vitiated by theological intrusions, but it did not exist apart from a theological frame of reference:

Great intelligence attains again and again to great verity. The Duce and Kung fu tseu equally perceive that their people need poetry; that prose is NOT education but the outer courts of the same. Beyond its doors are the mysteries. Eleusis. Things not to be spoken of save in secret.

The mysteries self-defended, the mysteries that can *not* be revealed. *(Guide,* pp. 144-5.)

One of the Chinese ideograms which figure largely in the *Cantos* is the one representing the Chinese word "Ming." In explaining this ideogram (in *Confucius,* p. 20) Pound shows that he finds a relation between Confucian thought and that of the neo-Platonists and their followers:

The sun and moon, the total light process, the radiation. reception and reflection of light; hence the intelligence. Bright, brightness, shining. Refer to Scotus Erigena, Grosseteste and the notes on light in my *Cavalcanti.*

Grosseteste and Cavalcanti were inheritors of the neo-Platonic tradition which conceived all creation to be substantially unified with its creator. According to Grosseteste, the essence of all bodies is light. In the lower bodies, that light may be less pure, less simple, less spiritual than in the higher bodies; nevertheless, it is, of all bodies, the essence—"things which are, are many through the multiplication of light itself in different degrees."

In his *Canzone* "Donna mi prega," which Pound translates as his thirty-sixth canto, Cavalcanti appears to identify Love with the Intellectual Light under discussion. Of Love, he says, in Pound's translation, that it

Descendeth not by quality but
            shineth out
Himself his own effect unendingly . . . .
and
    He himself moveth not, drawing all
            to his stillness . . . .
and
    Nor is he known from his face
    But taken in the white light that
            is allness . . . .

Thus Grosseteste in his philosophical treatise and Cavalcanti in his poem about love express a metaphysic not in the least repugnant to that expressed by Kung in a sentence held in high esteem by Pound: "The celestial and earthly process can be defined in a single phrase; its actions and its creations have no duality. (The arrow has not two points.)" *(Confucius*, p. 183.)

Ovid's *Metamorphoses*, neo-Platonism, Confucianism, and certain elements of Catholic thinking. It would, on first thought, seem impossible to bring these materials into any sort of coherence. But underlying and directing Pound's eclecticism is a hierarchy of values which enables him to discern the similarity between Oriental and Occidental thought, to select those elements which are meaningful to him, and out of them to build not a philosophical system but a philosophical point of view serving as the means toward the civilized life. And, further, he can mold these heteroclitics, in his poem, into a single ideogram which comes very near to summing up his total position. He does so, as it seems to me, in the following passage from Canto 74:

and this day the air was made open
    for Kuanon of all delights
        Linus, Cletus, Clement
                        whose prayers
the great scarab is bowed at the altar
the green light gleams in his shell
plowed in the sacred field and unwound the silk worms early
                                        in tensile
in the light of light is the *virtu*
            "sunt lumina" said Erigena Scotus
                as of Shun on Mt Taishan
and in the hall of the forebears
                    as from the beginning of wonders
the paraclete that was present in Yao, the precision
in Shun the compassionate
in Yu the guider of waters
4 giants at the 4 corners
        three young men at the door
and they digged a ditch round about me
        lest the damp gnaw thru my bones
            to redeem Zion with justice

*The *ming* here is an error; according to Pound, it should be supplanted by *hsin*—the tensile light.

sd/ Isaiah. Not out on interest said David rex
                                          the prime s.o.b.
Light tensile immaculata
        the sun's cord unspotted
"sunt lumina" said the Oirishman to King Carolus,
            "OMNIA,
all things that are are lights"

Here are brought together an oriental goddess of mercy (Kuanon); a quotation from the prayer in memory of the Saints in the Catholic mass; an assimilation of the priest in green vestments into the scarab of green stone over which Egyptian prayers were said; allusion to an early Chinese fertility ritual; the Chinese ideogram representing light, fortified by allusions to Erigena; reference to three early Chinese emperors, to the Christian trinity, and to three compassionate young men who eased Pound's hardships in the concentration camp; and allusions to two texts in the Old Testament upon which Pound can look with favor. Miss Barbara Charlesworth, who has done a complete explication of the passage, has said, and, it seems to me, with justice:

> ... it is my belief that when the *Cantos* has been completed and all the parts that make up its single vast ideogram have been sorted out— when, in short, anyone is in the position to make a valid géneralization on the theme of the entire poem—the theme that is decided upon may well be the one that is found in this passage. For no matter where one begins the study of the *Cantos*, one is always brought, sooner or later, into the presence of the creative and beneficent Light whose vision orders, harmonizes, and fulfills all things. *(The Tensile Light,* pp. 136-7.)

The situation, to sum up, is this. Pound lives in a time when civilization seems to him to have gone to seed. As a poet-teacher he accepts as his responsibility the job of pointing out this fact to those who believe that the scientific and technological triumphs of the past century equate with a triumphant civilization. In this respect he serves as a destroyer of stereotypes. But he is a constructor, too, and, learning from a study of history that no civilization has existed which did not rest upon a religious base, and, further, concluding that the religion which has served Europe in the past no longer functions satisfactorily, because vital belief has become devitalized dogma, he has studied the religious beliefs which were regnant in times when high civilizations existed and has discovered that beneath dogma, ritual, and other excrescences, certain basic truths have been common *semper ubique.* When these have been recognized and acted upon, civilizations have prospered; if they were now to be recognized, the foundation for a present civilization would be laid. Among the beliefs which he has seized upon as being fundamental are the following.

In the life of man some things merely occur; some things occur and then recur in changed form. But behind occurrence and recurrence exists a Permanent. Of this Permanent we have moments of awareness, moments of such clarity of vision, that we cannot doubt that, as Kung said, "The spirits of the energies and of the rays have their operative virtù." Given these moments of awareness, we can accept them and arrive at an assurance, a faith, which can incite us to benevolent action, which can give us reason for, and assist us in, organizing our lives; or, unfortunately, we can generalize the unique experience into a Universal Truth which we can tyrannically impose upon our fellow-men. Exemplary of the former way of acting is a tolerant polytheistic Hellenism; of the latter, intolerant monotheistic Hebraism.

In becoming aware of the Permanent, man also becomes aware of its two basic activities: that of creation; and that of ordering the things created. As far back as the historian of civilization goes, he finds in every successful culture images representing these principles: *e.g.*, Osiris and Ra, and Koré and Apollo. These basic principles can be presented in a more sophisticated terminology than that common to primitive myth (as Kung presented them, and the neo-Platonists), but without harmful consequence so long as what has been experienced or intuited—this victory of the imagination—is not rationalized into a coercive structure of logical propositions.

Now, since Christianity, both Catholic and Protestant, has gone far in the latter direction ("the theologians who put reason (logic) in the place of faith began the slithering process which has ended up with theologians who take no interest in theology whatsoever"—*A Visiting Card*, p. 23), its images of the mysteries no longer have life and poetical validity. But in his search for the bases of religious faith common to various cultures, Pound has discovered images that—for him, at least—possess that life and validity. He has found them in Greek and Egyptian, Chinese and Japanese myth particularly, and he has made them his own. In so doing, he has expunged from his records the *personae* of Jewish myth and history which have figured so prominently in Christian literature. And when, in his poem, he "philosophizes" his myth, he uses the terminology of Kung and of the neo-Platonists (the latter of whom, in imagizing their theory of the emanation of light, used figures from Greek mythology).

Briefly, Pound has tried to awaken his readers to the living religion which underlies the dead cerebralization of contemporary Christianity by compelling their attention toward those epochs when, in the Mediterranean basin, it was alive, and toward the conditions under which such life is possible. In this, he functions as Kung in his equally decadent era functioned.

In a way, too, his activity in this regard is not dissimilar from that of the Deists, three hundred years ago, who, weary of Reformation and Counter-Reformation, endeavored by a comparative study of religions, to show that men agreed in basic articles of faith and were foolishly fighting one another over trifles. Deism is regularly written off (especially by Christian apologists) as being, because of its superficiality, not worth serious regard. The same attitude has greeted Pound's exposition in the *Cantos* of what he considers a tenable faith.

T. S. Eliot, for example, published the following criticism:

> He (Pound) retains some mediaeval mysticism without belief, this is mixed up with Mr. Yeats's spooks (excellent creatures in their native bogs); and involved with Dr. Berman's hormones; and a steamroller of Confucian rationalism (the Religion of a Gentleman, and therefore an Inferior Religion) has flattened over the whole. So we are left with the question (which the unfinished Cantos make more pointed) what does Mr. Pound believe?
> ("Isolated Superiority," *Dial*, 84 (Jan. 1928), 7.)

This is a very supercilious piece of criticism and in egregious error. I know of no evidence proving that Pound disbelieves the medieval mysticism (the neo-Platonic doctrine of light) which appears in his poem; none of Mr. Yeats's spooks are incorporated; Dr. Berman's hormones are nowhere evident; and to refer to Confucianism as the Religion of a Gentleman is about as valid as to refer to Christianity as the Religion of Adulteresses and Tax-Collectors. (Oddly, a major criticism of the Anglo-Catholicism to which Eliot was converted is that it has become a monopoly of the aristocracy and upper middleclass.)

Eliot has made a further dissent in his comment upon Cantos 14 and 15 (the Hell cantos, in which Pound depicts the infernal state of English minds in 1919-20). He holds, he says, a

> considerable objection to a Hell of this sort: that a Hell altogether without dignity implies a Heaven without dignity also. If you do not distinguish between individual responsibility and circumstances in Hell, between essential Evil and social accidents, then the Heaven (if any) implied will be equally trivial and accidental. Hell, for all its horrors, is a perfectly comfortable one for the modern mind to contemplate, and disturbing to no one's complacency: it is a Hell for the *other people*, the people we read about in the newspapers, not for oneself and one's friends. *(After Strange Gods,* pp. 46-47.)

This reasoning seems specious on several counts. First, it assumes that we have here a *total* hell. But Pound says *(Letters,* p. 293), ". . . that *section* of hell precisely has *not* any dignity. Neither had Dante's fahrting devils." (Pound is referring to the *Inferno*, Canto XXI, in which there is certainly neither dignity nor tragedy.) Second, if Hell and Heaven are opposites, a Hell without dignity must (Eliot to the contrary) imply a Heaven with it,

Third, Eliot's argument assumes Pound's denial of individual responsibility. But Pound: "I certainly do *not* deny individual responsibility.
I do deny the right of any man to shut his mind and accept the
unmitigated . . . . of the present econ. system, artificially maintained by
the most god damned . . . and liars . . . ." *(Letters*, p. 293.) Fourth, it is not
a Hell for the *other* people; Pound has, like Dante, depicted himself as
being in it and escaping from it. Fifth, it is only the intellectual who is
himself damned who can find Pound's hell a "perfectly comfortable one
. . . to contemplate," and his degree of complacency before the hellishness
of hell is a measure of his degree of damnation.

> Our generation was brought up in absolute economic illiteracy. Only
> the most tortured and active among us have been driven to analyze
> the hell that surrounded us. Monetary infection has penetrated the
> inmost crannies of mind; the virus has been so subtle that men's
> minds (souls—call 'em souls if that concords with your religion)
> have been strangled before they knew it. How, indeed, can an animal
> be aware of its death, if it is first narcoticized, if the death comes as a
> gradual sleepiness, then sleep, a creeping *first* into the very organs
> of perception? *(Polite Essays*, p. 99.)

Pound laments *(Letters*, p. 293) that "the Protestant world has *lost* the
sense of mental and spiritual *rottenness*. Dante has it: 'gran sacco che fa
merda.' The real theologians *knew* it." Eliot knows it too, but as a loyal
party member, he must define terms according to the party line and deny
Pound the right to define according to *his* party line. That is, Eliot demands that hell represent a separation from an Anglo-Catholic God,
whereas Pound sees it as a separation from "the process," considering
this not less a *poena damni* than the other. And Eliot believes that only
the Church can save man, but Pound believes the artist can.

> There are things I quite definitely want to destroy, and which I think
> will have to (be) annihilated before civilization can exist, i.e. any-
> thing I shd. dignify with the title civilization, last vestiges of which
> probably went by the board in the counter-reformation . . . . Hu-
> manity is malleable mud, and the arts set the moulds it is later cast
> into. *(Letters*, p. 181.)

D. S. Carne-Ross, applauding Eliot's "penetrating criticism," agrees that
Pound's "good is excellent but never radical. And his evil is of the same
sort. Primarily monetary, issuing in usury and the corruption of the will
which usury produces, it gives no hint of the permanent essential Evil
underlying this or that manifestation." *(Examination*, p. 151.) But he,
like Eliot, errs in taking the effect, usury, as the cause. The underlying
cause of this particular manifestation is man's perverse violation of the
human-divine relationship. Pound notes of Dante's treatment of Ulysses:

> Re punishment of Ulysses, no one seems to note the perfectly useless,
> trifling unprovoked sack of the Cicones in the *Odyssey* . . . . there

> was no excuse handy, it is pure devilment, and Ulysses and Co. de-
> served all they got thereafter. . . . It gives a crime and punishment
> motif to the *Odyssey*, which is frequently overlooked. . . . Dante
> definitely accents the theft of the Palladium, whereon one could turn
> out a volume of comment. It binds through from Homer to Virgil to
> Dante. *(Polite Essays, p. 45.)*

And it binds through to Pound, who over and over again demands the
restoration of "the Palladium" (the Aphrodite at Terracina, the altar in
the garden, etc.) as a symbol that Wagadu (see p. 130) is now once more
incorporated in men's hearts, or that men are once more united with "the
process." In the beginning was the word, but the word was falsified.
"Clean the word, clearly define its borders and health pervades the whole
human congeries, *in una parte piu e meno altrove.*" *(Ibid.,* p. 52.) As for
Carne-Ross's complaint that Pound does nothing about an assumed "permanent essential Evil," it is doubtful that Pound would grant the
assumption. But if he did, he would still direct his attention to an evil
which can be remedied, not to one for which no remedy is possible. Which
seems at least pragmatically sensible.

If Eliot and Carne-Ross find Pound's Hell unsatisfactory, they must
find Dante's equally so. For Pound's damned are exactly those who would
appear in Dante's cantos XVII to XXX: they are the usurers and the
fraudulent who exploit others for their own gain by cheating their hopes
and using their fears, by corrupting language, by merchandising the
sacramental, by deforming knowledge, by selling justice, by sacrificing
truth to expediency, by teaching fraudulent practice, by sowing discord
for personal profit, by perjuring and counterfeiting. Pound has skipped
over the sins in Dante's earlier cantos because they are primarily the
effects of the great sins of the later cantos, the sins of those who misuse
money-power or who sell themselves to those who have it, and who conceal
their maleficent activities by directing popular attention to the minor
sins, particularly that of Lust. (Pound laments that the only popularly-
known incident in the *Inferno* is that of Paolo and Francesca; in his own
Hell, he has purposely avoided the possibility of sex's stealing the spotlight from fraud.) This does not mean that Pound's evil is "primarily
monetary." In 1916 he was saying, "Religion is the root of all evil, or
damn near all" *(Letters,* p. 98). Later, it is true, he came to emphasize
usurious practice to a greater degree. But it remains a symptom, not the
disease. The root of evil is here: in not looking straight into the heart;
or not carrying the "know thyself" into action; or in directing the will
against sincerity, fidelity, humanity; or, in fine, in not coming to rest in
equity and in impeding the possibility of someone else's doing so. Perhaps
it does not over-simplify to say that good and evil are a matter of *directio
voluntatis,* with money-power merely representing the most powerful
leverage for evil will.

It is not fortuitous that Pound in his explanation of the ideogram for *will (Confucius,* p. 23) directs attention to *Odyssey,* I, 34, the story of Aegisthus who, though warned by the gods of the consequences, persisted in his evil courses ". . . how vainly," Zeus moralizes upon the situation, "mortal men do blame the gods! For of us they say comes evil, whereas they even of themselves, through the blindness of their own hearts, have sorrows beyond that which is ordained." Zeus might have been speaking directly to Carne-Ross with his theory of a permanent essential Evil (is he a Manichean?) underlying its various manifestations.

As for Pound's "good," it seems "radical" enough. He asks (as Socrates and Kung did) that a man know himself and act upon that self-know-ledge; that he have respect for intelligence; that he inculcate in himself and others the right attitude toward the fecundating mysteries; that he participate in the effort of ordering society by achieving order within himself; and so on. The *Cantos,* concerned with the building of cultures and their degradation, sets up a social ideal to be striven for: the equitable distribution of natural abundance among a whole people. And Canto 2 (among others) shows clearly that this ideal can be realized only if the proper man-god relation obtains. It is not that the undivided Light does not continually pour *(i.e.,* that there is not a permanent essential Good); it is that we do not open our eyes to it.

I can only conclude that Eliot's (and Carne-Ross's) inability to recog-nize the essential quality of Pound's Good lies in the fact that Pound does not present it in a single image called God, but presents it in several images according with its several manifestations, and, further, that as Pound finds the Christian symbols empty of meaning, Eliot so finds the Greek (that is, that as, for Pound, Eliot's angels are "spooks," so, for Eliot, are Pound's gods and spirits).

It would seem to me evident that Pound is not quite so superficial in his religious comprehension as his critics have maintained. Interesting evidence supporting this assertion is to be found in some remarks made by Alfred North Whitehead, a thinker with whom many (both scientists and theologians) may disagree but whom few would describe as being superficial. Yet in the quotation with which I shall close this chapter, no sentence will be found to be at odds with Pound's own attitude toward religion.

It was a mistake, as the Hebrews tried, to conceive of God as creating the world from the outside, at one go. An all-foreseeing Creator, who could have made the world as we find it now—what could we think of such a being? Foreseeing everything and yet putting into it all sorts of imperfections to redeem which it was necessary to send his only son into the world to suffer torture and hideous death: outrageous ideas. The Hellenic religion was a better approach, the Greeks conceived of

creation as going on everywhere all the time *within* the universe; and
I also think they were happier in their conception of supernatural
beings impersonating those various forces, some good, others bad;
for both sorts of forces *are* present, whether we assign personality to
them or not. There is a general tendency in the universe to produce
worth-while things, and moments come when we can work with it
and it can work through us. But that tendency in the universe to
produce worth-while things is by no means omnipotent. Other forces
work against it.

God is *in* the world, or nowhere, creating continually in us and
around us. This creative principle is everywhere, in animate and so-
called inanimate matter, in the ether, water, earth, human hearts. But
this creation is a continuing process, and "the process is itself the actu-
ality," since no sooner do you arrive than you start on a fresh journey.
In so far as man partakes of this creative process does he partake of
the divine, of God, and that participation is his immortality, reducing
the question of whether his individuality survives death of the body
to the estate of an irrelevancy. His true destiny as co-creator in the
universe is his dignity and his grandeur. *(Dialogues,* as recorded by
Lucien Price, pp. 370-371.)

Chapter 2

When, in 1919, the idea of a League of Nations was broached, Pound commented emphatically:

> I have no interest in any country *as a nation*. The league of *nations* appears to me about as safe and inviting for the individual as does a combine of large companies for the employee. The more I see of *nations*, the more I loathe them; the more I learn of civilization, the more I desire that it exist . . . . *(The New Age, 26 (18 Dec. 1919) p. 106.)*

From this remark can be inferred the argument of the *Cantos*. A civilized society is preferable to an uncivilized one. But 20th century Europe is anything but civilized.

> The present accounting system murdered five million men between 1914 and 1918. It has done its utmost to suppress all the arts. It has maintained slums and poverty for twenty years when there was absolutely NO need for the continuance of these infamies. *(Polite Essays, p. 107.)*

The question therefore is, what shall a man do to save his own society? And the answer is, as we have already noted, study history—study with the particular view in mind of determining where and when a civilization worthy of the name has flourished and of analyzing the conditions which have been favorable to its growth and those conducing to its decay.

Obviously, if we are to search through time or space for civilized societies, we must know the characteristics of a proper civilization. Broadly speaking, a civilization occurs when the relations between man and god, man and nature, man and man, and man and himself are harmonious. More narrowly, a civilized society will be characterized by "Intellectual Honesty, the Abolition of Violence, the Fraternal Deference of Confucius, and Internationalism." And if we wish to determine whether a given society is erected upon these four pillars, we need only observe the arts; the study of architecture, sculpture, painting, music, and the language arts will show quite clearly the state of health of any society. For when there is good government, art flourishes; when there is not, it declines. And by directing our attention to the arts, we will not be misled by the falsifications and half-truths of official apologists and white-collar white-washers.

But this of course represents only the initial step. If a healthy art is the effect of a healthy government, what is the cause of the healthy government? We must resort to the historians. And here problems arise. Which historians are to be trusted? What account of the past based upon a philosophy of history is other than a non-Euclidean exercise in ingenuity? What account of the past lacking a philosophical frame of reference can compel disconnected facts to cohere meaningfully? What can be learned from a study of history save that history itself is a lie we have agreed to believe?

Pound has considered these questions and not found them unanswerable. He rejects, to begin with, the chronological ordering of fact commonly adopted by historians:

> We do NOT know the past in chronological sequence. It may be convenient to lay it out anaesthetized on the table with dates pasted on here and there, but what we know we know by ripples and spirals eddying out from us and from our own time. (*Guide*, p. 60.)

The chronological narrations which purport to give us historical truth fail in two ways: they give us knowledge without understanding; they tend to focus attention so strictly upon the minutiae of the past that the relation between past and present is minimized. But the only reason for studying the past is, by proper understanding, to improve the present:

> . . . it does not matter a two-penny damn whether you load up your memory with the chronological sequence of what has happened, or the names of protagonists, or authors of books, or generals and leading political spouters, so long as you understand the process now going on, or the processes biological, social, economic now going on, enveloping you as an individual, in a social order . . . . (*Guide*, pp. 51-52.)

Historians are, of course, quite as aware as Pound of the deficiencies of the strictly chronological method of narrating history. They have probed for cause-and-effect relationships, have inferred patterns from their study of events, or, as the Ptolemaic-Thomistic philosophers did upon the natural world, have imposed an arbitrary form upon the human. Thus, in terms of the doctrine of progress, history has been depicted as a straight line ascending to the admirable present; in terms of the doctrine of primitivism, as a descent from a golden age. It has been pictured as a series of cycles and as a pendulum swinging back and forth. Emphasis has been placed upon the actions of great men and upon the struggle of the proletariat.

Pound will not object to a pattern-izing of history, so long as the pattern emerges from a study of historical events, that is, is not an *a priori* interpretation to which data must be coerced into conformation. (Pound remarks of Spengler: ". . . . it may be urged that authors like

Spengler, who attempt a synthesis, often do so before they have attained sufficient knowledge of detail; that they stuff expandable and compressible objects into rubber-bag categories . . . ." *(Polite Essays,* pp. 156-7.) And insofar as Pound thinks it possible to interpret social rise and fall as the result of a single, discernible cause and discovers that these rises and falls recur with a certain regularity, he can be said to be a pattern-izer.

It is, indeed, the historian who out of mental laziness is disinclined to order his facts that Pound despises. His subject is "teacher" in the following quotation, but "historian" will serve as well:

> Until the teacher wants to know all the facts, and to sort out the roots from the branches, the branches from the twigs, and to grasp the MAIN STRUCTURE of his subject, and the relative weights and importances of its parts, he is just a lump of the dead clay in the system. *(Polite Essays,* p. 118.)

And beyond the merely lazy historian is the dishonest one, the apologist whose every ramification of thought has been corrupted by a vicious economic system.

A primary purpose of the *Cantos* is precisely to break down existing historian concepts and to tease or browbeat the reader into investigating for himself significant documents which Pound thinks have been falsified or concealed for partisan reasons by professional historians. His criticism of the syllogistic method of reasoning applies to the writing of history.

> The so-called "logical" method permitted the methodist to proceed from inadequate cognizance to a specious and useless conclusion . . . . This is *not* good enough for the age of Marconi . . . . The scientist today heaps together his facts and has to find organizations that fit them. He must consider his field of reference. *(Polite Essays,* p. 106.)

Pound, then, reads the history books and finds there conclusions about, for example, Malatesta. He does not rest upon the conclusions of others, whom he suspects, apparently, of being "methodists," but himself reads Malatesta's letters, decisions of the papal court—the requisite documents. And instead of wraping the facts to a conclusion, he educes (as he believes) a conclusion from the facts. This is the method of science; it is also the ideogrammic method, involving, as it does, the examination and juxtaposition of particular specimens, or "confrontations between facts relevant to the subjects discussed" *(Polite Essays,* p. 115) without concealment of or evasion from those which appear to be heteroclitic. (He says it in another way in *Guide to Kulchur,* p. 51: "The ideogrammic method consists of presenting one fact and then another until at some point one gets off the dead and desensitized surface of the reader's mind, onto a part that will register.") Now if the facts about Malatesta are relevant, they may be made to confront the facts about Jefferson or

Mussolini, and it is not unlikely that out of such confrontations a pattern in historical events will be revealed.

Thus, though Pound has dispensed with the "logical" method, he has not dispensed with order. He has merely shifted emphasis, from deduction to induction. (A favorite statement of Pound's is that made by K. Bruhns in describing von Humboldt's "art of collecting and arranging a mass of isolated facts, and rising thence, by a process of induction to general ideas.") And he does have a method, one which is, or at least appears to be, based upon that of the provocative 18th century historian Giambattista Vico. The latter's technique was to depict an event which has just occurred and to consider it in terms of various events distant in time or space; that is, collapsing time and space so that a field of reference is formed in which parallels or recurrences may be simultaneously observed. The result may be confusing for the confirmed chronologist, but often for the reader who is willing to accede to Pound's imperative to "renovate, dod gast you," the result will be "suddenly to see" when he snaps out a remark "that reveals the whole subject from a new angle." Further it may be convincingly argued that such a method makes for that intensity which for Pound differentiates poetry from prose.

But a more profound influence than Vico (if Vico was an influence) was the American historian Brooks Adams. Pound has complained that his generation was reared in total ignorance of the economic causes of historical events. His own ignorance was dissipated when he came upon *The Law of Civilization and Decay*, Adams's study of the effect upon society of the accumulation of money. Adams's thesis is that before a given society becomes consolidated, men of imaginative and of martial temperament hold the ascendancy. But with consolidation occurs a profound intellectual change. "Energy ceases to find vent through the imagination, and takes the form of capital; hence as civilizations advance, the imaginative temperament tends to disappear, while the economic instinct is fostered, and thus substantially new varieties of men come to possess the world." (P. 243.) And, says Adams, "nothing so portentous overhangs humanity as this mysterious and relentless acceleration of movement, which changes methods of competition and alters paths of trade . . . ." Pound may or may not have been awakened by Adams to the concept of economic determinism. But here he found a book which did not anesthetize facts upon a table but did show the facts alive as part of a process which has occurred and is occurring, a book, furthermore, that connected the status of the arts with the current use of money. And for supporting evidence he could and did turn to the books of Alexander Del Mar, whose *Barbara Villiers or a History of Monetary Crimes* opens with a sentence which is thematic in the *Cantos:* "The insidious crime of secretly or surreptitiously altering the monetary laws of a State—than which no more dastardly or fatal blow can be struck at its liberties—is not a new one." (In Canto 97 *(Hudson Review,* vol. 9), Pound paraphrases Del Mar at some length.)

At a given time, Pound was keenly interested in Platonism, Hindemith, and "all exploding gunrunnin gunselling jawbreaking and eviscerating and . . . amputating money." To find his interest in the former two incompatible with his interest in the latter would be the greatest of errors. For because of (or, at least, like) Adams he had discovered in the use of money a pervasive influence which conditioned history, lacking consideration of which neither Platonists nor Hindemith could be properly studied. The single book in which he most effectively shows the reciprocal impacts of art and economics remains the famous (or notorious) *Guide to Kulchur,* which may be described as the prose complement of the *Cantos,* save that it lacks the heightened sense of compassion and humility which distinguishes the later-written Pisan section of the *Cantos.* The same puzzled and ambivalent reaction which the *Cantos* has met with greeted this book on its first publication and occurred again on its recent reissue. A review in the *New Yorker* (by Albert Hubbell) serves as a typical example:

> It is a farrago of marginal comment on the state of contemporary letters and Western culture, which is always set forth as failing to measure up to the culture of the East. It is occasionally obscurantist, and occasionally tasteless and embarrassing, but it isn't dull. One pictures Pound prowling around his study muttering imprecations on the people he didn't like (they are legion), engaging in dialogues with himself on Bach, sound money, the "hirelings and boors" who run American universities, the virtues of Mussolini, and every now and then delivering himself of some of the acutest literary criticism of our day. Reading his book is an experience as baffling as it is stimulating. It also gives one something of a pain. (Oct. 4, 1952, p. 121.)

The book is not a farrago, and its comment is anything but marginal. If in any book Pound gets to the heart of his obsessing subject—namely, what makes for and what militates against civilization—it is here. He is saying very much what he has said in earlier books and in his *Dial* and *New Age* articles: that philosophy has been mistaught as "an arid and futile quibble over abstractions" and history as a series of names and dates to be memorized. The idea that the study of history and philosophy might prove at all beneficial in eliminating loan-sharks, bureaucrats, monopolists, prissy snoopers, and the like has been carefully avoided. Leading, Pound says, to "dessication of culture." For "not only is the truth of a given idea measured by the degree and celerity wherewith it goes into action, but a very distinct component of truth remains ungrasped by the non-participant in the action." *(Guide,* p. 182.)

What Pound offers in the place of "The Old Teaching" is "The New Learning." The New Learning requires of the philosopher that he abstain from spinning metaphysical structures out of his bowels and that he consider profoundly the best methods of producing and making available honey and wax. It requires of the historian that he write of the past not to overload his reader's memory but to provoke him to thought and action toward the improvement of the present; that, as Leo Frobenius did, he treat cultures as living organisms, see "through the debris of a civilization its paideumic structure which somehow is never lost and which is ripe for rejuvenation and influence from the best of other cultures, provided the nature of error which ruined it can be known and removed." (Guy Davenport, "Pound and Frobenius," *Motive and Methods in the Cantos of Ezra Pound*, p. 39.) It requires of the reader that he act not merely as passive receptor but also as a philosopher and historian in his own right, that he get for himself the real knowledge enabling him to tell a Goya from a Velasquez, knowledge differing both in kind and degree from that which he would get if he "copied a list of names and maxims from good Fiorentino's *History of Philosophy* and committed the names, maxims, and possibly dates to . . . memory." *(Guide*, p. 28. That is, it requires reading the *Cantos* instead of books like this.) It requires that the gap between the classroom or study and the market place or town hall be closed. It modifies Huey Long's old slogan "Every Man a King" to "Every Man a Philosopher-King"—or perhaps "Every Man a Kung."

Pound objects as much to the method of the old teaching as to its content. The *Guide to Kulchur* (like the *ABC of Reading* before it) exemplifies his idea of an effective text-book. The style, conversational but not chatty, brings him as teacher into close contact with his pupils: he is a sharer rather than a pontiff. His language is never highfalutin nor jargonistic, but he never gives the impression of talking down. As there must be in every good teacher, there is a good deal of "ham" in Pound, and he has not concealed it, as many text-book writers do, on the assumption that to distill out personality is to achieve objectivity, objectivity equaling Truth. Style and personality give the book a vividness and hitting-power not often encountered in academic works. But a more interesting technique is what might be called the Edgar Wallace method of development. According to Pound, "life has mysteries toward the elucidation of which comes, twenty years later, a witness." Orthodox text-books tend to collapse the twenty years, to give the solution of the mystery without endeavoring to recreate the atmosphere of puzzlement and doubt, of patient fitting together of obstinate facts, and the like. That is, they give only the triumphant last chapter. The *Guide*, on the other hand, is developed like a detective story—or, more accurately, like the notes taken by an investigator during the actual investigation. A hunt

plus an exact historiography are involved. What we are looking for is clear
enough:

> One wants to find out by a study of historical evidence what sort of
> things endure, and what sort of things are transient; what sort of
> things recur: what propagandas profit a man or his race; to learn
> upon what the forces, constructive and dispersive, of social order,
> move; to learn what rules and axioms hold firm and what sort fade,
> and what sort are durable but permutable, what sort hold in letter,
> and what sort by analogy only, what sort by close analogy, and what
> sort by rough parallel alone.
>
> *(Patria Mia*, p. 68. This is a very good paragraph to bear in mind
> when reading the *Cantos.)*

The *Guide to Kulchur*, by its broken flow, its ellipses, its disjunct paragraphs, creates the illusion that we are participating in a process—we are,
with Pound, as we read the book, forced to consider evidence, to probe
for a motive, to venture hypotheses, to nose out red herrings. A fact merely
noted at an early point gets developed later when other facts show it to
be significant; facts heaped together in apparent fortuitousness later are
shown to flow into a meaningful pattern. It is only rarely that a researcher
gets across to his reader the fun and excitement of the search for and
discovery of historical evidence. Pound gets it across by making his
reader participate with him in the search.

To reduce Pound's reading of history to order is to risk falsification.
But the risk must be taken. Leading ideas seem to be these:

(1) History tends toward the episodic and cyclical; there is not a steady
ascension toward an ultimate and permanent civilization, nor has there
been a decline from a time when man lived in peace and in accord with
nature. Civilizations have risen; civilizations have fallen. Pound does
not balance a "good" past against a "bad" present. The three great
collapses of civilizations are these: the fall of Alexander's Macedonian
empire; the fall of the Roman empire; the collapse of Italy after 1500.
(Polite Essays, p. 192.)

(2) Without Eleusinian energy civilizations would not rise, without
Kungian order they dissipate themselves. Civilization occurs and maintains itself when the two forces—the striving and the ordering—approach
equipoise.

(3) The two most useful axes of reference in determining the health of
any society are examination of financial practice and examination of the
arts—particularly the language arts. The misuse of money and the misuse
of language are certain symptoms of social illness.

(4) For 20th century occidentals, the Italian Renaissance serves as the
best study of the vicissitudes which any civilization must undergo. The
action is sufficiently localized to be perceived in its entirety, the back-

ground is not incomprehensibly or distractingly exotic or distant in time; the evidence—in the form of artistic monuments as well as historical documents—is plentiful and relatively familiar. And, since we ourselves are involved in the results of actions which produced and debilitated the Italian civilization, it is a particularly relevant study.

(5) However, what has occurred in the Mediterranean basin should not be studied to the exclusion of what occurred more remotely but no less significantly in the other center of culture-dispersion, China. In fact, the greater scope of China's history and European unfamiliarity with it require that it be given in the *Cantos* more detailed and elementary treatment than is devoted to the Italian Renaissance.

(6) The United States, as an experiment in social regeneration occurring when Europe was accelerating its decline (an experiment that failed for clearly ascertainable reasons) and as an archetype of the 20th century with its peculiar problems, must receive especial attention.

(7) Study of history shows that states have been governed in these four ways: (1) by active but insufficiently responsible individuals; (2) by the representative system; (3) by monopolistic financiers; and (4) by enlightened banker-rulers.

(8) The function of the historian in the 20th century is to assist in effecting a change in political organization from the existing (3) to the desiderated (2) and (4). And the historian's responsibility is immense because "As the present is unknowable we roust amid known fragments of the past 'to get light on it,' to get an inkling of the process which produced what we encounter." *(Guide to Kulchur*, p. 129.)

A philosophy of history can be inferred from the *Guide* or the *Cantos*, it is clear; but no more than we have an *Odyssey* or a *Commedia* are we to have a historical narrative as organized by a Spengler or a Toynbee. For Pound's conception, it has been implied, is that "All knowledge is built up from a rain of factual atoms." *(Guide*, p. 98.) And "real knowledge goes into natural man in titbits. A scrap here, a scrap there; always pertinent, linked to safety, or nutrition or pleasure." *(Guide*, p. 99.) Pound admits that an "underlying purpose or current" might be established beneath a series of facts so that education could be expedited, but he fears the method as necessitating too free use of generalization and thus leading away from education to indoctrination. His effort will be to steer a middle course: factual atoms will be rained upon the reader, ideas will be traced, the growth of concepts will be explored, the quality or tendency of a given time's sensibility will be isolated, parallels in history will be pinpointed—all these things will be done, and done as vividly as possible by focusing upon historical figures who will serve as *exempla* and upon epitomizing incidents.

So in the first 51 cantos, which emphasize the Italian renaissance and its aftermath, particular attention will be paid to the governors of various cities who exemplify the types of government mentioned earlier. The first and most completely portrayed of these (in Cantos 8-11) is Sigismondo Malatesta, ruler of Rimini, a city significant only in that Malatesta ruled it. Seen alongside the latter (in Cantos 20, 21, 24, 26) are the Estes (Niccolo III and Borso), and the Medicis, and various condottieri, all men who upheld certain values and brought a kind of order to Italy.

> For if Rome was a conquering Empire, renaissance Italy evolved the doctrine of the balance of power, first for use inside the peninsula. Italy produced notable peacemakers who based their glory on peace tho' it came by the sword. Nic. Este, Cosimo, Lorenzo Medici, even Sforza condottiero, all men standing for order, and, when possible, for moderation. (*Jefferson and/or Mussolini*, p. 79.)

Venice, ruled by an oligarchy (or committee), has, of course, no central figure to exemplify its form of government; attention is directed instead (in Cantos 25-6) to the acts of the governing body—acts which trace the evolution of Venice's form of government, which reveal the Republic's effort to maintain the balance of power, and which suggest its inevitable decline from greatness. It is a declined Venice to which we are first introduced in Canto 3, a 20th century city "where gondolas cost too much." This comment is juxtaposed with passages suggesting parallel failures of Spain, Portugal, and Mantua. But that Pound recognized the Republic's earlier glory is made evident in Canto 17, where, ascending from hell and purgatory under the guidance of Plotinus, Pound comes to an earthly paradise described in terms of Venice's architectural remains.

> There, in the forest of marble,
> the stone trees—out of water—
> the arbours of stone—
> marble leaf, over leaf,
> silver, steel over steel,
> silver beaks rising and crossing
> prow set against prow,
> stone, ply over ply,
> the gilt beams flare of an evening.

Venice was alive and progressing toward the Renaissance when the "forest of marble" took shape; in this canto (19), Pound in person comes to Italy when a new renaissance under Mussolini is under way. Thus the image deriving from what has been is used logically for the present-day parallel. How permanent Mussolini's governmental reforms would prove Pound did not at the time know. He did know that the Venetian oligarchy had increasingly divorced itself from the populace in the 15th century and after. So in Canto 26 and elsewhere we observe Venice on its way to becoming a spawning-ground for Shylocks. With the Shylocks, of course, usury, and with usury, as Pound sees it,

with usura the line grows thick
with usura is no clean demarcation;

Titian superseded Bellini at a time when the Pope wanted "TAXES to build St. Peter's . . . . Thereafter art thickened. Thereafter design went to hell. Thereafter barocco, thereafter stonecutting desisted."

It is in the fifth canto that the third form of government—that by financiers—is first mentioned. (But only obliquely.) Here Pound tells the story of two assassinations—that of Giovanni Borgia, whose throat, in 1407, was cut and his body thrown in the Tiber; and that of Alessandro de Medici, who was murdered in 1536 by his cousin Lorenzino, who thought or pretended to think himself a liberator ridding Florence of a tyrant. (He was received at Venice by Filippo Strozzi with the title of "second Brutus.") Pound's attitude toward the two assassinations is made clear by his interlarding the stories with references to certain poetasters—Barabello, a rhymester who asked to be crowned with laurel in the capital; whose request was, as a joke, granted; who was placed upon the Pope's elephant among fireworks; and who got no laurel because the frightened elephant refused to move. And a certain Mozarello, who, as Pound says

> for ending
> Is smothered beneath a mule,
>   a poet's ending,
> Down a stale well-hole, oh a poet's ending.

In Pound's estimation, bad poetry and social disorder are the results of misgovernment. And misgovernment may be defined as that in which the rulers misuse the wealth of the state. The Medici had made a reasonably good start (see Canto 21); learning and letters flourished under their patronage. But the time came when their banking practices deteriorated—when, specifically, they began to lend money to the princes for their wars, instead of making it available to the mass of people who produce goods. The necessary result was the blasting of the promise which the Medici had offered.

And, in general, things got steadily worse in Italy after the Quattrocento. The Church leaders loosened the restrictions on usury and lost their hold on the people; painting degenerated into baroque; the fine Latin style of a Laurentius Valla deteriorated; the truly poetical was superseded by the deceiving rhetorical; etc., etc. Side by side with these cantos stand those (7, 12, 14, 15, 28) which deal with the ultimate degeneration of the Renaissance—the 20th century scene in England, France, and the United States. And the first thirty cantos are followed by eleven which describe the attempts in France and America to halt the forces of degeneration, again with side-glances at Victorian and contemporary Europe to show their failure.

Before coming to Canto 31, Pound has treated three important matters:
(1) he has expressed an ethic and put it in what he conceives to be a
proper relation to the mysteries which underlie religious faith; (2) he
has introduced his reader to the high civilizations of Homer (Canto 1),
Provence (e.g. Canto 6), and the Quattrocento; (3) he has shown the
end-result in 20th century Europe and America of the decline which
followed the perversion of the ideals of the Renaissance. The focus has
been upon 15th century Europe. The question arises why he should leap
(in Canto 31) so suddenly from that continent to the New World and over
the three centuries intervening between Malatesta and Jefferson.

The answer has three parts. First, if the leap is a startling one geo-
graphically and temporally, it is not ideationally. For like art-works, political ideas have the right to rebirth and recurrence, and it was in the
American Revolution that the ideas of the Italian Renaissance had their
next chance of realization. Second, Canto 30, closing with a Pope's death,
has suggested the end of an era, the era of the Church's domination; Canto
31, focusing on Jefferson, the Deist, shows one significant result of the
Reformation, a Protestant America. Two great schisms are involved:
that in the Church; and that which separated England from Europe to
make it "an annex or an outlying province" (ABC of Reading, p. 101),
and which led to the development of an English-speaking New World.
In a sense, we are closing out the "Catholic" cantos and opening the
"Protestant" cantos. And since, in Pound's belief, Protestantism and
financial malpractice are closely related, our attention will henceforth be
diverted from the defects of centralized government to the defects of
government controlled by the financial interests—defects which have, to
some degree, already been explored.

Third, there is a good deal of truth in the remark of a TLS reviewer to
the effect that Pound "is always enthusiastic about the fresh start, and
he is often bored by the mature development" (Review of Guide to Kulchur, no. 2,649 (7 Nov. 1952) p. 724). Having described the springtime
of the Renaissance and its December in some detail, he has not felt it incum-
bent upon him to devote equivalent space to the interim seasons. They
will not be altogether slighted; but our attention will be first directed to
America's springtime, and dropping the metaphor) the European situation will be seen not in terms of itself but modified by the recollection
of the American effort to avoid that situation. Since we know already that
the effort will fail, the sense of tragic irony is heightened by the inter-
polation at this point of the hopeful four American cantos. And, further,
the poem's texture is thickened, since we witness not merely the European
decline but an American decline (after an exciting birth) paralleling it.
From the French and English points of view, Pound's treatment of history
will seem cavalier, for he has ignored the periods of Racine and Corneille

and of Shakespeare and Milton. But one must remember that this is a corrective poem, that one of its purposes is to correct conventionally received ideas. British historians (particularly the Whiggish Regius professors) have so successfully cornered the intellectual market, have so incessantly advertised the virtues of Shakespeare and his contemporaries, that Americans (in particular) have, Pound thinks, very nearly been bilked of a great part of their heritage. One of the poem's purposes is to break that monopoly.

So in these four American cantos (31-4) Pound ignores or plays down the fact that the colonies developed out of French and English settlements and directs attention to their ideological relation with the Italian Quattrocento. If a distortion of historical perspective is involved, the effect is to rectify a previous distortion.

The relation between Canto 30 and 31 has already been established. But themes in 29 (Cunizza's freeing of the serfs), 28 (the pioneering courage of Pound's grandfather and the Yankee pragmatism of Pa Stadtvolk), and 27 (the "Tovarisch" or revolutionary theme) are also developed in these four cantos. A specific link between Jefferson and Malatesta is made in the first line of Canto 31. And 11. 6-17 (on building a canal system) foreshadow a line in 49 to establish a relation between these American cantos and the Chinese cantos (52-61) to follow.

Thus Pound brings Italy, the United States, and China into one frame of reference. Having noted that there are differences among culture-heroes since "The exact historical parallel doesn't exist," he goes on to show what they have in common: ". . . the opportunism of the artist, who has a definite aim, and creates out of the materials present. The greater the artist the more permanent his creation. And this is a matter of WILL. It is also a matter of the DIRECTION OF THE WILL . . . . this phrase brings us ultimately both to Confucius and Dante." *(Jefferson and/or Mussolini,* pp. 15-16.)

Lines 65-72 of Canto 31 suggest one reason why Pound has chosen to treat the American instead of the French revolution. (The gloss appears in *Ibid.,* p. 14) :

> Jefferson participated in one revolution, he 'informed' it both in the sense of shaping it from the inside and of educating it. He tried to educate another . , . . While fat Louis was chewing apples at Versailles, Lafayette and Co. kept running down to Tom's lodgings to find out how they ought to behave, and how one should have a French revolution.

And the line on Bonaparte's "knowing nothing of commerce," permits a development in succeeding cantos of the Napoleon theme and brings into a single frame Malatesta, Jefferson and Adams, Napoleon (who was "cwushed"), and Mussolini (who was to be "cwushed").

Canto 31 is divided about equally between Jefferson and Adams; 32 is exclusively Adams's; 34 and 37 will introduce Quincy Adams and Martin Van Buren. In these four cantos, we have Pound's economic history of the United States:

> The true history of the economy of the United States, as I see it, is to be found in the correspondence between Adams and Jefferson, in the writings of Van Buren, and in quotations from the intimate letters of the Fathers of the Republic. The elements remain the same: debts, altering the value of monetary units, and the attempts, and triumphs of usury, due to monopolies, or to a "Corner." *(Introduction to the Economic Nature of the United States,* pp. 7-8.)

It may seem odd that, having written the history here, Pound should repeat it in Cantos 62-71, and equally odd that, having devoted a prose work to Jefferson and none to Adams, he should in the *Cantos* give a disproportionate amount of space to Adams. The reasons for both "oddities" appear in the *Guide to Kulchur* (p. 254) :

> The tragedy of the U.S.A. over 160 years is the decline of Adamses. More and more we ed., if we examined events, see that John Adams had the corrective for Jefferson.
>
> In Italy the trouble is not too much statal authority but too little. Liberalism is a running sore, and its surviving proponents are vile beyond printable descriptions . . . .
>
> In our time the liberal has asked for almost no freedom save freedom to commit acts contrary to the general good.

That is, in these four cantos (31-4) we have the history of a construction, in which the four men played such preeminent roles (Van Buren acting as Jefferson's ideological successor to balance the two Adamses). Jefferson is a particularly apt figure to emphasize here, because he serves as an archetype of the initiator, and because, as behind-scenes teacher of French revolutionaries, he pulls together the American and European efforts to combat tyranny. Adams, though a co-partner in Jefferson's initiating activities, more realistically planned toward the maintenance of what had been accomplished by the Revolution.

> John Adams believed in heredity. Jefferson left no sons. Adams left the only line of descendants who have steadily and without a break felt their responsibility and persistently participated in American government throughout its 160 years. *(Jefferson and/or Mussolini,* p. 19.)

But the forces arrayed against Adams were too powerful. The later Adams cantos, then, serve as the first act of a tragedy; and simply because the Adams family continued important in the developing action, Pound has a means of tying the later acts with the first as he could not have done if he had made Jefferson his major figure.

As to the second "oddity," it would be inaccurate to say without qualification that Jefferson represents Eleusis and Adams, Kung. Pound notes that Jefferson, like Odysseus, was *polumetis,* but he also notes that "T. J. had a feeling of responsibility and he knew other men who had it." But he erred in this: ". . . . it didn't occur to him that this type of man would die out." He did not foresee, as Adams did, the necessity of ensuring, by creating a sufficiently powerful statal authority, that responsibile government might endure. The result was that "Adams lived to see an 'aristocracy of stock-jobbers and land-jobbers' in action," and his descendants witnessed their total subjugation of the nation.

Adams and Jefferson had in common elements of Kung and Eleusis, Adams somewhat more of the one, Jefferson of the other. The rub is that contemporary liberalism speaks and acts in the name of Jefferson ("All men are created equal"; "that government governs best which governs least"). In view of his low estimation of liberal thinking, Pound's choice of Adams as the leading figure in his American cantos is seen to be completely logical. Liberalism, as Pound sees it, has got to be counteracted. Since the liberals have rallied around Jefferson (and a fake Jefferson at that, the liberals having misconstrued or falsified the true historical figure), the more successful attack can be made in the name of Adams than of Jefferson, use of whose name would tend to confuse the issue and render the propagandistic effort effective mediately rather than immediately.

Canto 33 breaks into two halves, the first showing the minds of Jefferson and Adams at work, the second (pp. 12 ff.) revealing the ultimate victory of the financial interests; 34 expatiates upon the theme of decline, Napoleon in Europe going to his destruction and, in America, a weak succession of presidents and legislators failing in their duty to the public interest. Allusion to Mordecai Noah's effort to build a haven for Jews in New York (p. 21) reintroduces a Jewish theme and leads to Canto 35, with its depiction of the ascendancy of the Jewish mode of thought which followed upon the defeat of Napoleon and the success of Rothschild. Allusions to 15th century Mantua and Venice show the roots from which the tree sprang. Sentimentality, "sensitivity without direction," a "general indefinite wobble," shrewd commercialism (even in the arts)—in a word, utter bourgeoisiedom—are the elements of Hebraism (as opposed to Hellenism) stressed here. Hyper-usury, or "kikery"—not limited, by any means, to Jews, but, for Pound, epitomized in the Rothschilds—triumphs to give the 19th and 20th centuries their peculiar character.

As if he were re-writing Arnold's *Hebraism and Hellenism*, Pound places next in bold relief the Cavalcanti canto (36). In 35, we are faced with what unfortunately is; in 36, with what has gloriously been—in Provence, in Italy, in colonial America, both in politics and in the arts— and what again can be.

Canto 37, a portrait of Van Buren *(Liberator Fisci)*, shows the Caval- canti mode of thought in operation on the economic, as opposed to the artistic or philosophical level; 38 intertwines paradisal (see p. 40's allu- sion to *Paradiso*, XXVIII, 16-19) and infernal threads, giving hope that the submerged conspiracy of intelligence can again see light; 39's first half re-states in mythological terms the themes of 35, and suggests (again) the means of escape ("been to hell in a boat yet?") : namely, study of history and of the Greek classics, maintenance of the monuments, etc.; 40 shows what happens when economic study is limited to Adam Smith and his successors (the simultaneous advent of Mr. Morgan and flaps, farthingales, unreadable volumes, etc.), but, an exit having been sought and found, leads to realization of the hope of 38, in the figure of Musso- lini, who appears in 41. Mussolini is here contrasted with his contempor- aries, and his place in the line of factive personalities is established.

Then Pound, having placed in view an end-result, reverts, as he so often does, to the point of initial departure, bringing seed and fruit, or root and branch, together. Cantos 42 and 43 describe in some detail the foundation and continued functioning of the Monte dei Paschi to give evidence that, though the Medici had failed as bankers, they had left a legacy which the conspiracy of intelligence (that "outlasted the hash of the political map") could make fruitful use of. "The real history went on," the fourth form of government (see p. 30) came into being; that is, they founded in Siena "A mount a bank a fund a bottom" which, because it was based on right principles ("there first was the fruit of nature/there was the whole will of the people"), has endured to the present time.

Canto 44 continues the intelligent-banking theme by describing a pro- cessional in honor of Pietro Leopoldo, who "declared against exporta- tion/thought grain was to eat." He is balanced against Napoleon who, in some respects a constructive civilizing agent (he gave "artists high rank" and left a code of laws), failed to achieve as much as he might have done, in part because the time was against him (and the Rothschilds and usuri- ous England) and in part because of his insufficient understanding of economics. Napoleon seems, essentially, a belated Malatesta.

The defeat of Napoleon, paralleling but not duplicating the defeats of Malatesta and Jefferson, and opening the question (without stating it) of whether Mussolini, with the same forces arrayed against him, will as certainly lose his battle, necessitates immediate and careful taking stock.

This procedure occurs in the next seven cantos (45-52), and the conclusion to which Pound comes is that we cannot get through hell in a hurry, that still further study of the evidence is indicated. Therefore the need for the subsequent Chinese cantos to which Cantos 45 to 52 serve as an introduction at the same time that they serve to conclude the earlier series.

"Wealth," Pound has said, "comes from exchange, but judgment comes from comparison. We think because we do not know." (A Visiting Card, p. 20.) Among the vaster areas, both in terms of geography and of culture, concerning which most Europeans and Americans know little and think confusedly is China. The Chinese cantos have their inevitable place in the Cantos at large not only because the Chinese culture requires to be known but also because a comparison of it with European culture affords the best basis for a judgment upon the latter. The comparison between China and Europe proves a particularly fruitful one for two reasons. First, the European scene is a confused one; viewing it compares with watching a multiple-ring circus, except, of course, that the ordinary confusion of the real scene is worse confounded than that in the metaphorical, since the performers move from ring to ring, new acts are tried while old ones go on, and the spectators are themselves performers. Chinese history has scope and duration, but it also has unity and continuity; it can be seen as a whole, its components falling into proper perspective, and it can be seen objectively. Secondly, and from Pound's point of view, more importantly, it reveals with admirable clarity what happens in a society which alternately affirms and denies the teachings of Kung. Pound has stated the ethic in Canto 13; now he validates the statement by showing that ethic in successful action and in inanition.

Fenollosa has said that "in Art, as in civilization generally, the best in both East and West is that which is common to the two, and eloquent of universal social construction." The Cantos testifies to the equation, and the transition from the European to the Chinese section is made in terms of it. The case against the destroyers of civilization ("helandros kai heloptolis kai helarxe") has been summed up in 45, the "usury" canto, and again in 46. The succeeding canto brings us full circle to Canto 1 by making explicit what the latter had imagized: the need to seek out the intelligence which will destroy the destroyers:

> First must thou go the road
>   to hell
> And to the bower of Ceres' daughter Proserpine,
> Through overhanging dark, to see Tiresias . . . .

And the greater part of this canto (47) is devoted (in the re-creation of the Tammuz-Adonis fertility rites) to the lesson that only by heeding this admonition can the desired renaissance be achieved. Canto 1, however,

not only imagized the means by which society might be made new but
also (in the *Hymn to Aphrodite* passage) suggested that, when intellec-
tion is divorced from fact to produce rhetoric, the renovating process
ceases. (See pp. 101 ff. for a full discussion of Canto 1.) The function of the
succeeding 46 cantos has been to explore the failure of the European
renaissance so briefly stated in Canto 1. Canto 47 sums the matter up
and thus represents a conclusion. But it also introduces a new theme, and
thus represents a beginning.

This new theme is stated only briefly and tentatively in 47 (p. 31, 11.
48-55) because it involves a learning too briefly and tentatively acceded
to by European intellectual leaders. Hence the failure of the European
renaissance. We must, then, embark upon a new voyage of intellectual
discovery, to question another shade who hath his mind entire and to
learn this: "The inborn nature begets this activity naturally, this looking
straight into oneself and thence acting. These two activities constitute the
process which unites outer and inner, object and subject, and thence
constitutes a harmony with the seasons of earth and heaven." (Confucius,
p. 179.)

The theme of looking straight into oneself and acting to achieve harmony with the seasons occurs in 47 in the translation of excerpts from
Hesiod's *Works and Days:* "Begin thy plowing/When the Pleiades go
down to their rest" *et seq.* It is varied fragmentarily in 48 (the expert
knowledge of the dog-breeder; of the trustees of the Salem Museum; of
the Polynesian boatmen), given full ideogrammic statement in 49, put
into relief by the depiction of its opposite in 50 ("In their souls was
usura and in their hearts cowardice"; "Italy ever doomed with abstractions"; etc.), fragmentized again in 51 (in the fly-fishing passage and
"That hath the light of the doer, as it were/a form cleaving to it"), and
finally given full exposition in 52 (the first of the block of ten Chinese
cantos) in Pound's translation of the Chinese Book of Days in which the
ordered process of life is gathered up into ritual.

In brief, the transition from the Occident to the Orient has been very
carefully made—how carefully is most clearly understood by a study of
45, 47, 49, and 51, each a passage of great lyrical intensity from which the
historical data that support the generalizations have been omitted. 45
reveals the sin, usura; 47 sets against it the active intelligence, Eleusinian
energy; 49 complements 47 by stressing the value of order, the dimension
of stillness. The teaching of 47 is not enough: the "splendour on splendour" of the light that "has gone down into the cave" (p. 32) needs to be
qualified by the light (p. 39) that "moves on the north sky line/where
the young boys prod stones for shrimp." In the two teachings exists the
potential of the culture which usury, social irresponsibility, distraction

from fact, and loss of faith have rendered null—the culture made up of:

(1) a direction of the will;

(2) certain ethical bases, or a general agreement on the relative importance of the various moral, intellectual, and material values;

(3) details understood by specialists and members of the same profession. *(A Visiting Card*, p. 21.)

In the *Guide to Kulchur*, Pound gives his interpretation of history in his own person and his own voice. In the *Cantos*, though the interpretation is Pound's the voice is the voice of the times being interpreted. He does not speak of Malatesta and his milieu from a 20th century point of vantage, that is, try to bring them forward through time to the stationary reader; his effort is to transport his reader back in time to become one of Malatesta's companions-at-arms. R. P. Blackmur and others have spoken of Pound's assuming a *persona* or adopting a mask—identifying himself now with one character and now with another. But more accurately speaking, Pound puts the masks on his readers; they make the quick changes from *persona* to *persona*.

For example, in Cantos 1, 2, and 4, Pound adopts no mask, and, in fact, speaks several times as himself. But with his translation of the *Odyssey* and *Iliad* passages, the description of Tyro's seduction, the Dionysus and Philomela stories, he induces the reader to become temporarily Greek and to participate in the primeval myth of the Mediterranean.

Cantos 57-61, the Chinese cantos, offer no great difficulty to anyone who is well-versed in Chinese history, or who has available the history books which Pound made use of. As for what these cantos teach, Pound himself has summed it up as follows:

> The dynasties Han, Tang, Sung, Ming rose on the Confucian idea; it is inscribed in the lives of the great emperors, Tai Tsong, Kao Tseu, Hong Vou, another Tai Tsong, and Kang Hi. When the idea was not held to, decadence supervened. (Pound's note, p. 189, *Confucius.)*

With the assistance of Mailla's *Histoire Générale de la Chine* or Pauthier's *Chine, ou Description historique, géographique et littéraire de ce vaste empire,* one can thread one's way through the confusion of names with a minimum of difficulty. Perhaps a brief outline will simplify the first reading for those who do not have such a source available:

Canto 52: Pound's translation of the *Li Ki* or Record of Rites, one of the *Wu Ching* or Five Classics, of which the other four are the *I Ching,* or Classic of Changes; the *Shu Ching,* or Classic of History; the *Shih Ching,* or Classic of Poetry; and the *Ch'un Ch'iu,* or Spring and Autumn Annals. These, plus the *Ssu Shŭ,* or Four Books (the *Lun Yü,* or Analects; the *Ta Hsüeh,* or Great Learning; the *Chung Yung,* or Unwobbling Pivot;

and *Mëng Tzü*, or discourses of Mencius) form the "canon" of Confucianism.

Canto 53: Pages 8-9 speak briefly of the following early Chinese leaders: (1) Yeou, a mythical king who taught house-building; (2) Seu Gin, a mythical successor of Yeou, who devised a method of accounting which involved knotting a string; (3) Fou Hi (2953 B.C.), first of the Five Emperors of legendary China; (4) Chin Nong (2838 B.C.) second of the Five Emperors—known as the Prince of Coroalo; (5) Souan yen, a favorite of Chin Nong; (6) Hoang Ti (2698 B.C.), known as the Yellow Emperor; all later princes of China claimed to be his descendants; (7) Ti Ko (2436 B.C.), successor of Tchuen-hio; Pound has skipped over Chao hao and Tchuen-hio; (8) Yao (2357), son of Ti Ko, an ideal emperor; (9) Chun (2255), another ideal emperor—an astronomer and regulator of religious ceremony (Chang Ti is the Ruler of Heaven); (10) Yu (2205), third of the ideal emperors. who controlled the floods of the Yellow River; he formed the First Dynasty, the Hia (or Hsia). Page 10 gives a passing nod to Kao-Yao, a minister under Chun; skips to Chao Kang (2079); adverts to the Five Emperors and associates them with the five elements of Chinese physics—wood, fire, earth, metal, and water; and then notes the founding of the second dynasty, the Shang (or Yin), which endured from 1766 to 1122 B.C. Though this dynasty had 28 emperors, only Tching Tang was noteworthy, as pp. 10-11 indicate. Pound skips 500 years to the advent of Wen Wang, whose son Wu Wang founded the third dynasty—the Tcheou, which existed from 1122 until 255 B.C. Tcheou Kong (adviser to Wu Wang), inventor of a compass, and able administrator, is memorialized here. For a time, after Wu Wang's death, Chao Kong (pp. 13 *et seq.*), another paragon among administrators, served as regent. Such men as these compelled Kung (p. 14) to say, "I am pro-Tcheou." After Chao Kong's time there were no strong rulers in the Tcheou dynasty, and China gradually dissolved into a set of feudal states. Into such a situation Kung (p. 18) was born, to teach and see his teachings ignored.

Canto 54: Page 21 describes the final fall of the Tcheou dynasty and the rise of the fourth dynasty—Tsin (221-206 B.C.); and the rise of the fifth—the Han dynasty (206 B.C.-22 A.D.). Kao Tseu (p. 22), whose example led to the adoption of Confucianism by his house, is a leading figure here, as are Kiao Ouen Ti (or Wen Ti) and Han Sieun. (Pound skips over Wu Ti—the Han Ou of p. 24—though "orthodox" historians pronounce his reign "glorious." The reason is obvious: he was influenced by Taoists so that the influence of Kung's philosophy declined, and he imposed China's first general property tax.) Page 27 leads to the fall of the Han dynasty; pp. 28-30 cover the period of the three Kingdoms (221-265 A.D.) and six minor dynasties (221-589 A.D.). Pages 30-31 cover the brief history of the 12th dynasty, the Soui (589-618 A.D.); p. 31 introduces the Tang (618-907 A.D.). Chief figure here: Tai Tsong (pp. 31-3).

Canto 55: Pages 37-9 show the decline of the Tang dynasty and the rise of the Five Dynasties (907-960 A.D.); p. 40 announces the arrival of the Sung dynasty (960-1279 A.D.). The chief figure is (pp. 42-4) Ouang-Ngan-che (1021-86 A.D.), who proposed a controlled economy whereby the state should take over the entire management of commerce, industry, and agriculture. Important features of this system were loans by the state to farmers so that they could avoid the usurious interest rates of private money-lenders; abolition of the conscription of labor by the state; the return of unnecessary troops to productive civilian life; a shift of emphasis in state examinations from literary style to the application of the principles of the Classics to current problems.

Canto 56: Here the Sung dynasty declines and China falls to the Mongols (1279-1368 A.D.). And (p. 53) the Ming dynasty succeeds (1368-1644 A.D.); its leading figure (pp. 54-7) is Hong Vou.

Canto 57: The history of the Ming dynasty is continued, a dynasty characterized by unity and internal peace, but lacking the originality, intellectual or artistic, of the Tang and Sung dynasties.

Canto 58: Between 1531 and 1598 the Japanese, under the energetic leadership of the commoner Hideyoshi *(Undertree* in the *Cantos)* invaded Korea. In the 17th century, the Nutche clans of the North were united (p. 63) under the leadership of Noorbachu of the Manchu clan and invaded China. Noorbachu died in 1626; his campaign was carried on by Tai Tsong (pp. 65 ff.) until the latter's death in 1643. In 1635 (p. 66) Tai Tsong assumed the style of Emperor of China (49 Mongol chiefs offered allegiance on condition that the King of Korea be forced to do likewise—pp. 67-8); but despite repeated efforts during the next nine years, he was unable to complete the conquest of China. In the meantime, the rebel Li Tseching (p. 68) became ruler of one third of China (destroying Kaifong in the process) and marched on Pekin. The Ming general Ousan invited the aid of the Manchus, who seized the opportunity to take China for themselves. Page 64 describes the efforts of the Italian Jesuit Matthew Ricci (later successful) to establish a mission in Pekin.

Cantos 59-61: These cantos describe the Ching or Manchu dynasty (1644-1838 A.D.) in which Confucian principles ruled, as is suggested by Pound's statement (p. 70) of the first Manchu ruler's opinion of the *Chi King.* The leading figure in Cantos 59 and 60 is Kang Hi (pp. 71 *et seq.)* who, a contemporary of Louis XIV, Peter the Great, and William III of England, was a ruler superior to any of them. Canto 61 considers the careers of Yong Tching (1723-65) and Kien Long (1736-96); hints of the imminent shift of attention from China to the United States appear on pp. 84 and 85.

The equally important histories of Europe and China have now been written, the complementary values of Eleusis and Kung have been described and affirmed. There remains a third area of study, one which offers peculiar advantages of its own. For both China and Europe have had long histories, their beginnings to be seen only as through a reversed telescope. But the history of the United States was initiated so recently, and with the advantage of such a wealth of historical witness, that it compares with an organism seen under a microscope.

Pound could, of course, have chosen to utilize a detail from Chinese history as a corollary to his panoramic view. There had been more than one Adams-like emperor. But Pound is an American; his audience is primarily English-speaking; the dilemma of the 20th century shows to best advantage in the English-speaking countries. To treat what has long ago happened in remote China can have but indirect propagandistic impact—although the Chinese cantos have effectively functioned to emphasize that the 20th century problems are not peculiar to a society conditioned by the new science and technology but are basic problems and to be met with perennially. For the problems of society cannot be solved by political acumen or technological genius. The radical change to be effected is in character, the altering agent is an enlightened ethic. The original sins are identical in China and the United States; the means of salvation have not changed. The decision to spotlight Adams in preference to one of the emperors has been made because of the tactical advantages the choice confers.

So there is no break in the chronological continuity which has held the Chinese cantos together. In 1735 YONG TCHING, "unregretted by scoundrels," died; in 1735 John Adams was born, who sought to bring into a single focus order and liberty. We proceed, as we have done in the immediately preceding cantos, from one dynasty to its successor. Constructive government through the great emperors had gone on in China up to the time of Adams; Adams is simply the next "full-size constructor." The single important difference now encountered is that where to this point the technique was treatment in breadth, now the technique shifts to treatment in depth. It would perhaps not labor the point too much to suggest that the distinction usually made between 52-61 and 62-71 be abandoned and the twenty cantos be considered together as the "Dynastic" cantos.

The character of Adams as interpreted by Pound (from Charles Francis Adam's edition of *The Works of John Adams*) emerges so clearly from these cantos that they do not need annotation to register an effect. It may be prudent, however, to quote at length a Poundian version of American history—one which he used in his broadcasts from Rome during World War II.

Allusion to the broadcasts, as a result of which Pound was confined in a concentration camp and later brought to the United States to be tried for treason, prompts one to remark that, though Pound expatriated himself at an early stage of his career, he has never been other than aggressively American. The recently issued but much earlier written *Patria Mia* perhaps shows his patriotism most obviously, but it is clearly revealed in both the *Guide to Kulchur* and the *Jefferson and/or Mussolini*. The house he wants most to set in order is the American house. The American cantos, therefore, precisely those least esteemed by most critics, are the most doggedly didactic cantos of the poem. He has stated the basic theme of these cantos in an "Introductory Text Book (in Four Chapters)" as follows:

I. All the perplexities, confusion, and distress in America arise, not from defects in their constitution or confederation, not from want of honour and virtue, so much as from downright ignorance of the nature of coin, credit, and circulation. *John Adams.*

II. . . . and if the national bills issued, be bottomed (as is indispensable) on pledges of specific taxes for their redemption within certain and moderate epochs, and be of *proper denominations* for *circulation*, no interest on them would be necessary or just, because they would answer to every one of the purposes of the metallic money withdrawn and replaced by them. *Thomas Jefferson* (1816, *letter to Crawford).*

III. . . . and gave to the people of this Republic THE GREATEST BLESSING THEY EVER HAD—THEIR OWN PAPER TO PAY THEIR OWN DEBTS. *Abraham Lincoln.*

IV. The Congress shall have power:

To coin money, regulate the value thereof and of foreign coin, and to fix the standard of weights and measures. Constitution of the United States, Article I, Legislative Department, Section 8, p. 5. Done in the convention by the unanimous consent of the States 7th September, 1787, and of the Independence of the United States the twelfth. In witness whereof we have hereunto subscribed our names.

George Washington
President and Deputy from Virginia.
(What is Money For? p. 15.)

It was in terms of this reading of American history that Pound made the broadcasts for which he was later charged with treason. In fact, the 8 June 1942 broadcast is merely an elaboration of this "textbook."

. . . This war started in 1696 . . . when Mr. Paterson got the idea for the Bank of England. That is, the angle of getting rich, a scheme whereby a few men were to get rich without working and by defrauding the general public. The bank gets interest on all the money which it creates out of nothing. All right, that was before 1700. What did it lead to?

Suppression of a Pennsylvania colony money. Sort of * money which had brung abundance to Pennsylvania. And that dirty old skunk in London shut down on that money and on other colonial moneys . . . . Bank of England, suppression of Pennsylvania colony money, then came the Revolution. Patrick Henry, George Washington, Samuel Adams, John Adams, with Mr. Jefferson writing the trimming and some of his best ideas being deleted . . . .

Well, Cornwallis surrendered and the Americans set up a government and no sooner had they won that Revolution than muckers began undermining it . . . .

In its ideology, in its principles, it was by God the best government system that the occident had up till then thought of. Despite its flaws and deficiencies, and those deficiencies were inside particular men, not in the conception of government. And that was the American heritage.

. . . then Jefferson and Jim Madison compromised to get the national capital transferred to the banks of the Potomac. God bless them. I thought for a while they hadn't ought to have done that. Well, they were good men, far above human average and they were right in at least one way. In those days it meant getting the government quite a few hours away from the banks of New York. But Lordy, John Adams was lacking in faith or maybe he was just strong in the confidence that the human mind can learn from experience. At any rate he [got] John Quincy Adams elected president . . . . Well, John Quincy was in some ways a Communist—wanted national ownership of most of the national land. Wanted the proceeds to go to education, including astronomy, wrote a thesis on weights and measures instead of . . . occupying his time with the question of money.

That was his error, that is, one of his errors. But he was no slouch . . . . 1700, 1750, and the American Revolution betrayed by Hamilton as far as he could betray it. Restored by Jefferson, Madison, Monroe. upheld by the Adamses. And then came the next fight not stressed in the American schoolboy's school books, the war of Biddle and his Goddamned bank against the American people. A war won by the American people, who [had] Mr. Jackson with Van Buren's assistance; and that friendship is the second great friendship in our history: John Adams and Jefferson, Jackson and Martin Van Buren. And then there had been Jeff and his circle and the tradition of those men was the American heritage. And then came the Civil War and the assassination of Lincoln. And that war was said to be about slavery and the American schoolboy's school books say very little about the effect of debts. Debts of the southern states . . . [to] the bankers of New York City. And if Calhoun's name is still in the text books, his most significant words do not receive emphasis . . . . Both sides upholding an evil, the south wanting to keep chattel slavery and the north wanting something cheaper than slavery . . . . (hired labor is cheaper than slave labor. And you don't really have to feed your employees whereas if your stock is in slaves you damn well have got to feed them.)

Rothschild, John Sherman, ** found the gold. Just put your name on those dynasties, just remember those family names which were not the names of the man who freed us from the shysters of London. Ickleheimer (?), Morton, and Vandergould and John Sherman and Rothschild . . . . And why did that war last long? Well, you can all look into that question, it is discussible. it is highly discussible, but the outcome was the shooting [of] Lincoln and the end of publicity for Lincoln's ideas. . . . "And gave to the people of this republic the greatest blessing they ever had. Their own [paper] to pay their own debts."

. . . how many people did not notice the quick one Sherman and Rothschild put over. The whole government of the United States handed over lock, barrel, and stock to a gang of kike bankers in 1863 by the Federal sub kike assister . . . "We cannot permit the

circulation of greenbacks because we cannot control them" . . . Here
are barriers that ruin the nation, buy the public officials, bleed the
whole nation . . . .

It is not paradoxical to assert that, had Pound not had the courage of
his Americanism, he would not have laid himself open to the ultimate
treason charge. As he said after his arrest, "If a man isn't willing to take
some risk for his opinions, either his opinions are no good or he's no
good."

Whether his opinions are or are not good, he has taken risks for them,
and he has reiterated them over many years in ways ranging from the
barbaric yawp of the broadcasts to the ideogrammically-structured utterance of the *Cantos*. And the risks he took, so he thought, were in a very
good cause: the rescue of a society which, under the misguidance of evil
and of ignorant men, was literally (in Pound's definition of the term)
hell-bent.

Chapter 3

Though Pound was engrossed, during the first world war, in what might be considered the proper studies of a poet-in-training, he found time to investigate the causes of the conflict, which in 1918 dwindled to a conclusion, and to consider the means by which future conflicts might be avoided. His association with A. R. Orage, editor of *The New Age* and a sharp critic both of the British conduct of the war and of the efforts to build a peace, brought him into contact with men whose chief preoccupation was political and economic theory. Among these was Major C. H. Douglas, the originator of the Social Credit theory. In one of the Rome broadcasts of 1942, Pound was to say: "No, I am not a social crediter, I passed by that alley"; but in the early 20's it seemed to him rather less an alley than a boulevard leading to an arch of triumph.

For Pound, the most fruitful of human rights was individual liberty—the right to do whatever harmed no one else. The paramount effort of the intelligentsia, therefore, needed to be directed toward "trying to kill not merely slavery but the desire to enslave; the desire to maintain an enslavement." *(The New Age, 21 (1917), p. 268.)* The tyranny of the common mind, the desire of the "provincials" to coerce everyone into uniformity, these had to be fought on every level. The proper strategy was to determine who profited by keeping the general mind common, to whose interest it was that the newspapers should deal in half-truth and distortion, that the publishing companies should deny their facilities to libertarian writers, that the universities should close their doors to the unusual man. Pound came to the conclusion that the enemy was not a political party, like the Tories, nor a social class, like the bourgeousie, nor a nation, like Germany, but a small, powerfully-knit group of manipulators who, in maintaining an economic system, used parties, classes, and nations (in part through their control of newspapers, publishers, and universities) for their personal aggrandizement.

In brief, Pound had come to an economic interpretation of history, not one, however, focusing attention upon the struggle between the classes or the slow, inevitable working out of an inverted Hegelian dialectic. The object of attention is money and the people who control its distribution. Since the Social Credit theory seems to have been an important step on Pound's *gradus* to his present theory, it seems advisable to quote

47

and paraphrase the standard Social Credit texts to show the kind of theorizing to which he was, in the early 20's, exposed.

The theory starts with a definition. Money may be defined as "any medium which has reached such a degree of acceptability that no matter what it is made of, and no matter why people want it, no one will refuse it in exchange for his product." *(ABC of Social Credit,* p. 15.) Clearly money is not wealth, and a nation's wealth does not consist in its possession of greenbacks or metal currency. "The *real* wealth of any nation is its ability to produce and deliver goods (including services) as, when, and where required. Similarly, the *real* credit of a nation is the belief in that ability, whereas the *financial* credit of a nation is quite simply the estimate of that ability expressed in monetary form. . . ." *(Ibid.,* p. 19.) Now, an industrial society cannot function without credit money. Indeed, the single function of Financial Credit is to set in motion and direct Real Credit. But there is a disharmony between Real Credit and Financial Credit which causes our economic difficulties. The source of Real Credit is the whole community, but Financial Credit is the monopoly of a few individuals.

> By 'cornering' Money, and by requiring that no Real Credit shall be employed save in so far as its employment 'makes money'; furthermore, by controlling the distribution of Money among producers and consumers alike, they are actually able to control, and they do, in fact, control, the whole of Real Credit, which . . . is a communal creation and possession. (C. H. Douglas and A. R. Orage, *Credit-Power and Democracy,* p. 165.)

The specific difficulty with the financial system is that part of the money put into circulation by a bank, as in a loan to a producer, fails to reach the consumer, and a shortage of purchasing power results. Interest on loans, for example, causes such a situation: the debtor is compelled to pay back more money than he was given; this money he takes from the community, which thereby loses "credit" for consumption goods. Thus the system, merely operating under its own momentum, must produce a society in which the majority "cling on to economic life by the eyelids." But the minority who increasingly control Financial Credit are in a position to increase or decrease that momentum as they wish, can flood industry with money or diminish the supply.

Obviously, the only remedy consists in restoring the control of Financial Credit to the government—which, not being a private business, need not be run for profit—in order to ensure an avoidance of the disparity between Real and Financial Credit and an end to the shortage of purchasing power. If this reform were to be put into effect, the Social Crediters believed, it would end labor troubles and internal disruption, would make possible the issuance of dividends by the state, and, more importantly, would change international trade from a "struggle for markets terminating in war, and differing from war only in the nature of the weapons used, into a friendly exchange of superfluities." (H. M. M., *An Outline of Social Credit*, p. 44.)

At the same time that Douglas and his group were propounding this remedy, the diplomats were meeting to form the League of Nations. The Social Crediters saw no hope there, as Douglas's ironic comment on Woodrow Wilson attests:

> . . . he heralded the entry of the United States into world politics by a series of speeches couched in the most silver eloquence, and embodying sentiments calculated to take the thoughts of men clean away from the facts of life; and then, in company with his fellow-conjurers, hatched out a treaty and a League of Nations expressly designed to reduce every one of these beautiful sentiments to a grinning mockery. "Open covenants openly arrived at"; Mr. Lloyd George goes down to Lympne to discuss policy with Sir Philip Sassoon prior to reshuffling the destinies of peoples with M. Millerand; "self-determination"—and admittedly the ordinary everyday liberty of the subject fell during Mr. Wilson's administration of the United States Government to a lower level than that of Russia under the Tsar. *(The Control and Distribution of Production*, pp. 139-140.)

Behind Wilson and George and Millerand stands Sassoon, a leader of the clever minority who are less concerned with making the world safe for mankind than making it safe for International Finance: Sassoon, the hidden hand of International Finance—and a Jew. Douglas takes note of an interesting possibility.

> . . . *The Spectator* recently started a symposium on the subject of 'the Jewish peril' . . . . Most people are no doubt familiar with the general legend, if legend it be. . . .

> It presupposes the existence of great secret organizations bent on the acquisition of world-empire. . . . Like *The Spectator* we have no means of knowing how much of this idea is pure moonshine, or even whether the whole matter is a malignant stimulus to anti-Semitism; but, with that journal, we can understand that it *might* have some foundation in fact, and that, as it puts the matter, we have a good many more Jews in important positions in this country than we deserve. And not only in this country but in every country, certain ideas which are the gravest possible menace to humanity—ideas which can be traced through the propaganda of Collectivism to the idea of the Supreme impersonal State, to which every individual must bow—seem to derive a good deal of their most active, intelligent support from Jewish sources, while at the same time a grim struggle is proceeding in the great international financial groups, many of which are purely Jewish, for the acquisition of key positions from which to control the World-state when formed. We do not believe for a single instant that the average British Jew would countenance such schemes . . . but in view of the curiously circumstantial evidence which is put forward to support such theories, and the immense importance of the

issues involved, we agree that it is very much better that as much
daylight should be allowed to play on the matter as may be necessary
to clear it up. *(Ibid.,* pp. 120-121.)

Douglas is hesitant and tentative in this paragraph, but there can be no
question that the Social Crediters hold Jews—or, at least Jewish bankers—
in low esteem. The *Social Crediter,* the official journal of the movement,
lists among books to be read by its members *The Protocols of Zion.* It
prints (as *The New Age* did) a good many anti-Jewish letters. In a brief
analysis of English history (in the book cited above, p. 55), Douglas
ascribes the depression extending from the Crusades to the Renaissance
to "the fact that the English nobles were all mortgaged to the Jews." And
the Hungry Forties of the 19th century were, he asserts, "no more due
to the Napoleonic Wars than the present industrial distress in this country
is due to the European War. They were due to the hold which financiers,
such as the Rothschilds, obtained upon this country, and the consequent
passing of the Bank Act Charter and other financial restrictive legisla-
tion . . . ." *(Loc. cit.)*

Granting that Pound eventually passed by the Social Credit alley, there
can be no doubt that reciprocal influences ran between him and the
Douglas-Orage group. He and Douglas, for example, shared the idea that
the key to an understanding of history is an understanding of how money
has been used; both agreed that the League of Nations was an instrument
of tyranny, that Wilson was a species of tyrant (Pound believes that the
Federal Reserve Act of 23 Dec. 1913 made the first World War possible
because it opened to international bankers the opportunity of having the
war without themselves having to pay for it); both found themselves in
some accord with what had been for several centuries the orthodox
Christian attitude toward Jews but which liberal thought was in process
of making unorthodox.

Though they had been forming in his mind, it was not till the 30's that
Pound began more or less systematically to publish in book or pamphlet
form his theories on economics. Between 1933 and 1944 came *ABC of
Economics*; *Jefferson and/or Mussolini*; and the six "Money Pamphlets."
His purpose in these books was precisely the one he advocated that
Hemingway adopt:

> . . . why don't you use yr. celebrated bean another 24 minutes and get
> to it that *all* them buggarin massacres are *caused* by money. What is
> money? How does it get that way? . . . .
>
> You seen a lot and unpleasant; but *why was it?* Because some sodo-
> mitical usurer wanted to *sell* the godamn blankets and airplanes. As I
> am trying to indicate in my poem . . . . *(Letters,* p. 283.)

He said it somewhat less disjointedly in *America, Roosevelt and the
Causes of the Present War,* first published in 1944:

Wars are provoked in succession, deliberately, by the great usurers, in order to create debts, to create scarcity, so that they can extort the interest on these debts, so that they can raise the price of money (i.e., the price of the various monetary units controlled by, or in the possession of the same usurocrats), altering the prices of the various monetary units when it suits them, raising and lowering the prices of the various foodstuffs when it suits them, completely indifferent to the human victim, to the accumulated treasure of civilization, to the cultural heritage. (P. 8.)

The great sin of this and preceding centuries has been avarice. The mechanism for setting avarice into action has been usury—usury being understood as "a charge for the use of purchasing power, levied without regard to production, and often without regard even to the possibilities of production." Among the great usurers Jews have been notable, but "usurocracy" is not by any means exclusively Jewish. An important consequence of usury has been the destruction of anything beyond a mere semblance of democracy:

It's so much waste of time to speak of this or that "democracy." The real government was, and is, to be found behind the scenes. The "democratic" system works as follows. Two or more parties, all under orders from the usurocracy, appear before the public. As a matter of form, and to reassure the simpletons, some honest men and one or two independent idealists are allowed to do a little clean work as long as they don't touch the various rackets. The biggest rackets are those of finance and monopolization, including the monopolization of money itself, both within the nation and in combination with the various foreign currencies. *(Ibid.*, p. 17.)

Strenuously opposed to usury, Pound spent a great deal of time and intellectual effort between 1934 and 1944

towards establishing a correlation between Fascist economics and the economics of canon law (i.e., Catholic and medieval economics), on the one hand, and, on the other, Major Douglas's Social Credit proposals together with those of Gesell, known as the "Natural Economic Order," or sometimes as "Freiwirtschaft." *(Ibid.*, p. 16.)

Of Douglas and Gesell, Pound has said elsewhere: "Two men have ended the Marxist era, Douglas in conceiving the cultural heritage as the great and chief fountain of value, Gesell in seeing that 'Marx never questioned money. He just took it for granted.' " *(Social Credit: An Impact,* p. 13.)

Gesell's effort was to increase the velocity of the circulation of money—that is, to counteract hoarding—and he proposed to do so by the issuance of "stamp scrip." Pound describes his theory as follows:

This should be a government note requiring the bearer to affix a stamp worth up to 1% of its face value on the first day of every month.

Unless the note carries its proper complement of monthly stamps it is not valid.

This is a form of TAX on money and in the case of British currency might take the form of ½d. or 1d. per month on a ten shilling note, and 1d. or 2d. on a pound. There are any number of possible taxes, but Gesell's kind of tax can only fall on a man who has, in his pocket, *at the moment* the tax falls due, 100 times, at least, the amount of the tax.

Gesell's kind of money provides a medium and measure of exchange which cannot be hoarded with impunity. It will always keep moving. Bankers could NOT lock it up in their cellars and charge the public for letting it out. It has also the additional benefit of placing the sellers of perishable goods at less of a disadvantage in negotiating with owners of theoretically imperishable money. (*What Is Money For?* pp. 8-9.)

A general summary of Pound's theory of money might read as follows: The AIM of a sane and decent economic system is to fix things so that decent people can eat, have clothes and houses up to the limit of available goods. Money is a freely-circulating measure of goods and services; its function is to get a country's food and goods justly distributed. When we do not hand over money at once for goods or services received we are said to have "credit"—another man's belief that we can and will some time hand over the money OR something measured by money. The state has credit. This credit rests *in ultimate* on the ABUNDANCE OF NATURE, on the growing grass that can nourish the living sheep. It is the business of the STATE to see that there is enough money in the hands of the WHOLE people, and in adequately rapid EXCHANGE to effect distribution of all wealth produced and producable. Distribution is effected by little pieces of paper. If you don't know how they are made, who makes them, who controls them, you will be diddled out of your livings. STATE AUTHORITY behind the printed note is the best means of establishing a JUST and HONEST currency. (The Chinese grasped that over 1,000 years ago, as we can see from the Tang STATE (not Bank) NOTE.) SOVEREIGNTY inheres in the right to ISSUE money and to determine the value thereof. Only the STATE can effectively fix the JUST PRICE of any commodity by means of state-controlled pools of raw products and the restoration of guild organization in industry. A nation whose measure of exchange is at the mercy of forces OUTSIDE the nation, is a nation in peril. STATAL MONEY based upon national wealth must replace GOLD manipulated by international usurers. (These sentences extracted from contexts in *What is Money For?* and *Social Credit: an Impact.*)

And in *Gold and Work* he has vividly described the society which would appear if such principles were put into effect:

On the 10th of September last, I walked down the Via Salaria and into the Republic of Utopia, a quiet country lying eighty years east of Fara Sabina. Noticing the cheerful disposition of the inhabitants, I enquired the cause of their contentment, and I was told that it was due both to their laws and to the teaching they received from their earliest school days.

They maintain (and in this they are in agreement with Aristotle and other ancient sages of East and West) that our knowledge of universals derives from our knowledge of particulars, and that thought hinges on the definitions of words.

In order to teach small children to observe particulars they practice a kind of game, in which a number of small objects, e.g., three grains of barley, a small coin, a blue button, a coffee bean, or, say, one grain of barley, three different kinds of buttons, etc., are concealed in the hand. The hand is opened for an instant, then quickly closed again, and the child is asked to say what it has seen. For older children the game is gradually made more elaborate, until finally they all know how their hats and shoes are made. I was also informed that by learning how to define words these people have succeeded in defining their economic terms, with the result that various iniquities of the stock market and financial world have entirely disappeared from their country, for no one allows himself to be fooled any longer.

And they attribute their prosperity to a simple method they have of collecting taxes or, rather, their one tax, which falls on the currency itself. For on every note of 100 monetary units they are obliged, on the first of every month, to affix a stamp worth one unit. And as the government pays its expenses by the issue of new currency, it never needs to impose other taxes. And no one can hoard this currency because after 100 months it would have lost all its value. And this solves the problem of circulation. And because the currency is no more durable than commodities such as potatoes, crops, or fabrics, the people have acquired a much healthier sense of values. They do not worship money as a god, they do not lick the boots of bloated financiers or syphilitics of the market-place. And, of course, they are not menaced by inflation, and they are not compelled to make wars to please the usurers. In fact, this profession—or criminal activity—is extinct in the country of Utopia, where no one is obliged to work more than five hours a day, because their mode of life makes a great deal of bureaucratic activity unnecessary. Trade has few restraints. They exchange their woollen and silk fabrics against coffee and groundnuts from their African possessions, while their cattle are so numerous that the fertilizer problem almost solves itself. But they have a very strict law which excludes every kind of surrogate from the whole of their republic. . . .

Inscribed over the entrance to their Capitol are the words: THE TREASURE OF A NATION IS ITS HONESTY. (Pp. 3-4).

Pound's attacks as a literary man upon usury, iniquitous taxation, governmental coercion, and the horrors of industrialism are nothing new. He takes his place with Emerson, Thoreau, Cooper, Howells, Clemens, Dickens, Morris, Ruskin, Carlyle, Shaw, the muckrakers, and so on as a writer who refused to evade or retreat from his social responsibilities. He may have arrived in London in 1910, as someone has said, a belated

member of the Pre-Raphaelite Brotherhood. He was to become the literary world's most outspoken critic of the "mob-minded money-lusting crew
that holds the world in fee." (Babette Deutsch, *This Modern Poetry*,
p. 117.)

There are still, as there have been over the past three or four decades,
complaints that contemporary poetry is written in a private language
to be understood only by a restricted coterie, and that, therefore, the poets
have failed in their obligation to society. Thus Robert Spector ("Pound
as Pound," *History of Ideas Newsletter*, Feb., 1958, p. 10) refers to Pound's
complete disdain and scorn in the mere matter of "communicating with
the more than 95 per cent of his 'uncultured' audience." But the fact is
that Pound pours out his disdain and scorn upon the 5% who are, as he
sees it, responsible for keeping the 95% "uncultured." Granted that Pound
has written a difficult poem, he has not made his attack upon the enemy
in a private language nor for the benefit of an exclusive minority. To the
contrary, he has been all too explicit.

Taking the foundation of the Bank of England (which "hath benefit
of interest on all the moneys which it, the bank, creates out of nothing")
as a point of departure, he traces the history of England

> . . . on through the ages of usury
> On, right on, into hair-cloth, right on into rotten building,
> Right on into London houses, ground rents, foetid brick work,
> (Canto 46, p. 27.)

He notes the accomplishments of the New Deal:

> FIVE million youths without jobs
> FOUR million adult illiterates
> 15 million 'vocational misfits,' that is with small chance for jobs
> NINE million persons annual, injured in preventable industrial
> accidents
> One hundred thousand violent crimes. The Eunited States ov
> America
> 3rd year of the reign of F. Roosevelt, signed F. Delano, his uncle.
> CASE for the prosecution. That is one case, minor case
> in the series/Eunited States of America, a.d. 1935
> England a worse case, France under a foetor of regents.
> (Canto 46, p. 29.)

He observes typical commentators upon the present scene:

> and the swill full of respectors,
>   bowing to the lords of the place,
> explaining its advantages,
>   and the laudatores temporis acti
> claiming that the sh-t used to be blacker and richer
> and the fabians crying for the petrification of putrefaction,
> for a new dung-flow cut in lozenges,
> the conservatives chatting,

distinguished by gaiters of slum-flesh,
and the back-scratchers in a great circle,
        complaining of insufficient attention,
the search without end, counterclaim for the missing scratch
                                        (Canto 15, p. 64.)

He considers a basic cause of the Civil War:

Debts of the South to New York, that is to the
banks of the city, two hundred million,
war, I don't think (or have it your own way . . .)
about slavery?   (Canto 46, pp. 25-6.)

And refers to an incident (not military but nevertheless significant) of
that war:

'62, report of committee:
Profit on arms sold to the government: Morgan
(Case 97) sold to the government the government's arms. . .
I mean the government owned 'em already
at an extortionate profit
Dollars 160 thousand, one swat, to Mr. Morgan
for forcing up gold.
"Taking advantage of emergency" (that is war)
After Gettysburg, down 5 points in one day—
Bulls on gold and bears on the Union
"Business prospered due to war's failures."
                                        (Canto 40, pp. 47-8.)

He describes a later version of this type of leader of the people:

                the ranked presbyterians,
        Directors, dealers, through holding companies,
        Deacons in churches, owning slum properties,
                Alias usurers in excelsis,
                the quintessential essence of usurers,
        The purveyors of employment, whining over their 20 p.c.
                        and the hard times,
                And the bust-up of Brazilian securities
                        (S. A. securities),
        And the general uncertainty of all investment
                Save investment in new bank buildings,
                        productive of bank buildings,
                And not likely to ease distribution
                                        (Canto 12, p. 55.)

And suggests, in a paraphrase of Adams, that a reason for the continued
success of their operations is

. . . . that despotism
or absolute power . . . unlimited sovereignty,
is the same in a majority of a popular assembly,
an aristocratical council, an oligarchical junto,
and a single emperor, equally arbitrary, bloody,
and in every respect diabolical. Wherever it has resided
has never failed to destroy all records, memorials,

all histories which it did not like, and to corrupt
those it was cunning enough to preserve.. . . . (Canto 33, p. 10.)

To find such passages as these esoteric seems to me perverse. The basic
sin is clearly isolated; the malefactors are named; the results are described. And possible solutions—quite down-to-earth ones—are suggested. As
in this paraphrase of C. H. Douglas (p. 40, Canto 38):

A factory
has also another aspect, which we call the financial aspect
It gives people the power to buy (wages, dividends
which are power to buy) but it is also the cause of prices
or values, financial, I mean financial values
It pays workers, and pays *for* material.
What it pays in wages and dividends
stays fluid, as power to buy, and this power is less,
per forza, damn blast your intellex, is less
than the total payments made by the factory
(as wages, dividends AND payments for raw material
bank charges etcetera
and all, that is the whole, that is the total
of these is added into the total of prices
caused by that factory, any damn factory
and there is and must be therefore a clog
and the power to purchase can never
(under the present system) catch up with
prices at large,

and the light became so bright and so blindin'
in this layer of paradise
that the mind of man was bewildered.

In brief, it is not Pound's obscurity but his clarity, not his avoidance
of responsibility but his vigorous acceptance of it—his translation of his
ideas into action—which lies at the root of most if not all criticism of
Pound both as man and as poet. It could scarcely be otherwise. He
attacked the sterility of academicism, the venality of the press, the monetary stupidity of Communist leaders, the maleficence of finance-capitalism,
the confusion and volitionlessness of liberalism, the dogmatism of Catholicism, the passivity and subservience of Anglicanism, the moral blindness
of Protestantism, the impercipience of publishing houses and of journalistic critics. That is, he attacked precisely the most articulate segment of
society, precisely those groups having most immediate access to the means
of reply, indeed, precisely those groups in control of those outlets.

Further, he praised Fascism and criticized Jews. Some acquaintance
with Pound's money theories is required for understanding the *Cantos,*
for they constitute an integral part of the poem's reason for being and
its meaning. And his attitude toward the Jews, since it seems primarily to
evolve out of his money theories and out of his reading of Brooks Adams's

study of history, needs to be discussed. However, save for isolated passages, his presumed Fascism has no bearing on the poem. It would not be necessary to discuss it at all had not so much been made of it on the journalistic level that it stands as a lion in the path distracting many readers from the proper object of study, Pound's poem.

Pound seems never to have been a "card-carrying member" of the Fascist party in Italy. The *Mercure de France* (1-IV-1949), after publishing an article in which Pound was charged with having become a Fascist and having broadcast under orders of the Italian government, received letters from Luigi Villari, "*Ancien fonctionnaire du Ministère Italien de la Culture Populaire, dont la radio dépendait,*" Carlo Scarfoglio, "*Journaliste antifasciste dès le début du régime de Mussolini,*" Camillo Pellizzi, "*professeur d'Université en Italie,*" Mrs. Dorothy Pound (the poet's wife), and others, all attesting that Pound had not been a Fascist, and that, after the United States' declaration of war against Italy, he had refused to make further broadcasts until he had been assured that he could continue to express his personal opinions freely and would not be required to make any remarks contrary to his sentiments of loyalty toward his country. In brief, he demanded, and got, even in war-time in a dictatorship, the privilege of free speech. (In the 19 April '42 broadcast, he said: "I have been offered the freedom of the microphone and I'm now going to take it, quite unsupported. . . .") He did, it is true, make use of that privilege to attack the policies of President Roosevelt, with particular reference to his allying the United States with England in a state of undeclared war regardless of the opinion of the citizenry; to his maneuvering in such a fashion in the Sino-Japanese situation that Pearl Harbor became an inevitability; to his allying the country with what Pound believed to be the real enemy, Communist Russia. In so doing, he was expressing an opinion of long standing, namely, that Roosevelt was endangering the Constitution of the United States. (Mrs. Pound notes in this connection that Pound had accepted from Fascist theory only that which was in conformity with the doctrines expressed in the Constitution.) Almost identical opinions of Roosevelt's policies were voiced by reputable (or at least exceedingly popular) newspapers both before and during the war without their editors' being arraigned for treason. Pound's error apparently lay not in his holding or broadcasting these opinions but in broadcasting from an enemy station. According to a statement in *Twentieth-Century Authors* (ed. Kunitz and Haycraft, 1942), Pound made plans to leave Italy for the United States at the outbreak of the war but was denied permission to leave by United States officials. If this is true, it was an ironic concatenation of events which placed the poet in St. Elizabeth's Hospital.

It would seem, then, that technically Pound might be charged with treason. It would also seem that, essentially, he should be charged only with having been for some years, and for well-defined reasons, an Italophile.

Early in the '20's, post-war London appealing to Pound as too miasmic to be endured, he moved on to Paris, where he employed his abundant energy in assisting all sorts of young artists to get a hearing—arranging for concerts, sponsoring literary reviews, writing letters and criticisms, reading and editing manuscripts, in brief, working like a doctor in an epidemic-stricken area to protect the "sound core." He studied sculpture with Brancusi and music with George Antheil, worked with Ford Madox Ford toward the publication of literary journals, advised Hemingway, fought for Joyce, assisted Eliot with *The Waste Land*, and so on.

With all his vitality, Pound could not go on forever at the pace which he had set himself, or which was set for him by the demands of the time, and he finally gave up residence in the "enervated center" for a home in a "reawakening Italy." (In the passage where he thus describes Paris and Italy, London is a "decadent wallow," and America "inchoate.")

Here, if anywhere, Pound touched home base. Not primarily because Italy was a vast art museum and thesaurus of historical remains, nor because Gods floated in the azure air (though both were important considerations), but because Italy after its long period of torpor was climbing uphill, while England and France were hastening their yoked descent and America seemed to be going simultaneously in all directions, "the betrayal of the constitution festering in every vein." Here Pound saw at first hand the effect which Mussolini had had upon the nation. His observation corroborated Lincoln Steffens's:

> Like the Russians, the Italians were worried and debating what to do until Mussolini came along, as Lenin did, and said, "Let George do it." . . . When Mussolini said that they, the people, might stop governing and go to work—he would do it all—it was almost as if all Italy sighed and said, "Amen." And the people did go back to work, and they worked as they had not worked before. *(The Autobiography of Lincoln Steffens, p. 818.)*

Of Mussolini, Pound wrote in those early days:

> I personally think extremely well of Mussolini. If one compares him to American presidents (the last three) or British premiers, etc., in fact, one can *not* without insulting him. If the intelligentsia don't think well of him, it is because they know nothing about "the state," and government, and have no particularly large sense of values. Anyhow, *what* intelligentsia? *(Letters, p. 205.)*

His admiration for Mussolini's active efforts toward Italy's revitalization was to increase in about a direct proportion to American liberals' antipathy. The question of whether Pound or the latter saw Mussolini with less distortion cannot yet be answered. It is not improbable that the characteristic liberal attitude was in great part shaped by, on the one hand, the British opinion-moulders, who recognized an active Italy as a threat to their hegemony over the Mediterranean, and, on the other hand, by the Communist propagandists, who were understandably bitter that Mussolini had anticipated and aborted their proposed *coup*. There is, accordingly, some likelihood that in the decades to come when all the parts of the picture fall into place, Mussolini will appear much less the tyrant or the buffoon than he was made to appear in the '30's. The case of Bloody Mary, who spilled very little more blood than Elizabeth (Good Queen Bess), is instructive here.

But these considerations, in the '20's, were things to come. What Pound saw was a man of tremendous energy and will, "an OPPORTUNIST who is RIGHT, that is who has certain convictions and who drives them through circumstance, or batters and forms circumstance with them" *(Jefferson and/or Mussolini,* pp. 17-18): an Italian "driven by a vast and deep 'concern' or will for the welfare of Italy, not Italy as a bureaucracy, or Italy as a state machinery stuck up on top of the people, but for Italy organic, composed of the last ploughman and the last girl in the olive-yards. . . ." *(Ibid.,* p. 34.) And Pound, always a proponent of "the Mediterranean sanity," supported this because

> EUROPE being what it is, the Hun hinterland epileptic, largely stuck in the bog of the seventeenth century, with lots of crusted old militars yelling to get back siph'litic Bill and lots more wanting pogroms, and with France completely bamboozled by *La Comité des Forges,* and, in short, things being what they are in Europe, as Europe, I believe in a STRONG ITALY as the only possible foundation or anchor or whatever you want to call it for the good life in Europe. *(Loc. cit.)*

After the first world war, Pound had diagnosed London as being "in terror of thought" and Paris as "tired, very tired," but Italy as being "full of bounce." *(Ibid.,* p. 49.) He quotes an Italian writer as saying ". . . . it is terrible to be surrounded by all this energy and . . . and . . . not to have an idea to put into it." Mussolini's achievement, so Pound has believed, was to make constructive use of that energy, to propound and to direct a "continuing revolution" with the material and immediate effect of

> *grano, bonifica, restauri,* grain, swamp-drainage, restorations, new buildings, and, I am ready to add off my own bat, AN AWAKENED INTELLIGENCE in the nation and a new LANGUAGE in the debates of the Chamber. *(Ibid.,* p. 73.)

(In the 20 April '42 broadcast Pound comments: "The Italians are the greatest kickers on earth . . . . Italian individualism; development of personality, reads to the point of exaggeration . . ." and argues that "Nothing less than the Fascist system would keep these people together."

In this broadcast he cites as progressive achievements the drainage of swamps; increased grain yield; an increase in living quarters for "dark race sectors of the nation's community"; an increase in electric power "so as they don't have to waste their substance buying dirty old smoke coal [from] England"; and the syndicalist method of representation.

So Italy, revitalized by Mussolini, suited Pound as neither London nor Paris before it had done. This is not to say that he had become converted to Fascism as one is converted to Communism or Catholicism as the single and universal means to salvation. As he says:

> Mussolini has never asked nations with a different historical fibre to adopt the cupolas and gables of fascism. Put him in England and he would drive his roots back into the Witanagemot as firmly as Douglas. *(Ibid.,* p. v.)

But the basic ideas, witness their similarity (in his estimation) to those of Confucius and of Jefferson, had, he thought, universal validity if, in their externals and in the means by which they were put into effect, they were conditioned by the particular scene of their operation and the problems indigenous to their culture. (He does not have much to say of Hitler or of National Socialism because, he says, he had no first-hand knowledge. He had, however, read *Mein Kampf* and found three points of Hitler's program to be sensible: the application of eugenic theory to human beings as well as to cattle—Pound makes no reference to Aryanism or Semitism here; the requirement that public officials be held personally responsible for their actions; and the suggestion to study history. See 18 May '42 broadcast.)

Apparently, then, it was not as an official Fascist propagandist, and not with treasonable intent, but as a dissenting American opposed to the course his country was embarked upon that he made the broadcasts which have sent him from concentration camp to treason trial to mental hospital. The broadcasts, as a matter of fact, are almost altogether reiterations of what he had been saying in prose and poetry for two decades—that materialism, usurious practice, the habit of conformity, and economic illiteracy were throttling civilization. As has been suggested, these are basic ideas in the *Cantos*, stated and stated again on various levels of language. It is a matter of remark that nowhere in the *Cantos* does Pound stipulate the adoption of the Fascist form of government as the salvation of any nation. There are a few sympathetic references to Mussolini, but he is a completely minor figure in the poem compared, for example, to Adams or Jefferson or Jackson.

If the evidence clears Pound of the charge of Fascism (beyond an admiration for Mussolini as a "factive personality" and a sympathy with his plans to re-vitalize Italy), the evidence is not so persuasive in the matter of anti-Semitism.

This is a ticklish subject. For many Jews, aware of the persecution of their group over the centuries, particularly aware of what has occurred in the past three decades, aware that for themselves the trivial irritations of today may become the persecution of tomorrow, any utterance not unqualifiedly anti-anti-Semitic may well be construed as anti-Semitic. It is a fact, therefore, that one must tread as though on egg-shells when writing of an alleged anti-Semite, as he need not in dealing with a person of anti-Catholic, Anglo-phobic, anti-Communist, or similar propensities. His very effort to be objective and dispassionate, to qualify and differentiate, is likely to be held suspect.

The question, I suppose, is this: are there degrees and kinds of anti-Semitism? Or is it the case that a man can no more be a little bit anti-Semitic than a woman can be a little bit virginal?

Pound himself is an inveterate differentiator. He has always striven for precision, for the unsquashable monad of thought. Early in his intellectual career he found a fellow-striver in Remy de Gourmont, author of, among other things, the essay *La Dissociation des Idées*. De Gourmont's method was to examine a concept ordinarily taken as a unit and to subdivide it into its overlooked or forgotten components. His finding was that man characteristically "associates his ideas, not in accordance with logic, or verifiable exactitude, but in accordance with his desires and his interests." Like de Gourmont, Pound functions as an exploder of stereotypes. (He was sufficiently interested in semantics at one time to write C. K. Ogden projecting the plan of writing a canto in Basic English.) As a matter of fact, the major confusion in the *Cantos* for the unknowing reader lies in the fact that in the poem he gets the shattered fragments (the overlooked or forgotten components) rather than the concept-taken-as-unit. Thus, in Canto 13, instead of a generalization about Kung's teaching, Pound offers these fragments, which the reader must himself put together:

And Kung gave the words "order"
and "brotherly deference"
And said nothing of the "life after death."
And he said
          "Anyone can run to excesses,
It is easy to shoot past the mark,
It is hard to stand firm in the middle."

And they said: If a man commit murder
          Should his father protect him, and hide him?
And Kung said:
          He should hide him.

No great difficulty obtains here in building a concept, since the subject of discourse is clearly delineated. But in a passage like the following, where one may not know who Commander Rogers, Giles, and young Jessie are, where there appears no obvious relation between Commander Rogers and Rossini, where no hint exists as to what sort of concept is supposed to be built, the difficulty is a good deal greater:

> Commander Rogers observed that the sea was sprinkled with
>   fragments of West India fruit
> and followed that vestige.
>   Giles talked and listened,
> more listened, and did not read.
>   Young Jessie did not forward dispatches
> so Fremont proceeded toward the North West and
>   we ultimately embraced Californy
> The Collingwood manned 80 guns.
>   "Those who wish to talk
> May leave now" said Rossini,
>   "Madame Bileau is going to play."

Pound can conceptualize, of course, can write a perfectly orthodox essay with normally generalized sentences, sentences logically and grammatically linked to one another. And the critics have invited him (vigorously) to return to this technique in the *Cantos*. He has not heeded their invitation.

But in the profile of the classic anti-Semite, a basic feature is the inclination, not to shatter stereotypes, but to formulate them. With reference to the Jews, one would expect Pound, unless in their case he has a blind spot, to undertake his usual differentiations. And so he does.

Considering the word "anti-Semitic" to be "idiot terminology," he dislikes its application to himself. He is not, however, averse to having substituted for it the phrase "anti-Kabal-system." What is involved here is a dissociation between the harmful and the innocent Jew like that made in the 1 June '42 broadcast: "Lay off the poor Jews, lay off Mike's [Michael Gold's] 'Jews without Money'; meet the Shatkans or Sassoons, they are amongst you and their money is working. . . ."

A similar dissociation had been made in the 30 April broadcast:

> Don't start a pogrom. That is, not an old style killing of small Jews. That system is no good, whatever. Of course, if some man had a stroke of genius, and could start a pogrom up at the top . . . there might be something to say for it. But on the whole, legal measures are preferable. The 60 Kikes who started this war might be sent to St. Helena, as a measure of world prophylaxis, and some hyper-Kikes or non-Jewish Kikes along with them.

With these comments Pound has at least dissociated himself from Dachau and Buchenwald, the gas-chambers and the cattle-trains. On the other hand, he has indicated here (and in other broadcasts and elsewhere) a belief that Jewish financial influence is such that it has had, over the past century, an effect as if a world conspiracy were in operation. In Canto 52, for example, he speaks of the "poor yitts . . . paying for a few big jews' vendetta on goyim."

It will be a rare liberal who will not wonder how such an opinion could emanate from a man so intelligent and well-read as Pound. It will not have appeared, save to be derided, in *The Saturday Review*, *The Partisan Review*, *Nation*, *The New Republic*, and other such journals of his acquaintance, and will, on the other hand, have 'appeared in various disreputable, almost illiterate "hate-sheets," of which he has some knowledge. He will perhaps never have read an intelligent, scholarly discussion of the evidence which might be found to support such a belief; but he will have encountered and properly discounted the unsupported exclamations of fanatical bigots. He will recognize no option, therefore, but to associate Pound with the latter. Or, at best, with the more literate and better-mannered but, in his opinion, almost equally illiberal elements which he finds in the Catholic Church. (And associates, in his mind, with the support of Franco, the ban on contraception, Mariolatry, Papal infallibility, and other vestiges of what he considers medieval superstition and tyranny.) And if he reads in Abram Sachar's *A History of the Jews* that the Montefiores, Salomons, and Goldsmids in England, the Pereires in France, the Bischoffsheims in Germany, and the Rothschilds everywhere in Europe became in the 19th century sufficiently powerful to influence history, he will agree with that author that such influence did not imply the formation of groups to control international finance.

But he is an American liberal reading a book written by the president of Brandeis University. A European Catholic of the landholding class, equally well-educated, might draw a quite different inference from the stated facts. Each has been conditioned; each has his bias; it is unlikely that either will make the exhaustive study necessary to test Professor Sachar's conclusion, which is merely stated, not supported by evidence. This is not to say that the liberal is wrong and the hypothetical landholder right but only that belief in the excessive power of Jewish financiers and even in their forming secret organizations is not *necessarily* the hallmark of the illiterate, the crackpot, or the man of ill will. Pound is no more to be thought associated with such groups because of his belief than is Paul Blanshard for his analysis of the power of the Catholic Church.

Brooks Adams, it will be remembered, made a sharp distinction between the society in which the martial and imaginative mind held ascendancy and that in which the usurious mind dominated. He analyzed the 19th century as follows:

. . . one of those vast and subtle changes was impending, which, by
modifying the conditions under which men compete, alter the com-
plexion of civilizations. and which has led in the course of the nine-
teenth century to the decisive rejection of the martial and imaginative
mind. *(Op. cit.,* p. 324.)

Or, as he puts it more specifically: "From the year 1810, nature has
favoured the usurious mind, even as she favoured it in Rome, from the
death of Augustus," a condition which, he argues, "marked the emas-
culation of Rome." And even more specifically: ". . . the acutest intellects
rose instantaneously upon the corpses of the weaker, and the Rothschilds
remained the dictators of the markets of the world."

Pound's analysis coincides with Adams's. And in his poem he has made
use of two historical figures to imagize these two types of mind as they
appeared in the 19th century: Napoleon for the martial and imaginative
(though, paradoxically, Napoleon is still praised by the Jews as their
liberator from medieval discrimination) ; and Rothschild for the usurious.
It is to be noted that this 19th century conflict of opposed minds has been
pre-figured in earlier cantos by the conflict between the martial and
imaginative Malatesta and the land-grabbing Church. Which is to say
that Pound attacks the usurious mind where he finds it—in Jews, in
Italian Catholics, in Protestant Scots and Britishers (as in his thematic
reference to the Bank of England's founders), in Americans (with special
reference to Nicholas Biddle), and so on.

His criticism of the Rothschilds appears to exceed in bitterness his
criticism of the others. At least, since certain lines in Canto 52 were
excised by his publishers, one must assume so. David Rattray ("Weekend
with Ezra Pound," *The Nation,* 185, 16 Nov., 1957) records him as saying:

> They wanted to leave the whole thing out without any indication of
> the omission, and I said, "Black lines or nothing" and so in went the
> black lines, so all my readers could see the censorship. I guess they
> were afraid of losing the support of the New York banks, if they pub-
> lished the truth about international finance."

However, in the summarizing passage which depicts the fall of Napoleon
(Canto 50), Jews are not singled out for particular attention; the most
opprobrious language is reserved for non-Jews:

> England and Austria were for despots with commerce
> considered
>   put back the Pope but
> reset no republics: Venice, Genova, Lucca
> and split up Poland in their soul was usura
> and in their hand bloody oppression
> and that son of a dog, Rospigliosi,
> came into Tuscany to make serfs of old Tuscans.
> S . . t on the throne of England, s . . t on the Austrian sofa

In their soul was usura and in their minds darkness
and blankness, greased fat were four Georges
Pus was in Spain, Wellington was a jew's pimp
and lacked mind to know what he effected.
'Leave the Duke, Go for gold!'
In their souls was usura and in their hearts cowardice
In their minds was stink and corruption
Two sores ran together, Talleyrand stank with shanker
and hell pissed up Metternich
Filth stank as in our day
      'From the brigantine Incostante'
for a hundred days against hell belch
Hope spat from March into June
      Ney, out of his saddle
Grouchy delayed
      Bentinck's word was, naturally,
not kept by the English. Genova under Sardegna. Hope
spat from Cannes, March, into Flanders.

And Pound has Napoleon account for his defeat in Brooks-Adamsian
terms:

                         'Not'
         said Napoleon 'because of that league of lice
         but for opposing the Zeitgeist! That was my ruin,
         That I ran against my own time, turning backward'

That there is a Jewish theme in the *Cantos* cannot be denied, nor that
he has unpleasant things to say of them. But not solely unpleasant things.
In Canto 22 Pound describes Jews in the synagogue and finds them to
be characterized by two of his favorite virtues, *hilaritas* and *humanitas*.
It is not Pound but a Mohammedan who speaks anti-Semitically here,
and the event, which was not fictitious, had enough impact upon him
to merit his recording it because "it was the first shock of coming on
Mohammedan prejudice—racial, not class." In Canto 36, Pound describes
the bourgeois Jews of Middle Europe in less favorable terms, commenting
upon "the intramural, the almost intravaginal warmth of/hebrew affec-
tions." But such a description is a common-place of Jewish novelists.

However, for the Jewish financier Pound has no warmth of affection.
The most outspoken passage appears in Canto 74:

      doubtless conditioned by the spawn of the gt. Meyer Anselm
That old H. had heard from the ass eared militarist in Byzantium:
      "Why stop?" "To begin again when we are stronger."
      and young H/ the tip from the augean stables in Paris
                  with Sieff in attendance, or not
                  as the case may have been,
                        thus conditioning.
         Meyer Anselm, a rrromance, yes, yes certainly
      but more fool you if you fall for it two centuries later
. . .

from their seats the blond bastards, and cast 'em.
the yidd is a stimulant, and the goyim are cattle
in gt/proportion and go to saleable slaughter
with the maximum of docility.

(P. 17.)

Questions that arise here are these: Did a Jew really make the statement "from their seats the blond bastards, and cast 'em" to "young H"
in Paris? And if so, does Pound expect his reader to infer from such
evidence a Jewish conspiracy? (It is interesting that in the *Guide* (p. 315)
Pound had been able to say of "Meyer Anselm" that he "had, let us say
a purpose, a race (his own race) to 'avenge.' He used the ONLY weapons
available for a tiny minority, for a lone hand against organized goy power,
pomp, militarism, rhetoric, buncombe." The rub, for Pound, is that the
minority, dramatically escaping exploitation, are in process of usurping
the earlier exploiters' place and characteristics.)

Now, a disengaged non-Jew might perhaps make the case that Pound's
axis is not anti-Semitic but anti-usural, that he does not hate all Jews
because they are Jews but some Jews, because they misuse money. He
could cite as evidence that in the *Guide* (pp. 242-3), after noting that "The
red herring is scoundrel's device and usurer's stand-by," Pound had specified race prejudice as a red herring and gone on to say that "It is nonsense for the anglo-saxon to revile the jew for beating him at his own
game." (In view of the perennial attacks upon Jews for "cosmopolitan-
ism," it is interesting to find Pound *(loc. cit.)* describing himself as
nomadic and remarking "It is not for me to rebuke brother semite for
similar disposition.") And, in 1954, Duarte de Montalegre, broadcasting
from the Vatican, did in fact make such a case:

> . . . Ezra Pound has been accused of racial prejudice and antisemitism.
> But those who make such absurd charges forget that the very logic
> of the broad humanistic culture of a poet and thinker like Ezra
> Pound makes racialism or antisemitism impossible. They also betray
> an ignorance of the writer's personal relationships, in which he assist-
> ed Louis Zukofsky and other Jews in their artistic and literary
> careers. They forget that in the Cantos XXII and LXXVI themselves
> he speaks of Jews with admiration, and that Jews such as John
> Cournos have spoken of him with interest and admiration in their
> biographies. . .
>
> The essence of Ezra Pound's teaching may be summed up in these
> words . . . *"He inveighed against usury."* This is why many people
> believed him to be an anti-semite, erroneously identifying a vicious
> practice with a whole race. Once this misunderstanding has been
> removed, no serious grounds for the accusation remain.

I think that a reader of the *Cantos,* where criticism of the Jewish financiers, though present, is only one, and a minor one, of many themes,

might come to some agreement with de Montalegre. He will remember, of course, that Pound considers the Old Testament an almost completely bad book and a deleterious influence; that he has remained firm in an early belief (similar to Santayana's) that Christianity has suffered insofar as it has permitted the Judaic element of its teaching to predominate over what had come in through Greece. But he will regard this as being no more an attack upon Jews as Jews than Pound's criticism of Aristotle in the *Guide* is an attack upon Greeks as Greeks.

When he encounters in the *Cantos* what appears to be an anti-Semitic comment, he will balance it against such comments as these:

USURERS have no race. How long the whole Jewish people is to be sacrificial goat for the usurer, I know not. . . . *(New English Weekly,* VIII, 6 (21 Nov. 1935), p. 105.)

. . . international usury contains more Calvinism, Protestant sectarianism than Judaism. *(British Union Quarterly,* 120 (4 June 1938), p. 13.)

Even Pound's anti-Rothschild remarks need to be read in the light of his question whether

anti-semitism, a red herring if ever was one, mayn't be a hidden war of the five Swiss protestant dynasties on the Rothschild, whom for all we know, they may never have forgiven for breaking into their Necker-created monopoly. Naturally THEY couldn't attack Rothschild as a taker of interest or a monopolist. There would in fact be nothing but a whispering campaign that could serve them. *(New English Weekly,* VIII, 5 (14 Nov. 1935), pp. 85-6.)

So, maintaining that uninvolved, non-Jewish stance, the dispassionate analyst might argue that several points of view toward Pound's alleged anti-Semitism present themselves:

1. He is, without qualification, anti-Semitic.

2. He is primarily anti-monotheist and therefore (insofar as he is "anti" at all) both anti-Christian and anti-Semitic.

3. He is not anti-Semitic but anti-usural.

   A. He is right in isolating Jewish financiers for special attack.

   B. He is wrong because Jewish financiers practice usury no more than non-Jewish and are greatly outnumbered by the latter.

   C. He does not isolate the Jews; they merely take their place in a pattern which includes French, Greek, British, American, German, and other bankers, cannon-makers, journalists, politicians, and so on.

4. He is anti-Semitic because, not being for the Jews, he must be against them.

5. He is not theoretically anti-Semitic, but in practical effect he has been, having given great aid and comfort to the anti-Semitic camp, who have used his statements without making his differentiations.

The analyst might show that these categories are not mutually exclusive, that one could adopt as a realistic position an assimilation of 3B or 3C and 5.

But what is possible for the reader of the *Cantos* is not possible for the reader of the broadcasts. It is true, as we have seen, that Pound is consistent in venting his wrath only upon the Jewish financiers—for their usurious practice and (surprisingly) for the support some of them are supposed to have given the Russian revolutionaries. (Pound's ironic summation of the attacks upon him is that he refused to "sign on the dotted for Marx and Rothschild SIMULTANEOUSLY.") But his apparent obsession with the subject, the contumelious tone of his references, and his refusal to admit any counteracting evidence of Jewish virtues make it very difficult indeed to discern any vestige of the broad humanistic culture referred to by de Montalegre.

In recent issues of *TLS*, Eliot has been charged with anti-Semitism (and Fascism). Mr. Albert Mardell cleared the air somewhat with the following differentiation:

> As a Jew I was . . . pleased to learn that he disavowed the charge of anti-Semitism against him. I did not myself call him an anti-Semite, and I do not believe he was one, even though he made some disparaging remarks here and there about Jews. Anti-Semitism means discrimination and even persecution. And of course Eliot does not believe in either. (20 Sept. 1957.)

This is a rather more restricted view of the meaning of anti-Semitism than is popularly held. Accepting it, however, despite its narrowness, and assuming that Pound has not persecuted or discriminated against Jews in the accepted senses of those words, one must nevertheless wonder whether a sufficient quantity of disparaging remarks does not in itself become the equivalent (by qualitative change) of persecution.

I have made somewhat more of this matter and of Pound's Fascist sympathies than I should have liked to do. It may be argued that, seen in their proper perspective and in strict terms of literary criticism, they are of minor importance. The critical evaluation of *The Faerie Queen* or of *Paradise Lost* does not hinge upon the anti-Catholicism or anti-monarchism of their authors. On the other hand, since the *Cantos*, like Spenser's and Milton's poems, is a poem of ideas, the subject could not be blinked. It needed to be faced, too, because the concept of Pound as "the mad, traitorous, Fascist, anti-Semitic poet" has been, recently, so widely disseminated. So far as the poem is concerned, my hope is that the reader will place these segments of Pound's thought in their proper relation to the other segments and to the totality of his thought and will forego preoccupation with the segment in favor of appreciation of the whole. So far as the poet is concerned, my hope is that the reader will recognize that, since Pound characteristically uses the dissociative and ideogrammic methods of approach to received ideas, his every qualification, his every differentiation, his every presentation of a "factual atom" must be isolated, probed for meaning, and permitted to give its shade or tone to the concept being evolved. It is just as easy and just as indefensible to formulate a stereotype of the Fascist anti-Semite as it is of the usurious Jew.

Chapter 4

Late in the first decade of this century, Pound became associated with a group of men, of whom Ford Madox Ford and T. E. Hulme were leading members, who were concerned with the problem of finding new values to supersede those which underlay the diluted romanticism of the 19th century. Hulme's statement of the need for a new classicism (in his well-known *Romanticism and Classicism)* could not but have been affirmed by Pound. In the second of the following comments, Pound is only more specific than Hulme:

> This period of exhaustion seems to me to have been in romanticism. We shall not get any efflorescence of verse until we get a new technique, a new convention, to turn ourselves loose in. (From *Romanticism and Classicism.)*

> In one's youth one discusses style—or one should. The poetical reform between 1910 and 1920 coincided with the scrutiny of the word, the cleaning-up of syntax. This should be tackled in addition to, almost apart from, the question of content: one should seek to define the image, to discover the truth, or a part of the truth, even before one has learned that it may not be the whole truth. *(A Visiting Card,* pp. 22-23.)

Hulme sets out to demonstrate that beauty may be in "small, dry things"; that the poet's aim must be "accurate, precise and definite criticism"; that "images in verse are not mere decoration, but the very essence of an intuitive language"; that "it must be an intense zest which heightens a thing out of the level of prose"; and the like. There is little in the essay with which Pound could not wholeheartedly agree.

This feeling of need for the hard, the definite, the precise, led to an interest in such Japanese verse-forms as the *hokku* and *tanka* and motivated the Imagist movement, of which so much has been written that it needs only the briefest mention. It was important, of course, that Pound was associated with the movement. His own technique was sharpened by his constant effort toward "definite image and clear speaking in a contemporary idiom"; he served as midwife for a respectable number of first-rate poems; he and his companions-at-arms made a "20th century" poetry possible; he originated one of the most important literary definitions of the time: "An image is that which presents an intellectual and emotional complex in an instant of time." But, in a sense, his most significant action in the movement was to leave it.

... at a particular date in a particular room, two authors ... decided
that the dilutation of *vers libre,* Amygism, Lee Masterism, general
floppiness had gone too far, and that some counter-current must be
set going ... Rhyme and regular strophes. *(Polite Essays,* p. 14.)

So Pound, having squeezed the juice out of Imagism, having broadened
his interests (to become active in music, painting, and sculpture), having
become associated with a new group—the notable members being Wyndham Lewis and Henri Gaudier-Brzeska made the important shift to
Vorticism. This movement has been passed over rather lightly by literary
historians as one of the "isms" of limited and temporary effect not worthy
of the consideration which must be given, for example, to Imagism. The
Dictionary of World Literature is typical in its comment that "the principles of the movement are not clear" and its erroneous opinion that with
reference to poetry "it is virtually another name for Imagism." Whether
or not the Vorticist group as a whole, or the movement as a movement,
has had a noticeable effect upon the arts, there can be no doubt that it
affected Pound (and, through Pound, at least poetry) and that the
Cantos have been shaped and colored by his tour of duty with the
Vorticists.

In the first place, the Vorticists endeavored to formulate an aesthetic
which would comprehend, not compartmentalize, all the arts. "Vorticism,"
wrote Pound, "is the use of, or the belief in the use of, THE PRIMARY
PIGMENT, straight through all of the arts." *(The New Age,* 16 (14 Jan.
1915) p. 277.) It thus differs from cubism, expressionism, and imagism,
which believe in one thing for painting and something else for poetry,
and it presents the possibility of a "correlated aesthetic which carries you
through all of the arts." *(Loc. cit.)* The relation between Vorticism and
Imagism consists in this, that "the primary pigment of poetry is the
IMAGE." *(Blast,* no. 1 (20 June 1914), p. 153.) And to stop here would
necessitate agreement that the two were virtually the same. But to stop
here would be to stop at the starting point. Imagism had had its uses:
it had emphasized the need for clarity of vision, for dependence upon
one's own vision instead of a literary predecessor's, for precision in rendering in words the thing seen, for using the contemporary idiom in that
rendering instead of the hand-me-down, and so on. But it had suffered
from the limitations of its virtues—and of its second-rate practitioners—
in tending toward the static and toward the miniature.

The defect of earlier imagist propaganda was not in misstatement
but in incomplete statement. The diluters took the handiest and
easiest meaning, and thought only of the STATIONARY image. If
you can't think of imagism or phanopoeia as including the moving
image, you will have to make a really needless division of fixed
image and praxis or action. *(ABC of Reading,* p. 52.)

Question was raised whether subservience to the Imagist virtues would not necessarily rule out the possibility of the broad view of contemporary life, of seeing it not only clearly but as a whole (and in its historical perspective); of whether excessive exercise of the imagizing process, which admittedly produced fine lyrics, might not lead to atrophy of the power to write the long poem of philosophical significance—the poem not to make people see but to make them think.

Vorticism was an answer. It consciously eschewed the static and mimetic for the dynamic and creative. Instead of receiving impressions, Pound says, the Vorticist directs "a certain fluid force aganist circumstance"; he conceives "instead of merely observing and reflecting." *(Blast,* p. 153.) He observes the 20th century, but he is not captured by it to become its servile flatterer, nor does he retreat from it to twilit hills where cows browse. As Wyndham Lewis said:

> The Art-instinct is permanently primitive. In a chaos of imperfection, discord, etc., it finds the same stimulation as in Nature. The artist of the modern movement is a savage; this enormous, jangling, journalistic, fairy desert of modern life serves him as Nature did more technically primitive man.

That is, he faces up to it; eventually he learns to exert over it a measure of control. Gaudier-Brzeska found will, decision, consciousness to be the 20th century's vortex. Of primitive man he writes:

> The paleolithic vortex resulted in the decoration of the Dordogne caverns.
> Early stone-age man disputed the earth with animals.
> His livelihood depended on the hazards of the hunt—
> his greatest victory the domestication of a few species.
>   Out of the minds primordially preoccupied with
> animals Fonts-de-Gaume gained its procession of horses
> carved in the rock.
>   (Quoted in *Guide to Kulchur,* p. 63.)

The modern artist's task is to win an analogous victory; to subjugate the machine (or, rather, to instruct the men who control the machines) to bring order out of chaos, plenty out of wilderness, peace out of quelled enmities. The poet's specific job is to observe the situation, come to a well-defined idea of what's right and what's wrong in it and what can be done to rectify the wrong, and then to put the idea into action. "The idea is completed by the word. It is completed by its going into action." *(A Visiting Card,* p. 37.)

What Vorticism emphasized, then, as Imagism had not, was the importance of will with direction ("The science of economics will not get very far until it grants the existence of will as a component; i.e. will toward order, will toward 'justice' or fairness, desire for civilization, amenities included" *(ABC of Economics,* p. 38) ; of action as opposed to passive reflection; of the poet as a dynamic civilizing force; of the poet in control of, not controlled by, both the environment which surrounds him and the matter of his poetry. Briefly, it set up the artist as a responsible, participating citizen with special gifts—clear vision and effective powers of communication—which society will refuse to recognize only at its peril.

> . . . the arts give us our best data for determining what sort of a crea-ture man is As our treatment of man must be determined by our knowledge or conception of what man is, the arts provide data for ethics. . . . *(Pavannes and Divisions,* p. 226.)

The artist and the scientist work together toward the betterment of their fellow-man, both as individuals and as members of a society; indeed, the "serious" artist is scientific in his attention to the data, his refusal to generalize without sufficient empirical evidence. ("Bad art is inaccurate art. It is art that makes false reports." *(Ibid.,* p. 222.) And "Bad writing, or a great deal of it, drips down from an abstract received 'idea' or 'generality' held with fanaticism (twin beast with personal vanity) by men who NEVER take in concrete detail." *(Polite Essays,* p. 51.) One may define more closely, considering the artist as medical scientist, art as social therapy:

> The cult of beauty is the hygiene, it is sun, air, and it is the sea and the rain and the lake bathing. The cult of ugliness, Villon, Baude-laire, Corbiere, Beardsley are diagnosis. Flaubert is diagnosis. Satire, if we are to ride this metaphor to staggers, satire is surgery, insertions and amputations. *(Pavannes and Divisions,* p. 225.)

But the scientist, particularly the social scientist, cannot work without historical perspective. He must, of course, report what he observes, but his report will be only partial if it is left unrelated to previous observa-tion. Kandinsky says it in broad aesthetic terms:

> The beauty and durability of art are possible only if they have their roots in the Principle of Inner Necessity. This arises out of three mystical necessities:
>
> 1. Every artist, as a creator, has to express himself (Element of Personality).
>
> 2. Every artist, as the child of his epoch, has to express what is particular to this epoch (Element of Style. . . .)
>
> 3. Every artist, as the servant of art, has to express what is particular to all art (Element of the pure and eternal qualities of the art of all men, of all peoples and of all times. . . .) *(Blast,* p. 119.)

Pound says it in more specifically Vorticist language:

> All history rushes into this vortex. All the energized past, all the past that is living and worthy to live. ALL MOMENTUM, which is

the past bearing down upon us, RACE, RACE-MEMORY, instinct
charging the PLACID, NON-ENERGIZED FUTURE.
The DESIGN of the future in the grip of the human vortex. *(Blast,*
p. 153.)

And he makes it very clear that Kandinsky's second "mystical necessity"
has validity only as it cooperates with the other two:

It is the artist's job to express what is "true for himself." In such
measure as he does this he is a good artist, and, in such measure as
he himself exists, a great one. . . . But the man who tries to express
his age, instead of expressing himself, is doomed to destruction.
(The New Age, 16 (14 Jan. 1915) p. 312.)

The discouraging thing for an artist is that when he emits an "abstract" or general proposition he can not sign it in the way he signs
a poem or a drawing, i.e., saturate it with his presence in cadence or
in proportion. *(The Exile,* no. 4, p. 1.)

In 1915, Pound published *Cathay,* with translations of Mei Sheng,
Rihaku, and others; in 1916 appeared his translations of the Japanese
Noh plays. This work led to one of the crucial events of his intellectual
life, the opportunity of editing Ernest Fenollosa's *The Chinese Written
Character as a Medium for Poetry.*

Fenollosa had been for many years an ardent propagandist for a rapprochement between East and West. His years of service had brought
him to the liveliest appreciation of the Japanese and Chinese civilization
in general and art in particular. He devoted his life to sharing that appreciation, by conversation, lecture, and the written word, with the American
and English public.

From his reading of history he concluded that there had existed, in
the past, two particularly active centers of art-dispersion: "one belonging
to the somewhat contracted regions about the east end of the Mediterranean. . . . The other . . . to some point of the many less defined Mediter-
raneans enclosed by the large islands of the western half of the Pacific
ocean." *(Epochs of Chinese and Japanese Art,* I, 3.) The former divides
into three sub-areas: the Mesopotamian plain, the northern Nile valley,
and the Greek Mediterranean. Each had influenced the other; Alexander's
conquest came close to merging them into a common "sea of forms."
Chinese art, he thought, had had the advantage of being the only significant form of world art that had combined creative "impulses" from the
Pacific and the Mediterranean. And he had descried an underlying unity
between occidental and oriental culture:

I say firmly, that in Art, as in civilization generally, the best in both
East and West is that which is common to the two, and eloquent of
universal construction. Translate China into terms of man's experience, and it becomes only an extension of the Iliad. *(Ibid.,* I, 2.)

He looks forward to the time when art-criticism will break through its provincial double standard, will recognize that "classification is only a convenience, valuable chiefly for chronological grouping," and see unfolded "a universal scheme or logic of art . . . which as easily subsumes all forms of Asiatic and of savage art and the efforts of children as it does accepted European schools." *(Ibid.,* I, xxxiv.)

The similarity between his thinking in this book and that of the Vorticists needs no comment. Nor does the fact that Pound must be considered as one pledged to carry on the missionary work (from East to West) where Fenollosa had left off. But it was *The Chinese Character* which most profoundly affected Pound. *The Epochs of Chinese and Japanese Art* had offered the invitation to become acquainted with Chinese and Japanese culture through the specific avenue of art-study. The *Chinese Character* was somewhat less an "art-and-culture" book. In the latter, Fenollosa wrote prophetically of the Chinese problem: "We in America, especially, must face it across the Pacific, and master it or it will master us." And he advised (in the first decade of the century) that "The duty that faces us is not to batter down their forts or to exploit their markets, but to study and to come to sympathize with their humanity and their generous aspirations." (Pp. 53-4.) The advice, of course, was not heeded, and the problem has not diminished. *The Chinese Character* makes the sympathetic approach through a study of Chinese poetry.

According to Fenollosa's analysis, the Chinese poet has several advantages over his Western counterpart. First, he enjoys the possibility of affecting his reader not only aurally but also visually. No picture inheres in the English written word "horse," for example; there is no necessary relation between the thing being spoken of and either the appearance or the sound of the word. The Chinese character for "horse" has at least the animal's four legs; further, it compels a certain activity of the eye (like that involved in viewing a picture), which produces the illusion that the symbol is in motion. As Fenollosa says, "In reading Chinese we do not seem to be juggling mental counters, but to be watching *things* work out their own fate." *(The Chinese Character,* p. 59.)

Thus, detached words are in themselves vivid, concrete, full of action (the character for "see" shows running legs under an eye); they tend to be descriptions of processes or actions instead of things—essentially verbal rather than nominative. And words combined into sentences are like motion pictures. Fenollosa finds this characteristic as important philosophically as it is poetically, because it reflects the true situation in nature that "things" exist in relation to one another as participating elements in a continuous process:

A true noun, an isolated thing, does not exist in nature. Things are only the terminal points, or rather the meeting points, of actions, cross-sections cut through actions, snapshots. Neither can a pure verb, an abstract motion, be possible in nature. The eye sees noun and verb as one: things in motion, motion in things . . . . *(Ibid.,* p. 60. And elsewhere: "The verb must be the primary fact of nature since motion and change are all that we can recognize in her." P. 69.)

This is not to say that the English language is necessarily divorced from nature. The sentence form ("a reflection of temporal order in causation" involving agent, act, and object) in English is precisely that in Chinese. But Western logicians have tended to compel a separation by insisting upon the virtue of the general and conceptual as opposed to the particular and perceptual. "The truth of all their little checker-board juggling depended upon the natural order by which these powers or properties or qualities were folded in concrete things, yet they despised the 'thing' as a mere 'particular', or pawn." *(Ibid.,* p. 62. *Cf.* Pound in *The Exile,* no. 4, p. 3: "We continue with thought forms and language structures used by monolinear medieval logic, when the aptitudes of human mind developed in course of biochemical studies have long since outrun such simple devices. By which I mean that the biologist can often know and think clearly a number of things he cannot put in a simple sentence; he can dissociate things for which there is as yet no dissociated language structure.") The logicians have invented a kind of linguistic non-Euclidean geometry, complete as nature is not complete, static as nature is not static—in short, a purely subjective and artificial construct. Evidence of the weakness of English resulting from the efforts of the logicians to remake nature after their minds' desire appears in the popularity of the intransitive sentence and the incidence of use of the copula "is." In our saying "the monkey is a mammal" instead of "monkeys bring forth live young," Fenollosa finds the language used devoid of descriptive quality and un-definitive because the action has been reduced to "the abstractest state of all, namely, bare existence." To have meaning at all, the intransitive sentence must depend upon adjectives and nouns, since its verb denotes only an equation. ("In all languages," Fenollosa says (p. 69), ". . . a noun is originally 'that which does something,' that which performs the verbal action.") But these are feeble substitutes; they cannot duplicate the sense of "transference of power" which is communicated by the sentence containing a strong transitive verb. And the English grammarian by isolating the noun as a part of speech at a remove from the verb to which it is related further "de-activates" it. "One is led to suspect from an analysis of the Aryan languages that such differences [between parts of speech] are not natural, and that they have been unfortunately invented by grammarians to confuse the simple poetic outlook on life." (P. 66.)

Against Fenollosa's line of thought the logician whom Fenollosa has condemned might argue that although vivid verbs and transitive sentences and pictorial writing may work satisfactorily in giving us information about the physical world in its gross aspects, they can scarcely assist us toward comprehension of "the greater part of natural truth," which is "hidden in processes too minute for vision and in harmonies too large, in vibrations, cohesions and in affinities." *(Ibid.,* p. 72.) But Fenollosa replies that the gap between the physical and the metaphysical, the seen and the unseen, can be effectively bridged by metaphor, "the use of material images to suggest immaterial relations." Unlike the classifying process of medieval logicians, the metaphoric process is not arbitrary, does not find in nature the non-existent black cat. To the contrary, it is founded upon observation; relations in nature exist, and they are "more real and more important than the things which they relate." *(Loc. cit.)* Poetry, like science, reveals what it finds. The poet, like the scientist, only more swiftly perceives (or by dint of harder work comes to perceive) than does the normal observer. Having perceived, he does not take the life out of his perception by isolating it in a category, by concealing its variety with an abstract name; his interest lies in its multiplicity of function, its potential for growth or change, its identity of structure with other things observed, its interactions with them. Or, as Fenollosa sums it up: "The cherry tree is all that it does" *(Ibid.,* p. 78) — a storehouse of forces, as nature is on a vast scale.

These, then, are the lessons to be learned from Chinese poetry: since the English poet cannot literally put pictures on his page, he must use highly charged words "crowding maximum meaning into the single phrase pregnant, charged, and luminous from within" *(Ibid.,* p. 78); he must avoid the intransitive verbs and use the active, vivid ones emphasizing not that things *are* but that they *do* ("Will is the foundation of our speech. We catch the Demi-urge in the act." *Ibid.,* p. 79); he must be alive to and make his reader alive to the metaphorical origins and the historically accumulated meanings of words; he must regard metaphor not as external decoration but as "at once the substance of nature and of language," the single device by which from disparate percepts an intellectual fabric may be woven. (Pound, it should be noted, not merely avoids the external decorativeness of metaphor; he avoids metaphor in the normal sense almost altogether. In his opinion, the mere location of one properly chosen fact next another satisfies the Aristotelian definition of metaphor as "setting the thing before the eye in action." Probably the greatest difficulty in reading the *Cantos* lies in discovering the similarities, and realizing the significance of the dissimilarities, between the two terms of Pound's un-articulated metaphors.)

Much of what Fenollosa had to say was not news to Pound but merely coincident with ideas which he had himself for a long time been propounding. But through Fenollosa he came to recognize how effectively the ideogrammic system might be used as a weapon against the tyranny of received ideas, whether they were expressed on the high level in chains of Aristotelian syllogisms or reduced for popular consumption to slogans.

"If," he writes, "I have made any contribution to criticism I have done so by introducing the ideogrammic system. True criticism will insist on the accumulation of these concrete examples, these facts, possibly small, but gristly and resilient, that can't be squashed, that insist upon being taken into consideration, before the critic can claim to hold any opinion whatsoever." *(A Visiting Card*, p. 36.)

Fenollosa's influence on Pound should not be misconstrued as merely aesthetic.

At Fenollosa's death in 1908 his essay was indubitably ahead of its time. . . . A new mode of thought was foreseen. A mode that would eliminate certain types of imbecility, in particular the inaccessibility to FACT glaringly lit up in 1935 by the peril of world conflagration caused by the type of mind which festered in the ideologues of the Wilson-Angell congregation. *(Polite Essays*, pp. 50-51.))

In showing that Jefferson's "All men are born free and equal" was not an *idée fixe* but an idea put somewhere in a definite space and time and subject to modification by time, Pound echoes the Fenollosa distinction between verb and noun and brings it into relation with Christian thought:

Again a little grammar or a little mediaeval scholarship would be useful, Albertus Magnus or Aquinas or some fusty old scribbler passed on an age-old distinction between the verb and the noun.
The verb implies a time, a relation to time. Be Christian, go back to the newer part of your Bible. Be Catholic (not Anglo-Catholic), consider the "mystery of the incarnation." *(Jefferson and/or Mussolini*, p. 22.)

That is, an idea, however old, expressed by the right man in the right way at the right time, does not remain "dead, set, stiff, varnished"; it becomes "organic and germinal, the 'seed' of the scriptures." Jefferson speaks and immediately the "drivelling imbecility of the British and French courts ceases to hypnotize all the pore boobs." *(Ibid.*, p. 21.)

Pound, then, will use the imagistic-ideogrammic method of structuring a canto. His primary pigment will be an image from which a prose statement can (sometimes surely, sometimes only tentatively) be inferred. Another image, whole or fragmentary, will be juxtaposed with the former. Again an inference may be drawn as to the meaning of the image. And, furthermore, something is to be learned from the fact of this particular juxtaposition, since it is not, of course, fortuitous.

Other supporting images will be added; the earlier images may be repeated (in whole or in part, in a variant form or in another language); image-motifs not applying primarily here but to be developed in later cantos may be introduced. Now and again it will be the case that a given canto is itself a single image. And a series of cantos (such as the Malatesta group, the Chinese cantos, the Adams sequence) will serve as a single image. Thus, within a canto, image is set against image; in a sequence, canto will comment upon canto; in the poem as a whole, sequence will elaborate sequence.

As for the metrical build-up of the image, it is probable that Rainer M. Gerhardt, in a radio-broadcast discussion of *The Pisan Cantos,* has given the most acute analysis. Since this broadcast has not previously been translated, I shall quote at some length:

First speaker: In contrast to the classical conception of verse as that of a certain symmetrical and metrical pattern, or of being constructed in accordance with such a pattern, modern verse is a matter of breathing, consequently, of speaking, of hearing. Notwithstanding the dangers one is exposed to, when defining things of one category in terms of another, one may say that modern verse requires the use of counterpoint and compositional skill in a way which is peculiar to modern music, or, even more obviously, to modern films—if they are good. The principle of the construction and the arrangement of verse consists in the relation of sound, rhythm and meaning of single terms to a certain line; and of the relation of each of these lines and their terms to one another. A certain parallel to Schoenberg's theory of twelve-tone composition can be observed. Contrary to traditional standards—as I said—the new pattern is a pattern of breathing, as long as it is not subjected to a metrical formation. (But the latter is adhered to by the great masters.) The unit of verse comprises all those successions of rhythm and melody, which normal bounds of speech can possibly comprise. Fundamentally, the length of these bounds is determined by their vocal content. The first breathing unit of a verse strikes up the theme. All the succeeding verses are dependent on or in a certain way related to it.

Fourth speaker: For example:

>   mint springs up again
>   in spite of Jones' rodents
>   as had the clover by the gorilla cage
>   with a four-leaf

First speaker: The theme:

Fourth speaker: mint springs up again

First speaker: Repetition of the theme:

Fourth speaker: in spite of Jones' rodents

First speaker: Variation extending the theme:

Fourth speaker: as had the clover by the gorilla cage

First speaker: Conclusion:

Fourth speaker: with a four-leaf

First speaker: Another example:

Fourth speaker: The Kakemono grows in flat land out of mist
                        sun rises lop-sided over the mountain
                              so that I recalled the noise in the chimney
                    as it were the wind in the chimney
                              but was in reality Uncle William
                    downstairs composing
                      that had made a great Peeeeacock
                        . in the proide ov his oiye
                            had made a great peeeeeeecock in the . . .
                    made a great peacock
                              in the proide of his oyyee

                    proide of his oy-ee
                    as indeed he had, and perdurable

                    a great peacock aere perennius
                          or as in the advice to the young man to
                    breed and get married (or not)
                              as you choose to regard it

First speaker: The first theme:

Fourth speaker: The Kakemono grows in flat land out of mist

First speaker: Repetition and variation:

Fourth speaker: sun rises lop-sided over the mountain
                        so that I recalled the noise in the chimney
                              as it were the wind in the chimney

First speaker: Summary:

Fourth speaker: but was in reality Uncle William

First speaker: Arabesque:

Fourth speaker: downstairs composing

First speaker: The arabesque is simultaneously functioning as an opening line. The second theme, closely related to the first one, is being varied rhythmically.

Fourth speaker: that had made a great Peeeeacock
                        in the proide ov his oiye
                    had made a great peeeeeeecock in the . . .
                        made a great peacock
                    in the proide of his oyee
                        proide ov his oy-ee

First speaker: After the end of the variation, the extension and conclusion of the cadence:

Fourth speaker: as indeed he had, and perdurable
                   a great peacock aere perennius
First speaker: The final variation, the arabesque, or, one could say,
    the farewell song:
Fourth speaker: or as in the advice to the young man to
                   breed and get married (or not)
                   as you choose to regard it.

First speaker: The first line of the final variation is expanded by the
second line, both being joined by an infinitive. Merely writing poetry
according to a certain recipe is not practicable. "First of all you have
to be a poet," said Duhamel and Vidrac. 'Or, as Benn expresses it,
"But if the right man does it, the first verse can be taken out of a train-
schedule, the second one out of a hymn-book, the third one may well
be a moron-joke; yet added together they will make a poem." But
also a poet of Benn's school of thought has to observe certain general
rules, which must remain essentially unchanged, in regard to the
succession of vowels. Units of breath and rhythm are permanently
valid, no matter what the verse looks like. It is possible to introduce
innovations of sequence, and to alter the subject and its way of
presentation. One may mould the language as one likes. No revolution, however, has yet produced a change in the sequence of vowels
and the laws governing certain relations of lines and verses. Units of
meaning were changed. But—with the exception of stopping the
nonsense of stupidly counting metrical feet—an essential alteration
of the parts, which make up the skeleton of sound, has not taken
place . . . .

(Die Pisaner Gesänge, eine Sendung, von Rainer M. Gerhardt; Eigentum: Hessischer Rundfunk, "Abendstudio," Frankfurt/Main, März, 1952.)

Gerhardt's effort here is to show how what Pound calls *melopoeia* and
phanopoeia cooperate to bind together apparently unrelated materials
and to produce a total "meaning" which, so to speak, glides beneath the
reader's conscious musings ere he is aware. Melopoeia emphasizes the
musical qualities of verse; phanopoeia, the visual images, which are
the "primary pigments" or the "form-motifs." Thus the reader of the
poem is confronted with a series of pictures, cohering in sound, and
producing a thought which no longer needs to be expressed.

In the *ABC of Reading*, Pound, trying to explain the purport of Fenollosa's essay, wrote:

The simplest statement I can make of his meaning is as follows:
In Europe, if you ask a man to define anything, his definition always
moves away from the simple things that he knows perfectly well,
it recedes into an unknown region, that is a region of remoter and
progressively remoter abstraction.
Thus if you ask him what red is, he says it is a 'colour.'
If you ask him what a colour is, he tells you it is a vibration or a
refraction of light, or a division of the spectrum.

And if you ask him what vibration is, he tells you it is a mode of energy, or something of that sort, until you arrive at a modality of being, or non-being, or at any rate you get in beyond your depth, and beyond his depth. (P. 19.)

Against this, Pound puts the Chinese method of defining red: putting together the abbreviated pictures of a rose, a cherry, iron rust, a flamingo to produce an ideogram. The method, he comments, is much like the biologist's when, from a large number of slides, he "picks out what is necessary for his general statement. Something . . . that applies in all the cases."

It is the latter method that Pound uses in the *Cantos*. Abbreviated images, each having what is necessary for Pound's general statement, are juxtaposed to produce that statement (or ideogram). It is a method altogether of a piece with Pound's general thinking, his prepossession for the hard, the definite, the precise; the observed specific object; the image as primary pigment; the individual's own experience, in religion; in ethics, the individual's gaze into his heart.

A good example of the method and of its difficulties for the reader occurs at the beginning of Canto 38.

> *il duol che sopra Senna*
> *Induce, falseggiando la moneta.*
> *Paradiso XIX, 118.*
> An' that year Metevsky went over to America del Sud
>   (and the Pope's manners were so like Mr. Joyce's,
>   got that way in the Vatican, weren't like that before)
>   Marconi knelt in the ancient manner
>   like Jimmy Walker sayin' his prayers.
> His Holiness expressed a polite curiosity
>   as to how His Excellency had chased those
> electric shakes through the a'mosphere.
>   Lucrezia
> Wanted a rabbit's foot,
>   and he, Metevsky said to the one side
> (three children, five abortions and died of the last)
>   he said: the other boys got more munitions
> (thus cigar-makers whose work is highly repetitive
> can perform the necessary operations almost automatically
> and at the same time listen to readers who are hired
> for the purpose of providing mental entertainment while they
> work; Dexter Kimball 1929.

Here the following images are brought together:

1. Philip the Fair's debasing of currency.

2. Sir Basil Zaharoff's (Metevsky's) sale of munitions.

3. A meeting between Marconi and the Pope.

4. Lucrezia Borgia's bad luck—if it is Lucrezia Borgia.

5. Dexter Kimball's time-motion study.

Each image is distinct enough. The question is whether the images, put together, produce an ideogram for black, for white, or, perhaps, for gray. It is certain that currency-debasing and munitions-selling are black. It is probable that the turning of human beings into automatons is black. But the Marconi-Pope image needs study: Do we have the irony of Science kneeling before medievalism? or the irony of medievalism's possible adoption of scientific methods? or the double irony? or none at all? And how does Lucrezia fit here—as a hint of an interesting historical parallel? But a parallel with what? Is it significant that she was the daughter of a Pope?

Notable among the images comprising the preceding ideogram is the quotation from Kimball. Pound's desire to be exact leads him to employ quotations constantly. In this instance, the quote is in English, Pound supplies the author's name, and the excerpt is complete enough to convey a meaning. Sometimes, however, he quotes from a foreign source a meaningless fragment which he leaves unidentified. He may soon after, or much later, give his own translation; soon, or later, complete the fragment so that it becomes meangingful; and soon, or later, identify the source. If not, the reader is in for some hard work. For example, in Canto 23:

"Et omniformis," Psellos, "omnis
   "Intellectus est." God's fire. Gemisto:
   "Never with this religion
   "Will you make men of the greeks.
"But build wall across Peloponcsus
"And organize, and . . .
   damn these Eyetalian barbarians."
And Novvy's ship went down in the tempest
Or at least they chucked the books overboard.

How dissolve Irol in sugar . . . Houille blanche,
Auto-chenille, destroy all bacteria in the kidney,
Invention-d'entités-plus-ou-moins-abstraits-
en-nombre-égal-aux-choses-à-expliquer . . .
La Science ne peut pas y consister. "J'ai
Obtenu une brulure" M. Curie, or some other scientist
"Qui m'a coûté six mois de guérison."
   and continued his experiments.
Tropismes! "We believe the attraction is chemical."

With the sun in a golden cup
   and going toward the low fords of ocean

"Αλιος δ' 'γπεριονίδας δέπας ἐσκατέβαινε χρύσεον
"Οφρα δὶ ὠκεανοῖο περάσας
      ima vada noctis obscurae
Seeking doubtless the sex in bread-moulds
"ηλιος, ἅλιος, ἅλιος = μάταιος

("Derivation uncertain." The idiot
Odysseus furrowed the sand.)
alixantos, aliotrephès, eiskatebaine, down into,
descended, to the end that, beyond ocean,
pass through, traverse

At first glance, this seems impossible. But given some understanding
of Pound's method, some knowledge of his prose, some recollection of
earlier passages in the poem, some willingness to do research, (and an
opportunity to consult the *Annotated Index*), even the classically un-
lettered can make it yield its message. The allusions to Psellos and
Gemisto Plethon suggest a reference to neo-Platonism. Recollection that
the fragment "Et omniformis" appeared near the name of the neo-
Platonist Iamblichus, in Canto 5, supports the inference. And research
may reveal that the Latin statement comes from Porphyry, still another
neo-Platonist.

Even the most superficial knowledge of French shows that, in the second
component of the ideogram, scientists are being quoted.

To unravel the third, it is useful to have a friend who teaches Greek.
He will from personal experience understand that Pound is presenting
himself in the act of translating a fragment of the Greek poet Stesichorus.

So neo-Platonism (or, more broadly, religion), science, and the translation of poetry form the ideogram. What is to be inferred from their
conjunction? Here some familiarity with the *Guide* will prove helpful.
The phrase "God's fire" and the word "Tropismes" indicate that Pound
has in mind his dissociation between two mystic states: "the ecstatic-
beneficent-and-benevolent" one of the neo-Platonists and "the fanatical,
the man on fire with God and anxious . . . to reprove his neighbour for
having a set of tropisms different from that of the fanatics. . . ." *(Guide,*
p. 223.) And on that same page (luckily) is to be found a paragraph which
elucidates the references to scientists and to Pound the poet at work and
ties them to the neo-Platonists.

> Man drunk with god, man inebriated with infinity, on the one hand,
> and man with a millimetric measure and microscope on the other.
> I labour and relabour the discipline of real theology or of any
> verbal combat or athletics that forces or induces him to define his
> terms clearly.

These images having been found to form an ideogram which can be
forced to yield a prose statement, there remains the task of determining
how this ideogram works together with the three or four others in Canto

23 to produce the canto's full statement and then to relate this canto with those that precede and follow. Hard work, of course—but very rewarding.

Among the significant images that Pound employs are persons drawn from history, mythology, and his own acquaintance. For if this is a poem without a plot, it is not without characters. In fact, the multiplicity of characters engenders another of the difficulties in interpreting the poem. In down-to-earth terms, the problem is to distinguish the good guys from the bad guys. And since any given character may represent an idea, a state of mind, some aspect of a historical epoch, or something else equally significant, he has got to be eyed with exceeding care, particularly since no congenial Vergil is nearby to assist in identification.

I do not intend to pin down all the characters in the poem like dead butterflies and produce a "linnaeus-map," but merely to indicate an approach.

To begin with, we know that Pound has strong negative feelings toward the usurer, the monopolist, the materialist, the monotheist, the dogmatist, the provincial, the snoop, the abstractionist, the synthesizer, the syllogizer, the warmonger, the "liberal," the impeder of communication, the obfuscator of history, the volitionless intellectual, the bourgeois, the fact-evader, and the de-sensitizer. Any character, then, who falls into any of these categories and has no redeeming virtues of sufficient moment will necessarily be considered a villain. And, on the contrary, any character who shows himself to be for peace, liberty, sound money, the rights of the individual, balance, the unbroken tradition, the inviolability of the mysteries, the revitalization of the arts, precise thought and expression of thought plus will to action, accurate dissociations, empirical observation, tolerance of variants, skill in the crafts, self-knowledge, respect for the folk-ways—such a character will be on the side of the heroes, even though he is not of wisdom all compounded.

To choose just forty five, then, who, regardless of their faults, are still on our side (or on whose side we ought to be) :

Kung, Mencius, Adams, Jefferson, Napoleon, Apollonius, Justinian, Malatesta, Drake, Hanno, Dante, Frobenius, Agassiz, Plethon, Erigena, Plotinus, Antoninus, Alexander, Cunizza, Eleanor, Cavalcanti, Pietro Leopoldo, T. H. Benton, C. H. Douglas, F. M. Ford, Mussolini, Varchi, Pisanello, Ovid, Yeats, Jackson, Randolph, Fremont, Van Buren, Homer, Valla, de Gourmont, Gesell, Richard St. Victor, Orage, Kati, Tching Tang, Chao Kong, Tcheou Kong, Sordello.

It needs to be noted that this list is only a random sampling, that the members of the group are not of equal stature, that many own grave defects of character. It will be the compleat reader's business to make the proper additions, differentiate the characters' strengths from their weaknesses (according to Pound's opinion, which may not be history's), and come to a proper recognition of Pound's estimate of their stature.

Separate from the historical personages are the various mythological figures used by Pound primarily as images of the various modes by which man confronts the mysteries, but also used to serve other functions. Some of these are discussed on pp. 112 ff.

Thus Pound has at his disposal a tremendous cast of characters to be used as images according to his need. Of some of them we learn a great deal, of others almost nothing. Or, to put it in musical terms, some serve as major themes to be developed at length, others are almost no more than recurring chords within the musical pattern.

Pound's method ought, of course, to be observed in practice in a full canto rather than generalized about, and I shall supply here an explication of Canto 3.

This canto is an appropriate one to use as an example because it is brief enough to manage in short space yet clearly illustrates Pound's method. It jumps about in time and space, brings into apparently chance relationship various human figures, historical and literary, introduces supernatural entities, and makes no generalization to explain what its burden is. Our problem is to dissociate one image from another; then to examine each image to determine its connotative potential; next to discover how they coalesce to form an ideogram; and finally to decide upon the prose statement which most adequately delivers the meaning of the canto. (No prose statement, of course, will be adequate; if it were, there would exist no reason for the poem.)

The ideogram of Canto 3 appears to be composed of the following components.

1. A reference to Pound's being in Venice in 1908—11.1-6.
2. A statement that the gods exist and have existed—11.17-19.
3. A recounting of an incident in the life of "My Cid"—11. 20-37.
4. Brief allusion to the story of Ignez de Castro—1. 38.
5. Description of the decay of Mantua—11. 38-42.

Given this analysis into recognizable parts to work from, the reader must now determine what the various allusions within each image have meant to Pound and come to an inference as to how he is using them here. Explication such as that which follows (which, though not complete, is complete enough for our present purpose) is the answer.

Canto 3

Line 1 *1:* Pound

1 *Dogana's steps:* Dogana di Mare, the principal custom-house in Venice.

2 *that year:* 1908. Pound went to Venice (erroneous myth has it that he walked there from Gibraltar) in that year and there published his first volume of poetry *(A Lume Spento).*

3 *"Those girls":* in an early version of this passage (published in *Poetry)* Pound addressed Browning:

> we can be where we will be
> · · · · · · · · · · · · · · · · ·
> Your "palace step"?

My stone seat was the Dogana's curb,
And there were not "those girls," there was one flare, one face.
'Twas all I ever saw, but it was real . . . .
And I can no more say what shape it was . . .
But she was young, too young.

Pound here compares himself with Browning, who broke off the story in Bk. III, *Sordello,* to "muse this on a ruined palace-step/ In Venice" and to reflect upon "those girls."

4 *Stretti:* a popular pre-jazz song. Recurs in Canto 27, p. 130.

6 *Koré's house:* quoted from D'Annunzio's *Notturno,* to which, in 1922, Pound turned *(Dial,* 73, p. 553) from the enervation of Parisian authors with relief, noting that the Italian "poet-hero" wrote simply, "lyricly," and without the decadent prolixity of Proust. In this essay, Pound is also concerned with the problem of establishing "some spot of civilization" and refers to the patronage of the Estes and of Malatesta and to Platina's "de litteris . . ." (see Canto 11, p. 51.)

7-16 *Gods . . . nipple:* in the original passage:

That should have taught you [Browning] to avoid speech
figurative
     And set out your matter
As I do, in straight simple phrases:
     Gods float in the azure air,
Bright gods, and Tuscan, back before dew was shed,
Is it a world like Puvis?
     Never so pale, my friend,
'Tis the first light—not half-light—Panisks
And oak-girls and the Maenads
Have all the wood . . . .

"It is not gone." Metastasio
Is right—we have that world about us.
And the clouds bow above the lake, and there are
folk upon them
Going their windy ways . . .
And the water is full of silvery almond-white
swimmers
The silvery water glazes the up-turned nipple.

Here Pound rebuked Browning for his sometime use of figurative
language and gave an example of the straightforward writing he
preferred. Since (as Pound sees it) usury and rhetoric go hand in
hand, a criticism of the Venice of expensive gondolas may be inferred. In *Pavannes and Divisions* (p. 102) is a comment which
applies to the above excerpt: "Time was when the poet lay in a
green field with his head against a tree . . . Metastasio, and he
should know if any one, assures us that this age endures—even
though the modern poet is expected to halloa his verses down a
speaking tube to the editors of cheap magazines. . . ."

17 *Poggio:* Poggio Bracciolini (1380-1459), papal secretary and
humanist reviver of interest in the classics. He unearthed a great
number of Latin manuscripts buried in monasteries: *e.g.,* twelve
plays of Plautus, Valerius Flaccus' *Argonautica,* Lucretius' *De Rerum
Natura,* etc. In *Pavannes and Divisions* (p. 31) Pound has a dialogue
between Poggio and Le Sieur de Manusier in which Poggio is made
to say of his time (1451):

Our blessing is to live in an age when some can hold a fair balance.
It can not last; many are half-drunk with freedom; a greed for taxes
at Rome will raise up envy, a cultivated court will disappear in the
ensuing reaction. We are fortunate to live in the wink, the eye of
mankind is open . . . . Men are prized for being unique.

18-19 *Green . . . cedars:* in the original passage, after asking "How
shall we start hence?" Pound suggests possibilities:

With Egypt!
Daub out in blue scarabs and with that greeny turquoise?
Or with China, *O Virgilio mio,* and gray gradual steps.
Lead up beneath flat sprays of heavy cedars . . . .

20-37 *My Cid . . . . Valencia:* a paraphrase of sections 3-10 of the
12th-century Spanish epic *Poema del Cid.* The Cid, whom Pound
calls "that most glorious bandit," is, in the sections paraphrased,
penniless and out of favor with his king, Alfonso of Castille. He
enters the town of Burgos, but the people, afraid the king will
punish them if they help the Cid, conceal themselves. A girl of nine
comes out to explain the situation. To obtain money, he sells two
trunks of sand to two Jewish merchants, who, because of the Cid's

reputation, think they are full of loot. Pound discusses the poem in
The Spirit of Romance, pp. 64 ff.
20 *Burgos:* Pedro I (see 1. 38) was born there.
23 *Una niña:* in Pound's original second canto "A girl child of nine."
25 *voce tinnula:* "Lisps out the words, a-whisper." The Latin phrase,
repeated and varied several times in later cantos, is taken from the
nuptial song by Catullus, *Carmen* LXI, l. 13.
34 *Raquel and Vidas:* the Jewish merchants. The author of the
Poema thoroughly approves of the Cid's action in cheating them.
38 *Ignez de Castro:* Pound takes this story from Camoens' *Lusiads*,
which he discusses in *The Spirit of Romance*, p. 218 ff. Pound's
précis:

Constança, wife of Pedro, heir to the throne of Portugal, died in
1345. He then married in secret one of her maids of honour, Ignez de
Castro, a Castilian of the highest rank. Her position was the cause of
jealousy, and of conspiracy; she was stabbed in the act of begging
clemency from the then reigning Alfonso IV. When Pedro succeeded
to the throne, he had her body exhumed, and the court did homage,
the grandees of Portugal passing before the double throne of the
dead queen and her king, and kissing that hand which had been hers.

Pound deals with this story at length in his original second canto
and concludes with this ironic comment:

What have we now of her, his "linda Ignez"?
Houtman in jail for debt in Lisbon—how long after?
Contrives a company, the Dutch eat Portugal . . . .

Pound apparently cites the *Lusiads* to make a point about the
Renaissance and about poetry of a certain sort. He says of Camoens
as a symptom of the Renaissance, "His work is utterly dependent
upon the events and temper of his time; and in it, therefore, we
may study that temper to advantage. A corresponding study in
architecture were a study of 'barocco.' " *(Spirit of Romance*, p. 215.)
He later quotes De Quincey's remark about "the miracle which can
be wrought simply by one man's feeling a thing more keenly,
understanding it more deeply than it has ever been felt before,"
and comments, "In this pass fails Camoens, for all his splendour,
and with him fail the authors of the Renaissance." *(Ibid.,* p. 219.)
Closely related to these points is this one:

If one were seeking to prove that all that part of art which is not the
inevitable expression of genius is a by-product of trade or a secretion
of commercial prosperity, the following facts would seem significant.
Shortly before the decline of Portuguese prestige, Houtman, lying in
jail for debt at Lisbon, planned the Dutch East India Company.
When Portugal fell, Holland seized the Oriental trade, and soon
after Roemer Visscher was holding a salon, with which are connected

the names of Rembrandt, Grotius, Spinoza, Vondel. . . ." *(Ibid.,* p. 221.)

The Pedro-Ignez story recurs in Canto 30.

39-42 *Here . . . Metu:* Pound briefly remarks on the decline of Mantua: founded by the Etruscans: the home of Vergil; as a free city led by Sordello to repel a besieging army commanded by Ezzelino; under the Gonzaga family, a center of wealth and culture attracting many scholars and artists. The city was sacked in 1630 and never recovered.

41 *Mantegna:* In the original passage Pound has these lines:

Send out your thoughts upon the Mantuan palace—
Drear waste, great halls.
Silk tatters still in the frame, Gonzaga's splendor
Alight with phantoms!

Mantegna worked for the Gonzagas, lords of Mantua from 1460 to 1506, adorning their palaces, chapels, and country-seats with now-ruined frescoes.

42 *Nec . . . Metu:* Neither in hope nor in fear.

1-42 This canto develops the themes of origin and decline started in Canto 2, but the emphasis here is upon the latter. We witness Pound at the embarkation-point of his career, but we must wonder with what prospect of success in "such a beastly and cantankerous age." Venice, once queen of the seas, is revealed as a tourist-trap; the Spanish hero subsists by cheating Jews; "The Dutch eat Portugal"; Homer declines into Camoens, and Odysseus' adventures into Vasco da Gama's; Mantua lies prostrate; Mantegna's frescoes peel.

Nevertheless, the gods exist; the possibility of renaissance remains. Saying that "Latin is sacred, grain is sacred," Pound then asks:

Who destroyed the mystery of fecundity, bringing in the cult of sterility? Who set the Church against the Empire? Who destroyed the unity of the Catholic Church with this mud-wallow that serves the Protestants in the place of contemplation? Who decided to destroy the Church itself by schism? Who has wiped the consciousness of the greatest mystery out of the mind of Europe—to arrive at an atheism proclaimed by Bolshevism, in Russia but not of Russia? *(A Visiting Card,* pp. 18-19.)

He gives a partial answer:

The Rothschilds financed the Austrian armies against Venice and Romagna. Naturally. The Rothschilds financed the armies against the Roman Republic. Naturally. They tried to buy over Cavour. Naturally. Cavour accomplished the first stage towards Italian unity, allowing himself to be exploited according to the custom of his times, but he refused to be dominated by the exploiters. *(Ibid.,* p. 29.)

Pound symbolizes the efforts toward Italian regeneration with the inscription

> R O M A
> O   M
> M   O
> A M O R

And he concludes: "Above all this, the substantiality of the soul, and the substantiality of the gods." Earlier in the same book (p. 7) he has said:

> We find two forces in history: one that divides, shatters, and kills, and one that contemplates the unity of the mystery. . . . There is the force that falsifies, the force that destroys every clearly delineated symbol, dragging man into a maze of abstract arguments, destroying not one but every religion. But the images of the gods, or Byzantine mosaics, move the soul to contemplation and preserve the tradition of the undivided light.

Thus the first three cantos are unified by the religious theme: Odysseus, assisted by Hermes, escapes swinishness; Cadmus, assisted by Athene, builds a city; Pentheus, repulsing Dionysus, is destroyed; Italy, foregoing the cult of fertility for the cult of sterility, is destroyed, but the potential for renewal remains—as the sea remains, from which rose Venus and Venice. The three cantos are also linked by the autobiographical allusions and by the thread of Renaissance history which runs through them. The story of Venice is developed in some detail in Cantos 25 and 26.

*   *   *

The explication done, the ideogram becomes clear enough, and a reasonably adequate prose statement can be made, as has been done. But there are further dissociations to be made, and further linkages, and there are other inferences to be drawn.

For example, reflection upon the explication leads to the conclusion that Pound uses literary figures and literary works as touchstones to indicate aesthetic judgments and that, sometimes, these aesthetic judgments suggest an attitude—positive or negative—toward a given epoch of a society's existence.

As another example, it requires no great effort of the imagination to realize that the girl howling "Stretti" does not have the life expectancy of the gods, her song will not endure as the Spanish epic or the classical works salvaged by Poggio have done. So, in this canto, there would seem to be images of the ephemeral, of the enduring, and of the permanent—the girl and her song, the art-works, the gods. Next, one may consider the destruction of beauty a hellish thing, the assurance of the gods' existence a heavenly thing, the decline of a hero a thing betwixt and be-

tween. One may infer, then, that Pound is indicating here paradisal, purgatorial, and infernal levels of activity. Finally, it has already been made
clear by the explication that autobiographical data, episodes from history,
and mythological elements are brought together.

These are provocative inferences, since they suggest a possible method
of structuring the poem as a whole, and the succeeding chapter will
investigate the matter.

Chapter 5

A brief summary is now in order. According to the data thus far collected, the situation is as follows:

1. Pound's didactic purpose in writing the *Cantos* is, negatively, to show that a civilization does not now exist in Europe or the United States and, positively, to show how one can be produced.

2. Necessary for both negative and positive purposes is comparison of our present society with various societies of the past—some equally squalid, others less so, still others contrastingly successful.

3. Comparison of our society with others, both occidental and oriental, reveals that certain constants are to be ascertained in successful societies: that, in them, a vital religion existed; that scarcity economics was not the order; that money was not misused and that, therefore, taxation was equitable, imperialism unnecessary, and the need for tyrannical rule inside the state and war outside the state were kept at a minimum.

4. Study of Kung and Mencius shows that the requirements for founding and maintaining such a society are available in their writings. Study of the vicissitudes of Chinese history offers substantiating evidence.

5. Study of American history shows that this country made a promising start, that its early government was relatively honest, just, and vigorous, but that in the 1860's control of our government passed into the hands of the usurocrats and has remained there.

6. Study of European history shows that Catholicism, which had recivilized Europe after the fall of Rome, lost its faith and therefore its *virtù* and vigor and was pushed into a position of secondary importance by an ascendant Protestantism, which was essentially an apology for the practice of usury. The Renaissance had its moment of glory and of opportunity, but the power of avarice (both Catholic and Protestant) aborted the moment and forces were set in train to bring us to our present catastrophic century.

7. The study may focus equally well upon money practices or upon the arts: when money is misused, the arts decline; or, if the arts are found to be in a state of decline, nefarious monetary practices will be found to exist.

8. The poem, therefore, will study past and present, Orient and Occident, money and the arts; it will concern itself with the ephemeral aspects of life, with those that have a certain durability—that is, that recur—and with the Permanent that persists behind quotidian and recurrent.

9. It will make use of certain historical figures to exemplify or imagize given historical situations; it will use mythological figures to imagize various aspects of the permanent mysteries; it will use the author himself as a character in our own time experiencing the infernal, purgatorial, and paradisal states of mind possible to a 20th century man.

10. In this study of history, the effort will be to recapture the intensity of life being lived, and, instead of bringing history to the reader, to bring the reader into history. That is, the reader will not witness an event as an accomplished fact but will seem to be a participant in the event. He will therefore often receive fragmentary information, thus being as confused or ignorant or misled as the original actors. He will often have to speak the language of the time, the dialect of the place. On the other hand, though pressed into the action, he will simultaneously maintain his perspective as reader and will be able to draw inferences from startling juxtapositions of apparently divergent times, persons, places, events, ideas.

11. This confrontation of elements, some of them apparently heteroclitic, will produce ideogrammic structures by which Pound will be able to express his meaning without stating it; but the reader may be confident that Pound will make a sufficient number of flat statements to ensure that his message is not left obscure.

Having been (however briefly) introduced to Pound's characteristic thinking on the subjects of religion, history, and economics, having received from the preceding chapter some idea of how these materials are put together in a given canto, the reader's next question may very well concern the method by which the cantos at large are brought to a unity. A good many writers have failed to find in the poem a unifying principle. That there is one I hope to show in the present chapter.

*　　*　　*

In 1917, Harriet Monroe's *Poetry* published the first three of what have since become ninety-eight cantos—and the end not in sight. After a lapse of three years, between 1920 and 1922, *Dial* issued five more. It was in the latter years that Pound wrote to Felix Schelling who, one infers, was somewhat puzzled by what he had seen:

> The first 11 cantos are preparation of the palette. I *have to* get down all the colours or elements I want for the poem. Some perhaps too enigmatically and abbreviatedly. I hope, heaven help me, to bring them into some sort of design and architecture later. *(Letters,* p. 180.)

Before five years have passed, he has found his design:

> Have I ever given you outline of main scheme : : : or whatever it is?
> 1. Rather like, or unlike subject and response and counter subject
> in fugue.
> A. A. Live man goes down into world of Dead
> C. B. The "repeat in history"
> B. C. The "magic moment" or moment of metamorphosis, bust thru
> from quotidien [sic] into "divine or permanent world." Gods,
> etc. (Letters, p. 210.)

In the ensuing ten years his principle of organization does not change:

> Take a fugue, theme, response, contrasujet. Not that I mean to make
> an exact analogy of structure . . . . There is at start, descent to the
> shades, metamorphoses, parallel (Vidal-Actaeon). (Letters, p. 294.)

Pound has referred to the *Cantos* as an epic, defining it as "A Poem
including history," a delusively simple definition, meaningless until the
key-words are understood as Pound understands them. Of poetry he has
said it is "a composition of words set to music," and that it "withers and
'dries out' when it leaves music, or at least an imagined music, too far
behind it." *(Pavannes and Divisions,* p. 151.) This comment more specifically applies to melodic line than to musical structure, perhaps, but
Pound has never been one to ignore the relation between the two. As a
Vorticist, he tended to see form in all the arts in terms of music. The
following analysis, for example, serves to describe a relation both between
painting and music and poetry and music:

> The musical conception of form, that is to say, the understanding
> that you can use form as a musician uses sound, that you can select
> motives of form from the forms before you, that you can recombine
> them and recolour them and "organize" them into new form—this
> conception, this state of mental activity, brings with it a great joy
> and refreshment . . . .
> This "musical conception of form" is more than post-impressionism.
> Manet took impressions of colour. They say Cezanne began taking
> "impressions of form." That is not the same thing as conceiving the
> forms about one as a source of "form-motifs," which motifs one can
> use later at one's pleasure in more highly developed compositions.
> *(The New Age,* 16 (14 Jan. 1915) p. 277.)

Corollary to this conception of form are the following remarks on rhythm
and counterpoint:

> . . . former treatises on harmony dealt with static harmony, they may
> have defined harmony as simultaneous melody . . . but they did not
> consider that the lateral motion, the horizontal motion, and the time
> interval between succeeding sounds *must* affect the human ear . . . .
> The question of where one wave-node meets another, or where it
> banks against the course of another wave to strengthen or weaken its
> action, must be considered. *(Antheil and the Treatise on Harmony*
> (Paris, 1924), p. 10.)

. . . verbal rhythm is monolinear. It can form contrapunto only against its own echo, or against a developed expectancy. *(Ibid.,* p. 35.)

[In a comparison of Arabian music and Provençal metrical schemes]: One might call it a "sort of" counterpoint; if one can conceive a counterpoint which plays not against a sound newly struck, but against the residuum and residua of sounds which hang in the auditory memory. *(Ibid.,* p. 95.)

Given this conception of poem as non-representational composition, it becomes clear that the *Cantos* is probably not going to tell a story, at least in the Aristotelian sense of a straightforward progress from beginning through middle to end. Rather, there will be an organization of motifs, stated, repeated, answered by other motifs, the whole theoretically coalescing into a meaningfulness. Perhaps de Schloezer's description of Stravinsky's *Sacre du Printemps* has point here:

The unity of the Sacre is obtained not by symmetric structure and the return of one or several fundamental themes, but by perfect homogeneity of a clearly characterized melodic, harmonic, and rhythmic style. Each of the 11 episodes has one or two motifs of its very own, melodies or rhythmic formulae diversely treated with repetitions, rhythmic and harmonic variations, contrapuntal development. Certain themes more or less modified pass from one episode to another, thus 2nd theme of Mysterious Circles, appears first, reduced, in Earth Dance. Sometimes episodes follow each other without transition of any kind, or with sudden break off and violent contrast . . . . Elsewhere there is transition via a common theme . . . . ("Stravinsky: his Technique," translated by Pound in *Dial,* 86 (1929) p. 114.)

De Schloezer sums up by ascribing to the *Sacre* a "cellular structure," and referring to it as being "an assemblage of short episodes each having a characteristic melodic, rhythmic, and harmonic element."

If we bring these various matters together, we can arrive at something like this:

1. The *Cantos* has certain basic themes—nekuia, metamorphosis, and historic parallels. These are enunciated as themes in a fugue are and are to be varied and counterpointed. Since it is impossible to run the themes simultaneously as in music, the contrapuntal relation will exist among the lines being read, the memory of lines read earlier and a kind of prevision of what is to come (Pound's "developed expectancy").

2. Words, images, rhythms, or consonant-vowel harmonies repeated from an earlier passage and appearing in the lines being read will jog the memory with the effect that the two passages are working simultaneously upon the reader's sensibilities. Since the reader knows what followed the earlier passage, and since a phrase of that passage has recurred, he develops an expectancy of something to follow logically, which equally affects him.

3. The *Cantos*, however, is of the time of Stravinsky, not of Bach, and the poem will not have the symmetrical structure of a 17th century fugue; it will have the jagged break-offs and startling contrasts of the *Sacre* and will therefore seem episodic. But the episodes will be bound together by the recurrents, the echoes, the wave-nodes meeting one another; and there will be, as well, an over-all "homogeneity of a clearly characterized melodic, harmonic, and rhythmic style."

*   *   *

A relation between the poem and music undeniably exists. But this is a poem "including history." Perhaps a lyric poem—as opposed to an instructional poem—can be developed after the fashion of a musical composition, but one might think that history needs to be "narrated," as the example of historians shows. Such a concept, as we have seen, Pound rejects. As he has already been quoted as saying: "We do NOT know the past in chronological sequence . . . what we know we know by ripples and spirals eddying out from us and from our own time." What we will get instead of chronological narration is something like this. Historical facts have "rained" into Pound's consciousness. Some of these have seemed to him valuable as images illuminating a character, a time, a country, a civilization, and he has carefully filed them away for use. Had he wished, he could have organized them chronologically or according to some other of the schematizations conventionally used by historians. Instead, he has, in the poem, so manipulated them as to make them seem to rain into *our* consciousness. They do not, of course, merely rain; he has organized them into ideograms. But the impression of a raining is captured. This poem "including history" thus dispenses with (as a 20th century epic must, in Pound's opinion) both Aristotelian narration and Aristotelian logic.

A remark by T. S. Eliot in his *The Use of Poetry and the Use of Criticism* applies here. After listing several kinds of difficulty in poetry, he goes on:

> And finally, there is the difficulty caused by the author's having left out something which the reader is used to finding; so that the reader, bewildered, gropes about for what is absent, and puzzles his head for a kind of "meaning" which is not there, and is not meant to be there. The chief use of the "meaning" of a poem, in the ordinary sense, may be . . . to satisfy one habit of the reader, to keep his mind diverted and quiet, while the poem does its work upon him: much as the imaginary burglar is always provided with a bit of nice meat for the house-dog. This is a normal situation of which I approve. But the minds of all poets do not work that way; some of them, assuming that there are other minds like their own, become impatient of this "meaning" which seems superfluous, and perceive possibilities of intensity through its elimination.

It is necessary only to supply the word "narrative" in place of "meaning" to come pretty close to a description of what Pound has done in the *Cantos*—and Eliot, too, in *The Waste Land*.

These two poems seem at first glance quite unlike one another. *The Waste Land* is a poem; the *Cantos* is a poem including history. That is, Eliot merely dramatizes a problem and suggests a solution, whereas Pound, citing the facts and figures which specify the seriousness of the problem and describing the train of events which produced it, works not only as poet but also as social scientist and propagandist. Nevertheless, the two poems share obvious similarities:

1. Both poems ignore chronological and geographical gaps the better to bring historical parallels into a single complex or field of reference.
2. Both compress their materials by using the device of connotative allusion.
3. Both are episodic and eschew normal transitions between episodes.
4. Both make functional use of the nekuia: in the *Cantos* the descent is actually made, in *The Waste Land* it is implied in the role played by Tiresias.
5. Both use the meaningful image or objective correlative.
6. Both comment on the dark lustra of the 20th century, but both suggest a means of lightening the gloom.
7. Both intimate the need for a rapprochement between East and West.
8. Both stand at only one or two removes from allegory.

The last point needs to be developed. Eliot does not create a Red Cross Knight who equals the Anglican Church, or a Bower of Bliss which equates with the Temptations of the Flesh. But in his works appear a Fisher King, reference to whom suggests spiritual sterility, and a rose garden, which seems to serve as objective correlative for some sort of spiritual experience. Although a systematic allegory depicting abstract entities in physical form is not present, things and people in some of Eliot's poems are clearly more than things and people, so that when the reader encounters a leopard or a unicorn he must consider the strong possibility of its having an ulterior significance.

Pound goes no further in this direction than does Eliot. In his study of Dante's allegory, Charles Grandgent differentiates two types of allegory:

> . . . the one starts with an abstract concept and gives it a semblance of material form; the other takes something real and makes it stand for the quality it exemplifies. The first method, to portray despair, creates a giant on whom it bestows that name; the second borrows the classical figure of Medusa. One begets a character called Arrogancy;

the other, to embody that vice, introduces an arrogant Florentine, Filippo Argenti, notorious for his unbridled temper. *(Dante*, p. 272.)

If Pound is to be considered an allegorist at all, he must be so considered in terms of the second definition. Thus Malatesta could be construed as Renaissance in Flower and Kung as Responsible Government, or something of the sort. But it is definite that Pound did not intend the characters in his poem to have an automatic and restrictive two-level existence. True, Malatesta was a Renaissance man; and true, Kung taught the way to bring order into a society. But neither is a collective image, neither is even a type. One is reminded of the anecdote about W. H. D. Rouse who once read paraphrases of the classics to a group of pre-school students: "The headmistress asked a boy 'what story I had been telling last, when we were doing the Iliad.' 'Story?' he said, 'He isn't telling us *stories*. He is telling us *things*.' " And it may be said of Pound: "He isn't giving us *symbols*. He is giving us men."

Recognition that the *Cantos* is not a *Pilgrim's Progress* helps the reader to avoid some futile scrabbling. There is, for example, at the end of Canto 2 (which tells the story of Acoetes' conversion by Dionysus) a passage which reads

> And we have heard the fauns chiding Proteus
> in the smell of hay under the olive-trees,
> And the frogs singing against the fauns
> in the half-light
> and . . .

The too-earnest seeker after ulterior meaning or mythological underpinning might be misled by his own ingenuity into reading the second sentence as a cryptic allusion to the Latona story, in which Latona, coming upon a lake, was debarred from assuaging her thirst by a group of peasants. She said to them: "Why do you deny me water? The use of water is common to all. Nature has made neither sun, nor air, nor the running stream, the property of anyone." The peasants, however, jeeringly muddied the pool with their feet, whereupon the goddess turned them into frogs; as such they still "exercise their offensive tongues in strife." *(Metamorphoses*, Bk. VI, Fable 3.) The story fits nicely into Pound's general attitude; in Canto 4, we have Ran-ti saying, "No wind is the king's wind." And the frog song seems an obvious transition to the howling of the popular song "Stretti" at the opening of Canto 3, which implies something of the decline of Venice from its erstwhile state as mistress of the seas. But Pound has remarked of such an interpretation that "sometimes katz is katz and frawgs frawgs."

Therein lies yet another of the difficulties in reading the *Cantos:* determining when the katz is katz and when, as (for example) lynxes attendant upon Dionysus, they are cats with a symbolic significance. But the difficulty tends to disappear as one reads and re-reads the poem, discovers what images recur, and distinguishes the images associated with major themes from the others. It becomes quite obvious as one goes through the *Cantos* that, for example, the birth of Aphrodite and her sexual union with Anchises, if they do not "stand" for something, certainly impel the mind beyond the literal reference, that (in the Pisan cantos) the Hoo Fasa-City of Dioce juxtaposition possesses more than a surface meaning. Nevertheless there does not exist for the *Cantos* an "Aquinas-map" as there does for the *Commedia*. ("As to the *form* of *The Cantos:* All I can say or pray is: *wait* till it's there. I mean wait till I get 'em written and then if it don't show, I will start exegesis. I haven't an Aquinas-map; Aquinas *not* valid now." *Letters,* p. 323). And a good many readers, at least on first acquaintance, will believe that Grandgent's description of "latterday Symbolism" ("attempted allegory in which the relation of reality to emblem seems arbitrary and external" and in which in detail "It is impossible for the layman to distinguish mysteriously impressive symbols from dainty but insignificant bits of folklore") was made to order for the *Cantos*. However, Yeats's definition of symbolism needs to be considered here as a corrective to Grandgent's rather jaundiced view:

> Symbolism says things which cannot be said so perfectly in any other way, and needs but a right instinct for its understanding; allegory says things which can be said, as well or better, in another way, and needs a right knowledge for its understanding.

The *Cantos*, then, like *The Waste Land* disavows narrative continuity; no more clearly than *The Waste Land* does it make an effort toward allegorical continuity. We are left thus far with a general kind of ordering analogous to that discoverable in modern music and coinciding with a theory of how historical facts get ordered in the receptive mind. George Seferis describes the result in these terms:

> It is . . . an epic of man of today, without plot, without myth, tending to present, in a unity which is purely poetical, an endless number of ingredients, spiritual or historical, which go to make up the life of man. Tragic clash or catharsis, analysis of feelings, action; none of these exist, at least as we are accustomed to follow them in literary works. Only the *episode* exists—it does not matter what episode: it is enough that it is able to mobilise the rhythmic expression of the poet . . . . It is purposeless to demand from such a poetry, where the important and the trivial have the same value, historical or chronographical link. The only link which exists is the link of the poetical language. The first canto, for example, beginning with a paraphrase of the XIth book of the *Odyssey*, ends with the words "so that." But the second canto speaks to us, without any other transitive link, of Sordello. *(An Examination of Ezra Pound,* pp. 77-8.)

But Seferis over-states his case. The poem is, as he says, without plot, but it is not without myth; and it has unifying principles beyond "the purely poetical." Close examination of the first two cantos, spoken of by Seferis, shows clearly that the *Cantos* has greater unity and coherence than he credits it with, and that the episode does not merely exist, but exists for a reason which makes it matter what episode it is.

Canto 1 opens with a 67-line translation into English of a Renaissance Latin translation of the first part of Book XI of the *Odyssey*. It is followed by scraps, in part Englished, from a Renaissance Latin translation of the *Second Hymn to Aphrodite*. A number of questions arise: (1) Why does Pound open his epic with an excerpt from the *Odyssey*? (2) Why with this specific passage? (3) Why with a translation of a Renaissance Latin translation instead of one directly from the ancient Greek?

(1) Pound opens with an excerpt from the *Odyssey* simply because his poem is an odyssey—the story of a society (he has called his poem "the tale of the tribe") which, given favoring winds, has unloosed to its confusion adverse gales, has been lured by Sirens, seduced by Lotos-eaters, transformed to swine by Circes, punished for blasphemy by Apollo, etc., etc. But it is also, as the reader will discover when he gets on to later cantos, the *Odyssey* of Ezra Pound.

(2) He has chosen this particular passage for a number of reasons:

First, the descent is, as we have already seen, a main theme. It will be remembered that at this point in Homer's poem, Odysseus' crew, after a year as swine, have just been restored as men and are ready to continue their voyage to Ithaca. (Pound has spoken often enough of the swinishness of the 19th and 20th centuries. But he has also believed in the inevitability of an American renaissance: "Any agonizing that tends to hurry what I believe in the end to be inevitable, our American Risorgimento, is dear to me. That awakening will make the Italian Renaissance look like a tempest in a teapot!" *Letters*, p. 10.) Before the crew can embark, however, their leader must learn from the soothsaying shades what course to set, what dangers to avoid. So, too, in the *Cantos:* we (reader and Pound) descend into Hades—the past—to learn from the shades—that is, from an enlightened reading of history—how society may achieve its Ithaca.

But, unlike Odysseus, we do not immediately reascend; we stay in Hades for canto after canto, observing in action unmitigated evil, redeemable evil, and good. For Odysseus' nekuia implies (and this is the second reason for his choice of the nekuia passage) Dante's, and Pound has assimilated the one into the other. Thus we make our descent with Odysseus but our Odyssey with Dante, traversing hell, purgatory, and paradise. Pound's comment that his poem begins " 'In the Dark Forest,' crosses the Purgatory of human error, and ends in the light" misleads by indicating for the *Cantos* the same obvious straightforward narrative progression as occurs in the *Divine Comedy*. It does not obviously occur in the *Cantos:* the deep hell of Cantos 14 and 15 is preceded by Canto 13 which, if it does not depict a heaven, at the very least points the way to its attainment. (But there is no illogic in this. The original nekuia of Canto 1 is not a descent into hell but a descent into the historical past. In history, hellish and heavenly times may occur simultaneously or follow one another immediately or after long expanses of time. Further, even in hellish times, the historical record or the memory of other times persists, ready to be actualized. Still further, if the poem is taken as an intellectual biography of Pound, one recognizes that, though the general state of mind in England in the early '20's was hellish, Pound was enabled to escape into the heaven of Confucianism.) And the purgatorial areas which extend on either side of these three cantos are momentarily darkened by glimpses of hell and illuminated by insights into heaven. The poem is not an orthodox comedy opening in complication and moving steadily to resolution. It is an odyssey into past time in which we (carrying the present with us) voyage from island to island of historical significance, exploring some, merely circling others, often returning to landfalls earlier made. Past comments upon past and present, present upon past: out of such comment a future can be built.

One such comment may be inferred from Pound's use of the nekuia passage. It must be inferred, of course, because Pound does not here make expository statements. Nor will he, since the scope of his poem (involving all we have learned in the 600 years since Dante) is so vast, describe panoramically the rise and decline of historical epochs. He is compelled to focus, and the most effective method of focus is to choose and delineate a historical figure who is a microcosm of the strength and weakness of his time. For this purpose both the character Odysseus and his action in requesting advice of Tiresias serve perfectly. (This is the third reason for Pound's choice of this particular passage.)

Odysseus is, for Pound, "the live man among duds," what he is pleased to call a "factive personality," one whose will has a direction, and he lived in "a very high society without recognizable morals, the individual responsible to himself." *(Guide*, p. 38.) Pound says further of the Greek society even in a more sophisticated era: "Plato's *Republic* notwithstanding, the Greek philosophers did not feel communal responsibilities . . . . The sense of coordination, of the individual in a milieu is not in them." *(Loc. cit.)* Therein lay the weakness of Greek society. Its strength lay in its "honour of human intelligence." *(Guide*, p. 146.) It is significant that Pound follows this quoted opinion with Homer's line describing Tiresias:

"Who even dead yet hath his mind entire." Thus Odysseus' descent is an action based upon honor of human intelligence: and Pound's use of the episode is to be understood as a comment upon Greek civilization.

Note has already been made of Pound's belief that in historical research one must differentiate carefully among the casual or ephemeral, the durable or recurrent, and the permanent. The same differentiation must be made as one makes his way through the *Cantos*. Pound has chosen characters, events, spoken comments, and so on to represent the casual; he has chosen others to represent the recurrent; and still others to represent the permanent. An interesting analogy to the poem in this respect is to be found in the Schifanoia frescoes at Ferrara, the lower panel of which shows events from Borso d'Este's life, the middle panel shows signs of the zodiac with their reference to the recurring seasons, and the upper panel shows the triumphs of the immortal gods.

Now, the nekuia passage puts us, with Odysseus, into contact with the immortals, with the mysteries, that is, the permanent. But it also reveals Odysseus as a ruler of a certain sort, an image of a government of a certain sort. Thus we have in the first canto the simultaneous beginning of two patterns, the mythological and the historical. Clearly, since both patterns are swiftly and decisively initiated (the single passage serving double function), Pound's choice of the nekuia passage is an admirable one. And each start promises the possibility of complex development. For example, the repeat (or recurrent) in history, the similarity with a difference. Odysseus is a character of some importance in the *Cantos*, but he owns a greater importance in this: that he foreshadows the leading historical character of the first 50 cantos, the Renaissance condottiere and ruler of Rimini, Sigismondo Malatesta (who, in turn, foreshadows Thomas Jefferson, Napoleon, Benito Mussolini, and others).

The parallel between Odysseus and Malatesta is very close. Malatesta, too, is a live man among duds. Like Odysseus, he had his successes. Though he spent 30 years in the ceaseless Italian wars, he found time to build the Tempio Malatestiano, to gather in Rimini a little of the best in art, and to propagandize the work of Gemisto Plethon, one of the initiators of the Renaissance. But, says Pound, "The Tempio Malatestiano is both an apex and in verbal sense a monumental failure." And he goes on significantly: "It is perhaps the apex of what *one man* has embodied in the last 1000 years of the occident." He reiterates this: "All that a *single man* could, Malatesta managed *against* the current of power." *(Guide,* p. 159.) But granted his individual successes, he, like Odysseus—who, though he won through to Ithaca, lost his ships and his crew—stands as a failure—as does the type of government which he exemplifies.

I have spoken of the mythological and historical patterns. There is a third: the autobiographical. And again Odysseus serves admirably, for like Odysseus, Pound has been a wanderer, undergoing the most various vicissitudes while seeking his Ithaca; has besought the shades for their assistance; has knocked his head against the opaque stupidity of his crew; has suffered his grievous failures; and, like Sigismondo-Odysseus, has, a single man, managed much against the current of his time.

Sigismondo's failure brings us to the third question: Why does Pound use a translation of a Renaissance Latin translation instead of one directly from the ancient Greek?

(3) "In the year of grace 1906, 1908, or 1910," writes Pound, "I picked up from the Paris quais a Latin version of the *Odyssey* by Andreas Divus Justinopolitanus (Parisiis, In officina Christiani Wecheli, MDXXXVIII), the volume containing also the . . . *Hymni Deorum* rendered by Georgius Dartona Cretensis." *(Make It New,* p. 137. Divus' text and a variant translation appear on pp. 138 ff.) Of these two Latin translations he later wrote:

> . . . the Renaissance is perhaps the only period in history that can be of much use to one—for the adducing of pious examples, and for showing 'horrible results'; one seems able to find modern civilization in its simple elements in the Renaissance. The native ideas were not then confused and mingled into so many fine shades and combinations one with another.
>
> Never was the life of arts so obviously and conspicuously intermingled with the life of power.
>
> The finest force of the age, I think, came early—came from Lorenzo Valla. He had a great passion for exactness, and he valued the Roman vortex. By philology, by the 'harmless' study of language, he dissipated the donation of Constantine. The revival of Roman Law, while not his private act, was made possible or accelerated by him. His dictum that eloquence and dialectic were one—i.e., that good sense is the backbone of eloquence—is still worth considering . . . . Also, he taught the world once more how to write Latin, which was perhaps valuable. Seeing that they were drawing much of their thought from Latin sources, a lively familiarity with that tongue could not but clarify their impressions.
>
> At this time, also, observation came back into vogue. The thing that mattered was a revival of the sense of realism: the substitution of Homer for Vergil; the attitude of Odysseus for that of the snivelling Aeneas. . . .
>
> As Valla had come to exactness, it was possible for Machiavelli to write with clarity . . . .
>
> And in the midst of these awakenings, Italy went to rot, destroyed by rhetoric, destroyed by the periodic sentence and by the flowing paragraph, as the Roman empire had been destroyed before her. For

when words cease to cling close to things, kingdoms fall, empires wane
and diminish . . . . And, curiously enough, in the Renaissance,
rhetoric and floridity were drawn out of the very Greek and Latin
revival that had freed the world from medievalism and Aquinas.

Quintilian 'did for' the direct sentence. And the Greek language was
made an excuse for more adjectives. I know no place where this
can be more readily seen than in the Hymns to the Gods appended to
Divus' translation of the *Odyssey* into Latin. The attempt to reproduce
Greek by Latin produced a new dialect that was never spoken and
had never before been read. *(The New Age,* (11 Feb. 1915) ·pp. 409-
410.)

In the prose we have the editorial comment—the interpretation. In the
poem, such interpretation is tabu; we are given instead the thing—the
two pieces of evidence from which inference is possible: Greek straight
talk well-translated into Latin and re-translated into virile (Anglo-
Saxonish) English balanced against the rhetoric which evidences decline.

A reader used to careful transitions, indications of emphasis, the firstly-
secondly-lastly development of "normal" prose and poetry may very well
ask whether Pound is not expecting too much of him to come to Pound's
generalization without having undergone Pound's experience. Here he
is—the normal reader—with small Latin and no Greek; totally unaware
of who Divus or Dartona was; without knowledge of how either wrote
Latin; unread in the *Hymni Deorum;* just barely able to place the other
excerpt somewhere in the *Odyssey.* Can Pound expect him to make head
or tail of the canto? The answer—Pound's answer (he knows his "normal
reader")—is negative. But he can expect at least one among 50 such
readers to poke about in his other works in search of the hint which will
elucidate. Pound is not an obscurantist; he is a poet and teacher. As poet
he compresses and intensifies, he "imagizes" prosy generalizations. As
teacher, he is no "methodist" of the canned-lecture variety, but a titillator
of curiosity, an inciter to research, home-work, outside reading. In short,
he expects his reader to move from the canto to *Make It New* and back
again. And though he might expect it only of a minority of his students, he
would like them to make an even more extended journey; from canto to
Make It New to *Odyssey* and *Hymns* in English and Greek to Divus and
the Cretan and back again to the *Cantos.* As he says of Dante, "Dante
wrote his poem to *make people think* . . . . The style of a poem written
to that end . . . differs from the style suited to a 3000 dollar magazine
story. . . ." *(Polite Essays,* p. 33.) And so does the method. Style and
method must combine to coerce or persuade or irritate us out of cogitation
into meditation; we must not be permitted to receive the poem in an
exclusively passive state. We are to be moved to action—if only the action
of finding the prose parallel and comparing it with the poetic recreation.
This action is, indeed, an important one, since it involves observation of

"the word striving toward precision." Pound has distinguished prose from poetry thus:

> I am unqualified to speak of exalted sentiment, but I should say no idea worth carrying in the mind from one year's end to another, and no story really good enough to make me at least want to tell it, but chafes at the flatness of prose, but suffers from inadequate statement, but leaves me feeling it is but half said, or said in abstraction, defined in terms so elastic that any god's ape can stretch its definition to meet his own squalor or to fit his own imbecility, until it be conjoined with music, or at least given rhythmic definition even though one do not arrive at defining its tonal articulation. . . . Not the idea but the degree of its definition determines its aptitude for reaching to music. *(Polite Essays,* p. 24.)

But the reader who goes this far is unlikely to stop there. He will almost certainly make further progress toward fulfilling Pound's expectations of him. Among other things, he will come to some theories about the means employed by Pound to unify his poem—a subject from which we have been briefly diverted but will immediately return to. By fitting Canto 1 into the context of Pound's thinking some answers to the question of the poem's unity can be found.

I

There is, first, the over-all unity of the journey into the past—the exploration of islands of past experience in the effort to discover permanent values. But the poem is an odyssey, not an *Odyssey:* that is, we assume the position of ship-board participators in events (we see things in passing; our experiences are fragmentary; much of what we see and do can be understood only in part, cannot be fully assimilated) instead of the position of readers of an account of the voyage whose events have been digested, put into proper perspective, with irrelevancies discarded and cause-and-effect relations established.

The Dionysus story of Canto 2 is such an island of past experience, and we are enabled to observe it at some length and from quite close range. But its importance to us on shipboard may not come immediately clear. We may later understand the episode as a recognition of a Messiah, and the *Metamorphoses,* in which it is incorporated, as a Gospel; Pound makes no overt editorial comment upon the story but merely presents it. However, the language, rhythm, and imagery quietly work upon us; an emotional response occurs immediately; later, retrospectively, intellect will be enabled to determine the values of the experience and to infer a meaning. And, of course, reference to Pound's prose writings may reveal at once the significance of the canto as theme and of the doctrine of metamorphosis as part of Pound's structure of religious belief.

II

Secondly, there is the unity of the poem's analogy with Dante's *Comedy*. In his commentary upon the "Inferno," Pound remarks:

> There is little doubt that Dante conceived the real Hell, Purgatory, and Paradise as states, and not places . . . . It is therefore expedient in reading the "Commedia" to regard Dante's descriptions of the actions and conditions of the shades as descriptions of men's mental states in life, in which they are, after death, compelled to continue. . . . (*Spirit of Romance*, p. 117.)

This would seem a fair description of his own "commedia," save that, like Kung, he says "nothing of the 'life after death.' " The Catholic Church holds that "hell is a definite place, but where it is, we do not know." A sect known as Ubiquitarians have believed that hell is everywhere and that the damned are at liberty to roam about the universe carrying their punishment with them. Pound modifies both beliefs. He knows where hell is: it is precisely where the damned are at liberty to roam and obstruct knowledge and distribution. The tyrant's, the usurer's state of mind is infernal; and he can interfuse his hell throughout society as a squid inks water. However, as in the poem as odyssey we see things fragmentarily as participants in the actions and not as a whole as historians, so in the poem as commedia we see the damned, the redeemable, and the redeemed living and acting together, not carefully categorized after judgment and punishment have been decreed.

That is to say, the poem is not clearly marked off into three sections, one devoted to Hell, the next to Purgatory, and the last to Paradise. Or, at least, it is not so clearly marked off as is Dante's poem. It has been stated that the new *Rock-Drill* cantos initiate an entrance into Pound's Paradise. And there are certainly paradisal passages to be found there. But passages are to be found in much earlier cantos which appear to be on an equally high level; and I must confess an inability to determine where (if the 1-2-3 organization does obtain) Hell leaves off and Purgatory begins. I propose to wait for final clarification until the poem is finished and Pound has produced his "Aquinas-map."

The fact is that is it not necessary to draw a structural analogy between Pound's poem and Dante's to come to grips with its meaning. The real effort has to be devoted to differentiating the images representing the good from those representing evil *as they occur*, either as whole cantos, or as parts of cantos, or as lines or fragmentated lines, and, when "good" images tread on the heels of "evil" images, to understand why they are so juxtaposed.

III

Third, there is the unifying effect of Pound's interpretation of history.

This has already been discussed in Chapter 2 and need not be repeated here.

IV

The fourth unifying element is comprised by the mythological pattern. Since the nekuia and the doctrine of metamorphosis are integral parts of this mythology, it has already been touched upon, but it (especially with reference to the figures of the myth) needs somewhat greater elaboration. Pound has said that things acquire significance only in their relation to the gods. And at the time when the earlier cantos were being written and revised, he made explicit his theory of the gods. (Previously quoted on p. 8.)

In the *Cantos*, Pound first declares his belief in the continued existence of the gods in Canto 3:

> Gods float in the azure air,
> Bright gods and Tuscan, back before dew was shed.

But the statement has already been prepared for. Canto 1, as has been said, does initiate the voyage into the past, does imply an amalgamation with the *Divine Comedy*, does comment upon the glory and the failure of the Renaissance, does suggest a relation between Odysseus and Malatesta and their methods of governing their people, and does obliquely introduce us to Pound. More immediately, however, it plunges us into the world of gods and talking shades, of miraculous births and fruitful deaths.

Canto 2 keeps us in that world by dramatizing the manifestation of a god, the perils of ignoring his divinity, and the immediacy of contact between the human and the divine, and by differentiating the ephemeral (the sailors who cannot recognize the divine), the durable (Helen—who moves *like* a goddess and with whom doom of a great city goes in walking), and the eternal (the Eleusinian fructifying power of Dionysus). Canto 4 introduces the elemental creatures, reaffirms the doctrine of metamorphosis, again dramatizes the importance of right relations with the gods (Actaeon-Diana), states the theme of historic parallel (Actaeon-Vidal; Ityn-Cabestan), and brings into a single field of reference Greek, Chinese, and Christian mythology.

The introduction of Canto 5 makes a transition from the Homeric civilization by allusion to the epoch-ending conquests of Alexander and the sophisticated rendering of earlier myth by the Platonists. And this latter offers a point of entry into the Italian Renaissance, to which five of the six succeeding cantos are devoted. The mythological pattern becomes predominant again in 15, where Pound is led out of hell by Plotinus; continues in 16, where Pound, after bathing in acid to free himself of hell-ticks, travels to confront the Malatesta brothers; is varied in 20 by comment of the Lotophagoi on Odysseus as commanding officer, and here ascends to a climax in the description of a procession, the diminishing passage of which is described in the latter half of 21. Save for fragmentary allusions, the mythic element is submerged by historical and personal narrative until Canto 39, which is devoted to Circe and to "making the god." Canto 40 varies the odyssey theme into Hanno's periplus; 47 brings together the Adonis and the Odysseus stories; then the myth is dropped in the Chinese and American cantos, to emerge in the Pisan cantos, like Paradise, in fragments. In Canto 74, three significant elements are added: the Lute of Gassir (a folk-song collected by Frobenius in North Africa), the city of Dioce (the story of which is told in Herodotus), and the tale of Ouan Jin (an Australian folk-tale). In Canto 79 appears a long (five pages) address to the lynx, sacred to Dionysus; other components of Pound's myth (as on pp. 12, 16, 35-6, 53, 78-9, 90-91, 95, and 108 of the Pisan cantos) occur fragmentarily.

In Canto 90 (and those following) of the *Rock-Drill* group, the myth becomes of extreme importance. We seem to be witnessing the gradual but inevitable victory of the paradisal—a victory taking place in the heart and mind of Pound himself. Throughout these cantos, Castalia appears to be the objective correlative of the place in which Pound, through prayer, humility, agony, comes to union with the process. The union—or the approach to the union—is imagized by the return of the altar to the grove, the "substantiation" of Tyro and Alcmene, the ascension of a procession, and the upward climb of a new mythic component, the Princess Ra-Set. Where, in Canto 82, Pound was drawn by Gea Terra, and in 83 found no base under Taishan (a holy mountain whose summit is to be achieved, as the city of Dioce is to be built) but the brightness of Hudor, in the *Rock-Drill* cantos he has moved into air, into light, and beyond. And where, in Canto 80, the raft broke and the waters went over the Odysseus-Pound, in 95 Leucothoe has pity and rescues him.

I do not believe that the significance of the mythological pattern in the *Cantos* has been sufficiently recognized. Mr. Watts, in *Ezra Pound and The Cantos*, fails to consider it, and because of this failure he comes to his characterization of Pound as a "nominalist" who insists that "we cultivate the only garden that we can really hope to cultivate: the immediate one that the five senses make available to us . . . .", who is essentially "one of a company that locates truth and wisdom in the transient moment," who "denies that truth exists in a fashion different from that in which the moment exists." (P. 105.)

It is quite true that Pound, like the medieval nominalists, is skeptical of the generalizing and the categorizing and the synthesizing processes and that he has attacked a good many philosophers, historians, theolo-

gians, economists, and literary critics with Occam's razor. But in attacking
them, he has not denied a permanent truth, or a permanent beauty; he
has only denied that their concept of truth or beauty has been a valid
one. The trouble with official generalizers has consisted in this: that they
have uttered as truth what they did not know and have coerced belief in
that misrepresented "truth"; that in achieving their synthesis they have
arbitrarily leveled out those differences which would have made it recognizable as a falsification.

That is, the gods exist. There is not one all-enveloping oblong whirl
whose existence can be discovered by deduction and whose characteristics
can be delineated in terms of the needs of a ruling class. But there are
permanent verities which can be distinguished one from another—as
Artemis can be distinguished from Aphrodite or Aphrodite Urania from
Aphrodite Pandemos. Without intuited belief in these verities, no culture
can exist. The belief is necessary and action upon the belief is necessary,
so long as that action does not take the form of rationalizing the belief into
a dogma which permits no change within or competition without. "When
you don't understand it, let it alone"; Aristotle, the Stoics, Aquinas,
among others, have sinned against this maxim.

Pound quotes from Scaevola the latter's differentiation of three theologies: "the poet's anthropomorphic and false, the philosopher's rational
and true but not for use, the statesman's built on tradition and custom."
(Guide, pp. 124-5.) What the Cantos proposes is "a wisdom built of the
first and third theologies." The third, of course, is Kung's; the first is
Ovidian. Each states permanent truth, neither "locates truth and wisdom
in the transient moment."

In short, since, in Pound's opinion, a culture without a religious faith
is impossible and since the Cantos represents a guide to culture, the work
must be considered a religious poem. That it has not been so considered
has been in large part due to Eliot's false antithesis, of which Pound has
said:

> Mr. Eliot will reply, even in print . . . as if some form of Xtianity
> or monotheism were the sole alternative to irreligion; and as if
> monism or monotheism were anything more than an hypothesis
> agreeable to certain types of very lazy mind too weak to bear an
> uncertainty or to remain in "uncertainty." (Dial, 85, p. 400.)

Mr. Eliot has often been referred to as our century's most eminent religious poet; and there are those who believe his Ash Wednesday to be the
century's finest religious poem. He (and it) may or may not be. I do feel,
however, that before such statements are made (or received as gospel)
comparison must be made between Ash Wednesday and such a passage
as the following:

Then knelt with the sphere of crystal
That she should touch with her hands,
           Coeli Regina,
The four altars at the four coigns of that place,
But in the great love, bewildered
        farfalla in tempesta
under rain in the dark:
              many wings fragile
Nymphalidae, basilarch, and lycaena,
Ausonldes, euchloe, and erynnis
And from far
         il tremolar della marina
chh   chh
    the pebbles turn with the wave
chh   ch'u
        "fui chiamat'
           e qui refulgo"
Le Paradis n'est pas artificiel
           but is jagged,
For a flash,
    for an hour.
Then agony,
        then an hour,
           then agony,
Hilary stumbles, but the Divine Mind is abundant
          unceasing
          improvisatore
Omniformis
      unstill
           (Canto 92, p. 79.)

Or this one:

Not arrogant from habit,
    but furious from perception,
          Sibylla,
from under the rubble heap
        m'elevasti
from the dulled edge beyond pain,
        m'elevasti
out of Erebus, the deep-lying
    from the wind under the earth,
        m'elevasti
from the dulled air and the dust,
        m'elevasti
by the great flight,
        m'elevasti,
          Isis Kuanon
    from the cusp of the moon,
        m'elevasti
the viper stirs in the dust,
        the blue serpent
glides from the rock pool

And they take lights now down to the water
the lamps float from the rowers
          the sea's claw drawing them outward.
"De fondo" said Juan Ramon,
          like a mermaid, upward,
but the light perpendicular, upward
and to Castalia,
                    water jets from the rock
and in the flat pool as Arethusa's
                    a hush in papyri.
Grove hath its altar
          under elms, in that temple, in silence
a lone nymph by the pool.
                              (Canto 90, pp. 66-7.)

The comparison made, these questions may be asked: Which poet seems the more certainly to have participated in the religious experience? Which more effectively compels the reader to share the experience? And which, after the spell of the experience has been broken, induces the reader to consideration of the terms of the experience? The questions must be answered, of course, with full recognition that the possibility of an approach to the mystery is not monopolized by Christians and that there is a usable devotional vocabulary other than that to be found in the *Book of Common Prayer*.

But, to get back to Pound's use of myth. The mythological pattern which runs through the *Cantos*, taken in conjunction with the historical pattern, provides the wisdom in terms of which a culture can be achieved. Of the former pattern some description is possible:

1. It involves not one god but a pantheon of gods, the images of most of them being Graeco-Roman in origin.

2. Important in the pantheon are Dionysus (varied into Adonis, Tammuz, Manes), Koré, Demeter—agents of fructification; Apollo and Helios --symbols of precision of definition; Aphrodite—a symbol for the imposition of material form on concept; Diana, both cruel and kind—suggesting the dual nature of change; Kuanon—the merciful, contemplation of whom induces the peace that passeth understanding; Ra-Set, who, like Danae, represents a fruitful god-man relationship; Hermes, the emissary between the gods and men and thus eminently helpful; but perhaps representing, too, that the gods are not altogether predictable, that man must be very precise indeed in defining his relations with them; Athene—a symbol of Justice.

3. Among the minor personages will be such figures (borrowed or manufactured) as Odysseus, Elpenor, Tyro, Alcmene, Tiresias, So-Gioku, Ran ti, So-shu, Hathor, Nerea, Zothar, Aletha, Vanoka, etc.

4. Possibly Yao, Chun, and Yu. Their virtue was so great, they lived in an antiquity so remote that they may perhaps be accorded a status between the historical and the mythological.

5. Among the dominant themes in the myth are these:

a) the need to consult the dead (conserve the tradition)—nekuia (Canto 1)

b) the need to escape provincialism (to see many people, many places) —odyssey or periplum (Canto 40)

c) the need for rebirth in new form—metamorphosis (Canto 2)

d) the need for decorum in dealing with the mysteries—Actaeon (Canto 4)

e) the need to recognize the varied recurrent—Actaeon-Vidal (Canto 4)

f) the need for accord with natural process—Hesiod, *Li Ki* (Cantos 47 and 52)

g) fertility through sacrifice—Adonis, Proserpine, etc. (Canto 47)

h) the need to bring energy and discipline to equipoise—Zagreus-Kung (Canto 13)

i) the forming and informing of matter—Aphrodite (Canto 90)

j) the creative power of emanating light—Ocellus, Cavalcanti, etc. (Cantos 36, 91)

k) the ascension to higher levels of understanding—Ra-Set, the moving figures in the procession (Cantos 94, 20)

l) the ultimate building of the city—Dioce, Wagadu (Canto 74) (The figures named in the above list, and the cantos specified, are only exemplary; other figures and cantos serve a similar function.)

To summarize, the mythology functions in various ways:

1. The nekuia-odyssey theme serves both to get the poem off to an immediately dramatic start and to hold together the total poem within the single, all-embracing metaphor. It offers "By no means an orderly Dantescan rising/but as the winds veer . . . and the raft is driven" (Pisan cantos, p. 21) but nevertheless it leads from "NEKUIA where are Alcmene and Tyro/to the Charybdis of action," and beyond—to Ithaca.

2. The coalescence of the Homer and Dante stories plus the immediately succeeding metamorphosis theme label the poem unmistakably as an affirmation, a comedy. (*The Waste Land*, it will be remembered, was long misconstrued as a negation.)

3. Composed, as it is, of those archetypal elements of belief which have operated most powerfully upon men's minds, it asserts the existence of permanent values; it thus makes possible ethical comment upon historical events—contrapuntally harmonizes history and ethics.

4. The material of the myth is of such intrinsic beauty that it can be used to represent a paradisal state at any point in the poem.

5. It offers, because of the familiarity of the material, the opportunity of juxtaposing mythological fragments with historical fragments to produce a meaningful ideogram.

6. The "fundamentalism" of the mythic elements chosen makes possible an assimilation of Dante's, Kung's, and Hellenic values. (Milton's assimilation of Hellenic and Hebraic values in *Paradise Lost* is attacked by exclusion.)

7. The mythic figures can be used (as the neo-Platonists themselves used them) to give concrete form to a very subtle interpretation of the relation between the ultimate creating force, intermediary forces, and the thing created.

8. The myth is used to comment upon the state of mind of Pound himself at certain junctures of his personal history, thus bringing history, ethic, and autobiography into one frame of reference.

V

The last point brings us to the next and possibly most important of the unifying elements of the poem—its autobiographical development. For the poem is a Guide to Kulchur, yes, but it is also a history of how Pound got kulchured—a kind of *Prelude*, though lacking that poem's chronological arrangement, narrative continuity, and retrospective-meditative character. Pound is to be seen in his own person—in Venice, London, Rapallo, New York, Gibraltar, Vienna, Paris, the concentration camp, etc. The things that happened to him in these places are "incidents in the development of a soul" (Browning's description of *Sordello*). That is, Pound does at times adopt the first-person point of view, stand off from himself and depict himself in some action or another. So, for example, we see him in the earlier cantos toying with a translation of the Homeric Hymn (Canto 1); differentiating his poem from Browning's (2); in Venice in 1908 (3); commenting on his ability to achieve Dante's heights (5); recording Henry James's conversation, and reflecting upon Paris (7); meeting Baldy Bacon (12); experiencing and escaping from London's hellish state of mind (15); achieving an Ithaca in Italy (16, 17, 20); conversing with Hamish (18); and with Arthur Griffith, Steffens, and others (19); visiting "old Levy" (20); baiting an orthodox economist (Keynes), hearing a folk-tale, visiting Gibraltar (22); in the act of translation (23); in Paris, Venice, Milan (27); in Chiasso and elsewhere (28); in Vienna (38); in Siena (43); commenting on his poem, talking to Orage, editorializing (46); watching a mass and procession (48). And in the Pisan cantos he is omnipresent.

But, though it shows most clearly in the Pisan cantos, the total poem is autobiography--a record of the experience that swirled into Pound as vortex, of his undergoing the experience of having experience swirled into him, and of the operation of his mind when he formalized the experience to produce the poem.

A thorough reading of his prose will give detailed information about most of the experiences—intellectual and otherwise—which Pound has been involved in. Not all, of course. In Canto 7, there is no hint that (on p. 27) "The live man, out of lands and prisons," is Desmond Fitzgerald, the Sinn Feiner whom Pound met along with Arthur Griffith. (They appear again on pp. 84-5 of 19.) I have found no reference elsewhere to the story told Pound by an Italian hotel-keeper and recorded on p. 102, Canto 22 (the story of how Jesus came to make Adam's mate of a fox's tail) ; only the briefest reference to the succeeding Gibraltar incident; none to the sequence of reminiscences in Cantos 28 and 29. Many of the allusions threaded through the Pisan cantos will remain obscure until Pound's biographer ravels them out. However, the reason for Pound's use of these stories and reminiscences is usually plain. We already have the background of the "I mean, that is Andreas Divus." "I sat on the Dogana's steps" in 3 gives a time and a place when Pound saw vividly a declined culture and, simultaneously, the potential of regeneration; in 4, "Topaz I manage . . ." comments on Pound's poetical abilities and suggests influences on his work; 7 shows him in Paris discriminating the live from the dead; 12 also discriminates live men from duds—Jim X (John Quinn), for example, set against "the ranked presbyterians"; 16 shows the reckless waste of talent and genius which has produced the hell in London of 14 and 15, the cynical manipulation of uninformed and misinformed people which makes war and fruitless revolution possible,and the escape of Pound from this confused milieu to a reviving Italy; 17, 18, and 19 continue the themes of 16; 20 offers a contrast by showing the "conspiracy of intelligence" going on in the midst of the debacle: Emil Levy and Pound concerned with the permanent matter of achieving a precise definition; 21 ("Gold fades" et seq.) shows that Pound has discovered the peace with quiet not given those who "died in the whirlpool" "after many vain labours"; 22 contrasts the intelligence of Major Douglas and the creative energy of an unnamed Italian with the stupidity of Keynes and the torpidity of an English publishing company, and dramatizes the realism, the vitality, the down-to-earthness of those unorthodox economists, the Mohammedans and Jews of Gibraltar; 23 places Pound again in his earthly paradise of Rapallo; 27 ("England off there in black darkness" et seq.) contrasts the decadence of Paris in the early '20's with the communal vitality of faith of the middle ages, comments on communal activity (revolution) having, perhaps, faith but not knowledge and

thus building no *duomo*; 28 seems to describe persons who distract
the attention of workers (Pound, Rennert, Pound's uncle) and who must
be resisted to compel them to "dive and . . . flee"; 29, with its emphasis
on osmosis, suggests the result of failing to resist and thereby sinking in
the bourgeois mind, and contrasts such sinking with an ascension (such
as Cunizza's) into Paradise; 35 takes Pound to middle Europe and describes another (see 22 for the first) aspect of the Jewish character; 38
isolates Frobenius (and Pound) from the general European muddle and
describes the effect of Douglas's pronouncements upon Pound; in 43
Pound sees from his window the continuing good effect of a good banking
system; 46 adverts to the London scene and Pound's acquaintance with
Douglas, Orage, *et al*; in 48 occurs another statement by anecdote of the
utility of traditional knowledge in which the folk have faith.

Most of the anecdotal material of the Pisan cantos is self-explanatory
or can be explained by reference to the earlier, fuller telling of the story,
though one difficulty lies in dissociating what Pound was perceiving in
the camp from what he was recollecting out of the past. Some of these recollections are formally introduced, as in 74 with the line "Lordly men are
to earth o'ergiven/these the companions" (p. 10). Some are explained in
an earlier canto. For example, on p. 32

> So that in the synagogue in Gibraltar
>   the sense of humour seemed to prevail
>   during the preliminary parts of the whatever
> but they respected at least the scrolls of the law
>   from it, by it, redemption . . . .

is explained in Canto 22. And some, contrariwise, explain earlier allusions.
The opening line of Canto 39 is elucidated on page 36 of the Pisan cantos:

> this wind out of Carrara
> is soft as *un terzo cielo*
>   said the Perfetto
> as the cat walked the porch rail at Gardone
>   the lake flowing away from that side
> was still as is never in Sirmio . . . .

But most of the recollections of the Pisan cantos (particularly from 80
to the end) are to be considered as tied together by these lines:
(1) Dum spiro amo; (2) amo ergo sum; and (3)

> What thou lovest well remains
>   the rest is dross
> What thou lov'st well shall not be reft from thee
> what thou lov'st well is thy true heritage . . . .
>   (Canto 70; Canto 80; Canto 81.)

The distinctive feature of the Pisan cantos is their sense of immediacy.
In the earlier cantos we journey to past times and distant places or make

the grand tour through contemporary Europe as companions of Pound and distinct from him. But in the Pisan cantos, the distinction tends to vanish; we are drawn into and become one with Pound, experiencing and recollecting with him. If we have read well in the earlier cantos and in his prose, we can slip with almost his ease from one memory to another or from perception to associated recollection. For the materials of these cantos do not differ (save in details) from those which have already been stated at some length: the mythological, the historical, and the autobio- graphical. And the same principles of organization obtain. Only shifts in emphasis and of stance and of mood have occurred. The historian has given way to the self-biographer—the *Commedia* has swallowed the *Odyssey*; the poet is less aloof from his reader—in a sense, the teacher has swallowed the pupil; and the lyric as an expression of personal emo- tion supersedes the dramatic lyrics and the instructional poetry of the earlier cantos. But these cantos have changed only because the man and his situation have changed, and such change does not, of course, violate the unity of the poem considered as autobiography.

As for the recently published section, known as *Rock-Drill*, there are some personal comments (as "And there is something decent in the uni- verse/if I can feel all this, *dicto millesimo*/At the age of whatever"), but far fewer than in the intensely personal Pisans, and to these what has been said of the private allusions in the Pisan cantos applies. As has been indicated, however, in the Pisan and *Rock-Drill* sections, the auto- biographical and mythical levels are assimilated into one to a degree not the case in the earlier cantos. In the Pisans, Pound undergoing the dark night of the soul, out of harmony with the process (as Odysseus was with the gods) but surviving against odds to learn humility and compassion, is to be seen constantly in close relation with his mythic images. And in the *Rock-Drill*, as he approaches that harmony, the relation is even closer.

* * *

The argument that the *Cantos* does possess unity can be summarized as follows. Pound's mind is to be considered a vortex into which all experi- ence rushes—"all the energized past, all the past that is living and worthy to live." Pound as artist is obligated to impose form on this mass of material without falsifying it, laboring under the necessity of expressing himself (the Element of Personality), of expressing what is particular to his epoch (the Element of Style), and of expressing what is particular to all art (the Element of the pure and eternal qualities of the art of all men, of all peoples, and of all times). As vorticist poet, he will use only the primary medium (or pigment) of his art. Namely, the image. By means of his images he will define his ideas since "not the idea but the degree of its definition determines its aptitude for reaching to music."

And he will arrange his images and ideas so that they rain upon his reader and swirl into his vortex, employing, perhaps, Kandinsky's recipe:

> . . . the principles of concord and discord in all the . . . parts; the juxtaposition of the single forms, the interpenetration of one form with another, the distortion, the binding and tearing apart of the individual forms, the same treatment of the groups of forms, of the combination of the mysterious with the definite, the rhythmic with the non-rhythmic on the same plane, the abstract forms with the purely geometrical . . . . all these are the elements which create the possibility of a purely aesthetic counterpoint . . . . *(Blast,* p. 124.)

Using such a method Pound is better able (he believes) to vivify for the reader his own experiences than is, for example, Wordsworth with such vaguely emotive statements as "Bliss was it then to be alive"; better able to make learning a creative instead of a passively-receptive process than is the historian who coldly furnishes forth the funeral baked meats of history; better able to synthesize religious enthusiasm and ethical teaching than, say, Milton, whose spokesmen in *Paradise Lost* being formed in Milton's image evoke no awe and appear as special pleaders.

The method will not admit of narrative continuity in the traditional sense. But the apparently disparate components will be discovered to have their places in mutually cooperating patterns: the autobiographical, the historical, and the mythical; the infernal, the purgatorial, the paradisal; and the ephemeral, the recurrent, the permanent. And if the reader bring to bear upon it as needed the proper one of Richard St. Victor's three modes of thought (cogitation, meditation, and contemplation), the poem as a whole will be discovered to hold together both as a record of the development of a soul and as a pronouncement, in terms of the evidence, of the requirements of a good society.

Chapter 6

Unity exists beneath the surface diversity of the *Cantos* as it exists in the union of states which, despite the variance between a New Mexico and a South Carolina or a Texas and a Rhode Island, remains indivisible. The poem is neither a rag-bag as Blackmur has said, nor, as Tate has said, merely talk, talk, talk. And it has coherence as well as unity. There is, first, the method of indicating a relation between elements by a variation of language, rhythm, and melody. The first 67 lines of Canto 1 move vigorously forward, the strong beat of the alliterated lines producing an effect precisely right for the action being described—men's work being done by heroic men in a primitive time. The mood evoked by these lines is rudely broken by the prose statement of bibliographical data. "I mean, that is Andreas Divus,/In officina Wecheli, 1538, out of Homer," so that we are prepared (after "And he sailed, by Sirens and thence outward and away / And unto Circe," which pulls us back from the sphere of prose and reality to that of poetry and myth) for the broken rhythms, the disconnected harmonics, the sense of unsuccessful effort, of second rate versifying:

> Venerandam,
> In the Cretan's phrase, with the golden crown, Aphrodite,
> Cypri munimenta sortita est, mirthful, oricalchi, with golden
> Girdles and breast bands, thou with dark eyelids
> Bearing the golden bough of Argicida. So that:

The melopoeic contrast between the two passages is so great that we cannot doubt an attitude of affirmation on Pound's part toward the first and of relative negation toward the second.

Second, there is an ideogrammic connection between the two passages. The first (in itself a complete action) pictures successful future accomplishment resulting from present daring; emphasis is placed upon men imposing their will upon matter. The second (not an action, but a catalog of attributes) gives a rather unclear picture of a woman stagily posing; emphasis is placed upon the feminine, richly adorned and inactive. No comment is made, no analogy expressly drawn, the terms of comparison have been reduced to nothing. But the coalescence of the two pictures into a single ideogram says as clearly as would a declarative sentence: After strength, weakness; after rise, decline. It would be a mistake, of course, to find here a simple contrast of good and evil, white

119

and black. For the golden bough of the second passage contrasts favorably with the bronze lance heads of the first; Aphrodite's mirthfulness with "joyless region," "ill star," etc; and her journey over the sunlit ocean to Odysseus' over the "dark sea." So that one is justified in elaborating the above "declarative sentence" to read: in our beginnings are our ends; in our ends are our beginnings.

To repeat a previous statement, the melopoeic-ideogrammic method presents for contemplation a series of pictures, cohering in sound; these produce in the reader a thought which no longer needs to be expressed—if the reader is a sensitive, active receptor. The poem means without expressing a meaning. And it may be argued that it means more than it would if it expressed a meaning. For a statement of meaning appeals to the rational man as distinct from the total man of sense *and* sensibility the former always running the danger of taking the prose meaning and letting the poetry go.

Granting this to be true, there will be few readers, nevertheless, who are not going to demand intellectual coherence too. What is more, it is not so easy as the previous paragraphs implied to determine without reference to Pound's prose works what the components of his ideograms signify. A good example is Canto 30, which offers

1. A lyric in antique style—Artemis wailing against pity.

2. An allusion to the Venus-Vulcan-Mars triangle.

3. The general statement "Time is of the evil," followed by an allusion to the Pedro-Ignez story.

4. An allusion to a Madam ΥΛΗ, which may run three lines or five.

5. Allusion to a certain Messire Alfonso, who non-committally passed an unspecified place on his way to Ferrara.

6. An allusion to early type-cutting.

7. Allusion to a text of Laurentius and a codex of the Malatestas.

8. Statement that Pope Alessandro Borgia has died.

What is the even quite sensitive reader to make of this medley? He will take note that the first two components make use of archaic spellings and verb endings, that the burden is mythological, that Pound here uses rhyme as he rarely does in the *Cantos* and repetition and alliteration as he often does. He will wonder if the first component is a translation of one of Pound's touchstones (René Taupin thought it a rendering of Propertius) or whether it is original. He may wonder whether Pound intended an honest effect of beauty or, ironically, one of "pretty-pretti-

ness" like that contrived in the "poesie" which Stendhal made anachron-
istic. He will perhaps remember the Diana-Actaeon story of Canto 4 and
wonder whether Artemis equals Diana and whether a relation between
the two cantos is intended. He will wonder what the relation of this lyric
is to the other components of the ideogram—one or two of which (4 and
5) will mean nothing to him at all. (He will therefore consider very
carefully the language and rhythm of 4 and 5 and try, with uncertain
success, to determine whether positive or negative values are being expressed.) And he will wonder what the relation of this canto is to the one
which precedes and the one which follows—each quite different from it
(and from each other) in mood, language, and first-level subject matter.

He will do a lot of wondering. And though his sensibilities will offer
something in the way of conjectural answers, he will still remain uncertain
that he is responding as Pound intended. And if he discovers on further
study that he has not responded as some critic (offering no evidence) says
he should have, he will be distraught indeed.

No, most readers are going to demand the assurance of sense as well
as that of sensibility. And why not? One may cynically suspect that some
critics of the *Cantos,* favorable toward Pound but finding in the poem no
intellectual coherence, have concealed their failure by diverting attention
to its tonal or conversational or musical coherence. They need not have
done so, for the poem does not disappoint on the intellectual level.

Even the most superficial explication of Canto 30, for example, will
show this to be true.

1-18 *Compleynt . . . away:* In his discussion of the *Divine Comedy (Spirit
of Romance,* p. 125), Pound remarks, "When Dante weeps in pity for the
sorcerers and diviners, *(Inferno XX)* Virgil shows classic stoicism":

> Art thou, too, like the other fools? Here liveth pity when it is well
> dead. Who is more impious than he who sorrows at divine judgment?

Of this same passage Charles Williams *(The Figure of Beatrice,* p. 136)
has written: "Dante weeps . . . from sheer misery at the physical contortion
of the human form. . . . All is gone awry; all is perverted—and so much
so that his pity here has no place." Thus the Diana-Actaeon story of Canto
4 has its editorial comment here. Offenses against the verities must be
judged and punished. When sentiment, a lack of savagery in intellectuals,
a false tolerance interfere with the exercise of justice, all things are
"growne awry," as they are in this day when knowledge is perverted (as
Dante's Sorcerers perverted it) to the selfish ends of the individual or of
the privileged minority.

The passage is not "to be taken as a plea for setting up the inquisition
again 115 years after the last burning for heresy" *(Guide,* p. 185), since a

church believing its own dogma would not run to such excess. On the other hand, ". . . the elimination from protestant Europe, England and America of any sense of mental corruption and of any need to describe states of decaying mind by the analogous states of material rot and corruption, is the justification of theological hate." *(Loc. cit.)*

Pound was thinking specifically of the art of printing when he wrote this. He said further:

> Abomination of desolation and may hell rot the whole political ruck of the 19th century as lasting on into our time in the infamy which controls English and U. S. finances and has made printing a midden, a filth, a mere smear, bolted down by the bank racket, which impedes the use of skill and implements for the making of proper books or of healthy populations. The first step toward a new Paideuma is a clearance of every prelate or minister who blocks, by diseased will or sodden inertia, a cleaning of the monetary system. There is no mediaeval description of hell which exceeds the inner filth of these mentalities." *(Ibid.,* p. 184.)

Thus these lines and 11.44 ff. are to be taken together.

19-24 *In . . . warm:* in Pound's translation of *Donna mi prega,* (Canto 36) love takes its state where memory liveth, "Formed like a diafan from light on shade / Which shadow comes from Mars . . . ." He glosses the passage *(Make It New,* p. 388) : ". . . there is a Neoplatonic gradation of the assumption of faculties as the mind descends into matter through the seven spheres, *via* the gate of Cancer: in Saturn, reason; in Jupiter, practical and moral; in Mars, the 'spirited'; in Venus, the sensuous." The comment here seems to be upon love tamed, spiritless, gone to "bed with decrepitude" (Canto 14), usura having stayed "the young man's courting"; thus, perhaps, upon the Church's divorce from vigorous belief, leading to sterility.

25-36 *Time . . . her:* see note to 1. 38, Canto 3 (p. 89) ; an image of the decline of the Renaissance.

36-40 *Came . . . it:* Madame "matter"—Pound's name for Lucrezia Borgia whom Alfonso d'Este took from Rome to be his wife. Pound gives her this name because, with no regard to morality, she adapted (or molded) herself to circumstances. Though her behavior in Ferrara was respectable, her actions in Rome showed that she could habituate herself to such evil practice as was necessary to gain her ends.

41-43 *Is . . . O:* Alfonso chose Lucrezia for political reasons; "what kind of a press release would you expect from Alfonso? She was hardly the blushing bride." (She turned out, however, a good deal better than he expected.) The insistence on coming and going is not without point. So the Church, so the Italian city-states, so the Renaissance rose to splendor and declined. Ferrara recalls not only the Estes and Borgias but also the

meeting of the fathers of the Eastern and Western churches which Gemisto
Plethon attended.

44-62 *Whence . . . Malatesta:* an image of the durable which underlies
the transient. In this paraphrase of Soncinus's comment are brought
together: good printing; the Medici library (enlightened despotism);
Petrarch (Soncinus's remarks preface an edition of the poet); Malatesta
and his Tempio (good architecture); and, by implication, Gemisto
Plethon's good thinking.

63-4 *And . . . mori:* like d'Este, Alessandro came and went; and the
Church continued its descent toward the Reformation. But one must
remember that "An institution which has survived the picturesqueness
of the Borgias, the picaresqueness of the Renaissance, and produced
Pauthier, Lacharme and Don Bosco, has an inherent resilience." *(Guide,*
p. 259.)

1-64 *Compleynt . . . mori:* "In a Europe not YET rotted by usury . . .
Sigismundo . . . registered a state of mind, of sensibility, or all-aroundness
and awareness." *(Guide,* p. 159.) Lorenzo built a library. "Gemisto
Plethon brought over a species of Platonism to Italy in 1430." *(Guide,*
p. 224.) Soncinus and the printing press made their significant contribution to ushering in the Renaissance.

Canto 30, then, as this explication reveals, is a summarizing and a
transitional canto: Greek mythology, Catholicism, and neo-Platonism are
brought together, as are a Renaissance apex and a Renaissance decline;
government by the strong individual is alluded to. Thus, much of the
burden of the preceding cantos is here epitomized. But the Pope's death
and the allusion to printing hint at things to come in later cantos: the
rise of Protestantism, the shift from an Italy-centered to a Britain-centered
world—a Britain which will, in the course of time, originate a Bank of
England, making money out of nothing and assuming control of Britain's
destiny; which will develop colonies in North America and, because of
financial malpractice, lose them; which will, in the war against Napoleon,
come under the thumb of the Rothschilds, as the United States, after the
Civil War, likewise falls to the bankers.

Obviously, not all of this is in Canto 30 itself—it is in Canto 30 taken
in connection with other cantos. But this is a way of saying that canto
connects with canto—that they cohere.

A first step in revealing the intellectual coherence of the *Cantos* at large
is to construct an outline, organizing the 95 separate cantos into as small
a number of groups as is simultaneously convenient and meaningful. The
first and obvious organization is as follows:

Cantos 1-51: (1) a history of Europe from the Renaissance to the present, with special emphasis upon the Italian peninsula, and not neglecting

classical and medieval influences which gave the Renaissance its character. (2) a brief history of the United States's experiment in government. Note: Cantos 13 and 49 do not fit into this historical frame.

Cantos 52-61: a history of China.

Cantos 62-71: a full-length portrait of John Adams.

Cantos 72-73: not published.

Cantos 74-84: Pound's reflections upon the state of the society the history of which he has recounted; and a consideration of himself, leading to an awakened humility, which leads to a sympathy, which in turn leads to a possibility of union with "the process" previously remote.

Cantos 85-95: a clear re-statement of the bases required for a clean society; an evocation of the paradisal state of mind which can exist in such a society.

Now, in the Chinese cantos (52-61), Pound has adopted a relatively straightforward narrative technique; the reader will have no difficulty with them save, perhaps, for the psychological blocks raised (as in the Russian novels) by "all them furrin names." Since the Adams cantos (62-71) have their focal point in the single figure of John Adams and since their multifarious details conduce to bring that figure alive, these cantos are not particularly confusing, whether or not the reader is willing to consult the books upon which Pound has based his account. The Pisan cantos, in which Pound himself is the single speaker, are puzzling only insofar as some details of his life either prior to or during his confinement are not generally known; and insofar as he brings from the early cantos themes (particularly elements of his myth) which require explanation in terms of those early cantos; and insofar as the stream-of-consciousness technique always affords some difficulty in distinguishing the visual from the reflective, the significant from the trivial, etc. And the reader who can bring order out of the apparent confusion of the Pisan cantos will find no significant difficulties in the *Rock-Drill* if he has available copies of Couvreur's *Chou King*, Philostratus's *Life of Apollonius*, and T. H. Benton's *Thirty Years' View*.

But the first 51 cantos do not employ chronological narrative order, do not have a single speaker, do have various focal points; and, furthermore, they shift from history to myth to autobiography, and from continent to continent, and from time to time in a manner new to English poetry. These need further organizing—perhaps something like this:

Cantos 1-6: *Statement of basic themes:* a) nekuia—the need to respect human intelligence and to pursue historical studies; b) metamorphosis—the need to have faith in the gods (the mysteries, the verities) ; c) repeat in history—the need to recognize that change is constant, that cultures have their seasons; d) introduction of the

Eleusinian element. History, myth, and autobiography all under way; literary and historical values established.

Canto 7: A comment upon the dead men of contemporary Paris; one result of society's failure to regard the values stated in Cantos 1-6. Autobiographic and mythic (describing a circle of hell).

Cantos 8-11: A study of the Italian Renaissance and of its live men. Special attention to Sigismondo Malatesta.

Canto 12: A comment upon the live but misdirected men of contemporary New York; parallels Canto 7. Autobiographical and mythic (describing another circle of hell).

Canto 13: Introduction of the ethical element lacking (in various degrees) both in past and contemporary society; this element to be brought into harmony with the Eleusinian.

Cantos 14-15: A comment upon the hell-disseminating men of London, paralleling 12 and 7. Autobiographical and mythic (describing deep hell).

Cantos 16-17: Pound's escape from London's hell to Italy's earthly paradise. Autobiographical and mythic.

Cantos 18-19: Some observations upon the causes and results of Cantos 7, 12, and 14-15.

Cantos 20-26: History, autobiography, and myth almost inextricably intermingled here.

History: Italian renaissance—Nic. Este, 20 and 24; the Medici, 21; Venice, 25-6.

Pre-Renaissance Provence, 20, 23; late Rome, 20; Greece, 20; middle ages, 25, 26 (see also 27, 29).

Myth: in 20, 21, 23, 25.

Autobiography: in 20, 21, 22, 23, 26.

Cantos 27-30: Cantos 27-8-9 comment upon the middle and upper classes —their selfishness, materialism, and ineptitude, their division from the proletariat. (The exploited proletariat theme (see 18, 19, 25) is stated fully in 27.) Softness, sentimentality, vagueness, effeteness, etc. are set against the unity of conviction that built a cathedral, the active will of Cunizza, and (in 30) the strict justice of Artemis. Canto 30 brings to a close this section of the *Cantos* with its primary emphasis upon a Europe unified by a strong church.

Cantos 31-4: A shift from the Italian Renaissance to the American, seen through the eyes of Jefferson, Adams, *et al.* Side-glances from America at the French Revolution, the career of Napoleon, the general decline of Europe. (Canto 33 reaches beyond the period to the present to show the failure of the American experiment.)

Canto 35: Middle Europe and influence of the Jews.

Canto 36: The Cavalcanti or "Mediterranean sanity" canto: as 13 (the

Kung canto) stands in opposition to 14-15 and others, this applies the corrective totalitarian integrity of Cavalcanti to the "general indefinite wobble" of 35. More positively it makes a philosophical statement of the values exemplified in the actions of Jefferson and Adams (31-2) and Van Buren (37) and of Mussolini (41).

Canto 37: Van Buren's effort to maintain the Jefferson-Adams ideology.

Canto 38: Evidence in the contemporary scene of the defeat in the battle "between the public interest and the interests"; but also evidence (in Douglas allusions) that the war is not lost.

Canto 39: A mythological re-statement of 38: degradation followed by nekuia followed by regeneration.

Canto 40: Further statement of the perverted values of the late 19th century followed by an ascent out of its muddle (*via* Hanno's periplus).

Canto 41: The journey out of Victorianism brings us to Mussolini, contrasted with Hindenburg, Churchill, etc., and related to Cosimo I, Douglas, the mayor of Woergl, Adams, and Jefferson.

Thus, Cantos 31-41 bring together Jefferson and Mussolini and the American and Italian revolutions ("your revolution is our revolution; and ours was, and is, yours . . . ." *Visiting Card*, p. 10) ; and they simultaneously illuminate Pound's belief that "For more than a century after Waterloo, no force could stand up to the monopoly of money." *(Ibid.,* p. 9.) It would not falsify them to name them the *Jefferson and/or Mussolini* cantos.

Cantos 42-3: The preceding 10 cantos have described the thin line of sound monetary thinkers who endeavored, from 1775 to 1923, to withstand the forces of usury. These two cantos go back in time to the early 17th century in Italy to describe the foundation of a bank which incorporated the sound attitude toward money which those thinkers later (and independently) sought to initiate.

Canto 44: Introduces Pietro Leopoldo in Italy and Napoleon in France as two who (like Malatesta) struggled against but were swept away by the current of power.

Cantos 45-6: These state and rest the case against usury, the former "poetically," the latter in "a more natural language."

Cantos 47-52: Canto 47 restates the nekuia-regeneration theme as the condition for escaping the degradation of 45-6; and it adds another condition (*via* Hesiod's *Works and Days*) : the need to impose ritual order upon natural creative process (already, of course, implied in 13, the Kung canto). This condition, involving intuitive and experiential understanding of the processes of nature and the dangers of acting *contra naturam*, is imagized in fragments in 48, and given full poetical expression in 49, and is restated in 52 (first of the

"Chinese history" cantos) in Pound's translation from the *Li Ki*, a Chinese near-parallel with Hesiod's *Works and Days*. In other words, even after the extended journey already made, "yet must [we] sail after knowledge," this time in Chinese waters. The direct movement from 47 to 52 is only slightly interrupted by 50, which states again the sins to be redeemed. And 51, which, repeating 45 (the "usury" canto), brings this section to a close, modulates the "Hesiod-Li Ki" theme, compelling entrance into the succeeding section.

*   *   *

We have had, in these 71 cantos, a good many glimpses of Mr. Pound engaged in various activities. But there has appeared no solid attempt on his part to delineate a progressive growth of his soul. Our business has not been to investigate the reasons why the poet came to be what, in the 1940's, he was. We have been compelled to study history, not autobiography: we have compared successful societies with unsuccessful; considered the power of money; meditated upon the mysteries; involved ourselves in questions of artistic taste. But the time has come now, in the Pisan cantos and the *Rock-Drill*, to circle more systematically about the poet himself—a man in a concentration camp, in a mental hospital, making a determined effort to survive, and, beyond that, to come to such union with the process as was possible to him, he being what he was, the conditions afflicting him being what they were. An analogy exists between what is described as happening to Pound here and the neo-Platonic theory of the soul's purification.

According to the neo-Platonists, the soul descends into a body and must reascend from it at least once every cosmic cycle. It can do so only after a process of purification. Some souls undergo the process in Hades, but others avoid this. The avoiding soul first withdraws from the world of sense; then contemplates within itself the indwelling intellect; then Intellect above; and finally the One. But the last is accomplished only if the One sends into the soul of the philosopher or saint a special light which enables it to see the One.

Pound is certainly undergoing his purification in Hades; nevertheless, something similar to the steps described above takes place in the Pisans and the *Rock-Drill*.

It is possible only to conjecture how Pound would have carried his poem on to its conclusion had the war not intervened and had he not chosen to take an active part in it, with internment the necessary result of his decision. That is to say, it is possible only to conjecture whether these later cantos would have continued the strongly historical emphasis of the earlier instead of the strongly personal emphasis which now obtains, and, if so, what area of history would have been explored. But such conjectures would be both fruitless and without point. For the structure of the poem was sufficiently flexible, its basic philosophical generalizations of sufficient breadth and permanent validity, to allow its continuation no matter what happened historically. (Indeed, earlier cantos, portraying the strength of the forces of evil, had implied the near-inevitability of what did in fact happen.) Since use had been made of anecdotal materials from Pound's own life to illuminate states of mind or to discriminate gradations of ethical and aesthetic values, the shift of emphasis from historical to personal was easily made when necessity dictated. Thus, the Pisan cantos, however much they may differ from what might have been, fit into the general scheme as snugly as if they had formed an integral part of an initial plan. It does not matter that historical exposition has given way to diary. Either permits "statement and criticism, benediction and condemnation; the saints of the seven steps of the mountain of the blessed, as well as the inmates of purgatory and hell." (Gerhardt, *op. cit.)*

There are no mysteries in the Pisan cantos; there are only hiatuses which will be closed, presumably when a definitive biography of Pound or an exegesis of the *Cantos* has been published. Pound's hierarchy of values has not altered, the destroyers or perverters of that hierarchy remain what they have been, changed only insofar as their strength has increased.

Nevertheless, because of those hiatuses, this survey will of necessity be unsatisfactory. The temptation is strong to agree with Kenner that one should not be "too much obsessed with identifying Pound's materials" since "this labour is in one sense ancillary and in another quite unnecessary" and to recommend, as he does, the Pisan cantos "as a volume . . . to browse in." *(The Poetry of Ezra Pound,* p. 191.) But as Pound says, "Real knowledge does NOT fall off the page into one's stomach," and, though "the focus of poetic meaning does not lie *there"*—in Pound's materials—somewhat more than browsing acquaintance with them seems necessary to achieve that focus.

These materials will consist of:

1. Fragments of the historical data given at length in earlier cantos. (No solid blocks of history here.)

2. The things Pound saw, heard, smelled, tasted, felt in the concentration camp.

3. Pound's remembrances of things past, of friends, of acquaintances, of people in the news. (Pound's friends assume an importance here as they

have not done in the *Cantos* before and as they do not in the *Rock-Drill* to follow.)

4. Mythic images already introduced, and a few new ones.

5. Passages of self-analysis showing Pound fighting his way out of the hell in which he is imprisoned toward a paradisal state of mind.

6. Lyrical passages (some involving mythic images, some deriving their images from nature) indicating the steps in Pound's escape from the dark night and movement toward ultimate union with "the process."

Probably the latter two need closest attention, particularly since they represent something new in the poem. To determine the status of Pound's soul at any given point in these cantos requires the most precise possible definition of the mythic images and a clear understanding of the function of the lyric high points. However, though the poet is concerned with himself as he has not been before, his major interest is still in pointing out the requirements to be met in order to build a clean society. My emphasis here will be upon the latter rather than the former.

As Canto 74 opens, Mussolini is down, Pound is in prison, militarism progresses west, the Constitution is in jeopardy. Reason enough for undergoing a dark night of the soul. But "that state of things is not very new." If Mussolini is dead, greater leaders than he have died, but their vision of the city of Dioce lives in their successors' minds indestructible. If Pound must on occasion give way to despair, there are small things to restore his flagging spirits—a lizard, a wasp, an ant, herbs, the sparrow that Catullus had delighted in, the friendly gesture of a Negro. Even in the prison camp "amid what was termed the a.h. of the army," "all them g.d.m.f. generals" are unable to flatten out values or obliterate the monuments of the past. If Pound is, as Odysseus was, Noman in a cave (the sun gone down and luck not lasting), reason still exists to continue the poem, to state the credo which will ensure the recovery of his identity. Though the gods are desuete in name, eternity is of their essence.

So Canto 74 notes the present victory of the forces of evil but asserts the hope of their ultimate destruction. The key symbols here are a folk-song collected by Frobenius and Herodotus's account of the city of Dioce. In Book I of his history, Herodotus recounts the story of the unification of the Median tribes into a nation. For 525 years they had undergone Assyrian subjugation; they revolted and gained their liberty, but a liberty accompanied by a disunity and divided authority which made recourse to justice impossible. Out of this situation arose the figure of Deioces (d. 656 B.C.) to restore central authority, to unify the Median tribes, and to dispense justice.

Deioces was enamoured of sovereignty, and thus he set about gaining it. Being already a notable man in his own township . . . he began to profess and practice justice more constantly and zealously than ever . . . [When the Medes ultimately decided to enthrone a king, Deioces was the logical choice.]

He bade them build him houses worthy of his royal power, and arm him with a bodyguard . . . .

. . . having obtained the power, he constrained the Medes to make him one stronghold and to fortify this more strongly than all the rest. This too the Medes did for him; so he built the great and mighty circle of walls within walls which are now called Agbatana. This fortress is so planned that each circle of walls is higher than the next outer circle by no more than the height of its battlements . . . . There are seven circles in all; within the innermost circle are the king's dwellings and the treasuries . . . . the battlements of the first circle are white, of the second black, and of the third circle purple, of the fourth blue, and of the fifth orange; thus the battlements of five circles are painted with colours; and the battlements of the last two circles are coated, these with silver and those with gold.

The African folk-song fills out the ideogram—as this excerpt (translation mine) shows:

Wagadu appeared four times in the daylight in splendor; four times she departed, that men could not see her. Once through Vanity, once through the Breaking of Faith, once through Greed, and once because of the Schism. Four times Wagadu altered her name. Once she was called Dierra, next she was called Agada, then Ganna, and finally Silla. Four times Wagadu turned her face. Once she looked to the North, once to the West, once to the East, and once to the South. For Wagadu had, as often as they had been visible to man on earth, four gates: one to the North, one to the West, one to the East, and one to the South. From these quarters comes the strength of Wagadu and to these quarters it extends, whether Wagadu is imaged in stone or in wood or in earth or only exists as a shade in the mind and in her children's yearning. For the essence of Wagadu is not of stone, nor of wood, nor of earth. Wagadu is the strength that lives in the hearts of men. And she is knowable when the heart lets her be seen and the ears hear the strokes of the sword and the clanging on shields: but she cannot be seen when, oppressed and exhausted by the ferocity of Man, she falls asleep. Because of Vanity, Wagadu slept once, a second time for the Breaking of Faith, a third because of Greed, and the fourth time because of the Schism. But, if Wagadu is found again the fifth time, then she will live so strongly in the minds of men that she will never be lost to them, and Vanity, Breaking of Faith, Greed, and Schism will never again have effect on her.

Each time that Wagadu declined through the fault of Man, she rose with new beauty, more splendid than ever. Vanity brought with it the song of the minstrels which everyone imitated and values so highly today. The Breaking of Faith brought pearls and a shower of gold. Greed brought the craft of writing. . . . But the fifth Wagadu will bring from Schism the permanence of rain that falls in the South and the cliffs that rise from Sahara, for every man will bury Wagadu deep in his heart and every woman deep in her loins.

Ho! Dierra, Agada, Ganna, Silla! Ho, Fasa!

". . . with one day's reading," Pound says, "a man may have the key in his hands / Lute of Gassir. Hoo Fasa. . . ." Certainly one could do worse than seek a principle of organization in these cantos in terms of the African song's burden. Something like this, perhaps: At this moment Wagadu sleeps; but she has slept before and waked with increased splendor—and will wake again. The fundamental sins against her have been Vanity, Loss of Faith, Usuriousness, and Divisiveness. The immediate problem, then, is to reveal as clearly and mercilessly as possible the persons who promote disunity, so that the fifth coming of Wagadu may be made possible. Nor will evidences of Vanity, Loss of Faith, or Greed be ignored.

Analysis of Canto 74 into its components—dissociating personal experience from historical reference from mythological symbolism—will show whether the hypothesis is tenable.

The more important autobiographical references are as follows:

Page 5—Pound in the death cell remembering an evening at the Villa Catullo when the lake-water mimicked the Homeric description of the sea-sound, one of Pound's poetic touchstones; recognition that behind the ephemeral noisiness of man's war-making remains the permanence of natural process. Perhaps a recollection of Confucius:

Know the point of rest [being at ease in perfect equity] and then have an orderly mode of procedure; having this orderly procedure, one can 'grasp the azure,' that is, take hold of a clear concept; holding a clear concept one can be at peace internally, being thus calm one can keep one's head in moments of danger; he who can keep his head in the presence of a tiger is qualified to come to his deed in due hour.

5-6—a re-statement of the above theme in diminished terms: Pound and his fellow-inmates set against the "recur-ability" of butterflies, mint, and sparrows, and the durability of Villon and Catullus. Recollection of a Provençal journey.

6-7—Pound ascending out of the observational and recollective to the intellectual and undergoing, apparently, a mystical experience. The images imply unification: light like a silken cord; Egyptian, Catholic, and Chinese religious figures unified; the compassion of Shun linked to the ditch-digging of the young men.

8—a) a hanging, and an illuminating fragment of conversation. Pound later questions whether criminals have intellectual interests. It must be understood that, when he asks this question, he is commenting upon the intellectuals who support the interests of major criminals in whose regime based on grand larceny "petty larceny might rank as conformity." This *trahison des clercs,* instead of elevating, degrades all levels of society. b) Pound witnesses a natural glory, but a fit of despair follows.

9—Pound "amid the slaves learning slavery," recognizes himself as a "hard man in some ways." (On p. 5 he has related himself with Villon.)

10—an incident from an early trip to North Africa. This is perhaps an image of the banks making money out of nothing and is contrasted with the mating of chrysalids; but perhaps the two images cooperate to imagize the possibility of a renewal which under existing circumstances seems impossible.

10-12—an elegy upon Pound's earlier companions; and a discrimination between *(Guide,* pp. 82-3) "the fine flower of a civilization" and "a species of rot and corruption."

12—Pound's experience with Mr. Edwards re-emphasizes the text that "the greatest of these is charity." Edwards's act is covered by *Leviticus* XIX, 34 and *First Thessalonians* IV, 10; in each instance Pound cites the following verse, relating charity to non-usuriousness (in the former) and to not messing in others' affairs.

12-13—the preceding passage on charity is followed by Pound's credo— a statement of hope and faith.

13-14—a) Pound shares his tent with a grasshopper and is forcibly reminded of the earth's continuing fertility. b) Recollection of the French painters who, though they lived in a society which was "for fecal analysis only," brought a new splendor to painting; of his European travels; of men (Frobenius, Cocteau, Eliot, etc.) who "did something."

14—another period of despair (though with companions in misery).

15—recollection of Allan Upward who Pound thinks shot himself out of "feeling of utter hopelessness in struggle for values." *(Letters,* p. 284.) Pound may at the moment experience a similar depression, but not utter hopelessness. After the Dark Ages came Matteo and Pisanello to "make it new"; Kungian humaneness, often departed from by the Chinese, has always been renewed.

16-17—Pound, wondering whether we have struck the rock-bottom of hell, is reminded of Ugolino, who came very near it *(Inferno,* Canto XXXIII). But again paradisal fragments of experience uplift him. And if Athena (like Zarathustra, Jupiter, Hermes) is "desuete," her olive remains, the wind blows, the hawk soars. Or if the house of Oedipus is down, the house of Remus will rise. If Pound hears the Gershwin song, he can recollect the sharp song of Shun.

22-3—recollections of a time when Pound was in London, where the conversation was such that Sappho might be quoted against Cavalcanti, but where the distinction between the first-rate and the second-rate was too often blurred. Here Pound, Ford, Lewis, *et al.* planted the *semina motuum* toward the revolution of the word—not with total success since Pound's name is yet to come "for those who are to be."

24-26 —starting from the comment that certain recollections remain in the mind as resurgent icons, Pound brings together memories of various experiences—in Italy, New York, Spain, France, Tangiers, etc.—during the course of which he formed that hierarchy of values and stamped on his mind that imaged list of beautiful things of which he says, "I have not deflected a hair's breadth from my lists of beautiful objects, made in my own head and held before I ever thought of usura as a murrain and a marasmus." *(Guide,* p. 109.)

The reference here to usury leads us logically to a consideration of the historical references in this canto, since all of them state or imply its effect upon society and the individuals in it.

Page 3—an elegy upon Mussolini who, like civilizers before (Manes, Dionysus) is killed, but in whose death there is promise for the future. He is characterized as one who realized the inborn nature; as one who, like Adams and Malatesta, is of the company of "precise definers." The relation between him and Deioces is obvious. Elegy upon a man of this company is futile since, as Tsang said, when there was talk of regrouping after Kung's death: "Washed in the Keang and Han, bleached in the autumn sun's-slope, what whiteness can one add to that whiteness, what candour?" *(Analects,* p. 4.) Not, of course, that Pound conceived Mussolini to be of Kung's stature or anywhere near it. As he says, "You people in this country are so buggared by years of propaganda smear that Mussolini looks ten times his size."

4—an image of usury in practice and of the consequence in Europe.

7—the image of unity on this page is followed, on the historical level, by references to medieval witch-hunters and contemporary cannon-makers; these are ironically juxtaposed with references to the sound monetary policy of Athenian leaders and the common sense of Malatesta Jefferson *("Tempus . . . loquendi").*

9—reference to the usurers as obfuscators of history.

12—the line of clean thought running from the Old to the New Testament.

15—the pervasive influence of usury compared to the bewitching herb of Circe.

17-19—the Adams statement of p. 15 here introduces negative comment upon the Jews, though with implicit recognition that in the Old Testament ("Old test / an anthology / a collection of everything / NO thought save by ISOLATING the clean bits") are ideas such as Kung espoused. (Canto 53 should be read in connection with this canto.) Against the financiers (Jew and Gentile), with their rackets of usury and of change in the value of money, Pound sets the town of Wörgl, which issued its own money and dragged itself out of bankruptcy within two years. "All went well until an ill-starred Wörgl note was presented at the counter of an Innsbruck bank. It was noticed, all right . . . . The judaic-plutocratic monopoly had been infringed . . . . The burgomaster was deprived of his office, but the ideological war had been won." (*Visiting Card*, p. 15.)

19-20—the divisiveness of Aristotelianism contrasted with the unifying effect of Kungian thought. Pound says, "in the face of Aristotle's repeated emphases on experience, and of testing by life" that he (Aristotle) is the "Master of those that cut apart, dissect and divide. Competent precursor of the card-index. But without the organic sense." He quotes Rackham: "Hence the tendency to think of the End not as the sum of the Goods, but as one Good which is the Best. Man's welfare thus is ultimately found to consist not in the employment of all his faculties in due proportion, but only in the activity of the highest faculty, the 'theoretic' intellect." And he comments: "that leads you plumb bang down to the 'split man' in Mr. Wyndham Lewis' *Apes*. That is the schismatic tendency." (*Guide*, pp. 342-3.) Hence the deterioration of Japanese culture from that represented in the Noh plays ("a better fencer . . . ." *Cf. Guide*, p. 81) and the decline of Italy. But the hope for renewal remains ("4 times to the song. . ." and "Koré, splendor of splendor").

21—Von Tirpitz quoted upon the Jews.

Dissociated from the historical references, all of which assist toward developing the theme of usury, are the images of permanence. They are not dissociated from the autobiographical passages because they are used not only to represent the existence of the Permanent but also to suggest Pound's effort to come to terms with the process. The significant images, on the societal level, are the cities of Dioce and Wagadu to be reconstructed, the mountain of Taishan to be climbed, the Dantean rose (p. 27) to be formed from lifeless matter, the wisdom of Yu, Shun, Kung to be recaptured. On the personal level, earth or fertility images—Cythera (Aphrodite, Ixotta, Mary), Ge, Koré—own an especial importance, as do Kuanon, through mercy bringing peace, and the Charities, bringing grace. Alcmene, Tyro, and Odysseus imagize the voyaging rebel-hero theme. And pp. 6-7 sum up the tensile light theme as it is perhaps nowhere better summarized in the poem to this point. A kind of synthesis may be made of the foregoing: the rebel-hero, making his exploratory voyage, comes to an understanding that "light descending" (Kung's radiant intelligence, the neo-Platonists' creative emanation) and "earth producing" are the two forces to be celebrated. As for the progress of the soul, the requirement is *sinceritas*, precise defining of the heart's inarticulate tones. (In equating (p. 5) the Kungian *sinceritas* with the Christian paraclete, Pound introduces an Australian myth: Ouan Jin, a god's son, speaking the names of objects, created them; but, creating too many, his mouth was removed by his father. The point may be that the basic truths are everywhere understood, are not the monopoly of, for example, Christians.)

Now, if the canto opened in chaos, it closes in recognition of the potential of order—the ordering possible through memory by which such basic traditional truths as those cited above may be conserved and upon which the creative imagination may build the renovated society or re-form the disintegrated personality. It is the ideogram of p. 27 which represents the totalitarian or anti-schismatic factor. The preceding pages of memories and the comment that the muses are the daughters of Memory have prepared for it. For memory is not passive, not a mere receptacle—at least in the totalitarian mind. It is an agent; it functions inseparably with the other properties of the mind in, for example, the poetic process. It thus bridges the gap between present and past and, *via* art-work, present and future. Without memory, the tradition is broken; without the tradition (and its symbols—the altar in the garden, the statue at Terracina) loss of faith, rootlessness; without the tradition, equally, forfeit of the bases of comparison, with the probability that the forces of greed will set up false absolutes. The last thought provokes need for a dissociation. Pound thinks that Kung has been misinterpreted as, in emphasizing the past, deifying the emperors—setting up false absolutes (see pp. 3-4 of this canto) of the sort described by Pound in *The Exile*, p. 13: "theoretical perfection in a government impels it ineluctably toward tyranny. In ancient days it was the divine descent of the ruler; in our time, it is the theoretical justice or perfection of the organism, the to, for and by the plebs, etc. that puts this more moral fervour and confidence in so dangerous a place . . . ." But Kung's effort, in Pound's estimation, was not to produce a theoretically perfect government but to place government in the hands of "men of breed," an effort in which deification of emperors is not involved. ("One uses men in governing men." *Confucius*, p. 95.)

Memory is anti-schismatic in another way, since love takes its state "where memory liveth" *(dove sta memoria)*. The explicit tie between the present passage and Canto 36 is made in Canto 76:

        nothing matters but the quality
of the affection—
in the end—that has carved the trace in the mind
dove sta memoria

But consideration of the Cavalcanti theme in connection with the present
fountain image serves as a reminder of these related passages from Dante's
Paradiso (Canto XXXI) and "The Unwobbling Pivot" *(Confucius,* p. 99).

For the divine light pierceth with such power
    The world, in measure of its complement
    Of worth, that naught against it may endure.
This realm of unimperilled ravishment
    With spirits thronged from near times and from far
    Had look and love all on the one mark bent.

The main thing is to illumine the root of the process,
a fountain of clear water descending from heaven
immutable. The components, the bones of things,
the materials are implicit and prepared in us,
abundant and inseparable from us.

And the last line ("we who have passed over Lethe") suggests that a
relation exists with Canto XXVIII of the *Purgatorio,* with its discussion
of Lethe's function of washing out evil memories and Eunoe's of restoring
memories of good deeds; with Canto XXXI *(Purgatorio)* in which Dante
passes over Lethe; and with XXXIII, in which all his memories of good
are secured against oblivion.

                               *   *   *

For what seems to me sufficient reason, I have spent more time upon
Canto 74 than I propose to do upon the cantos which follow. D. D. Paige
has made the acute suggestion that

    the structure of the poem may be clarified if we refer to Richard of
    St. Victor's distinction between cogitation, meditation and contempla-
    tion. . . . I should hazard—and this is the merest speculation—that
    The Pisan Cantos and those yet to come are designed as the contem-
    plative centre from which Pound's thought radiates to illuminate not
    only these cantos but whatever may have remained obscure in pre-
    ceding ones. (In his review of Watts' *Ezra Pound and the Cantos.)*

I should like to adopt the suggestion, but with certain modifications. It
would seem to me that several "contemplative centers" have already been
posited—or, perhaps more accurately, that several earlier cantos taken
together (say Cantos 1, 2, 4, 13, 30, 36, 39, 40, 45, 47, 49, 51, 52) have
formed a center, and that Canto 74 with its important mythological additions joins with them and, indeed, since it has the advantage of being
approached by readers who have already in their minds the contents of
those earlier "central" cantos, possibly does more effectively than any

other single canto the job of radiation and illumination. Certainly a
thorough understanding of 74 facilitates the reading of its successors, as a
quick survey illustrates.

Canto 75

Canto 75, which seems to say little or nothing, does in reality suggest
a good deal to the student of Pound's prose. It comments upon the
dangers of divisiveness (e.g., in poetry, of dividing words from music) ;
upon the virtue of a writer's giving *the thing* instead of a reference to it
(as Pound, in Canto 38, instead of giving an abstract of Douglas's Social
Credit theory, gives Douglas speaking in his own voice) ; upon the durability (recurrent vigor) of the excellent, the substance of which maintains
its validity regardless of a change in its accidents; upon the importance,
therefore, of conserving the tradition; upon the value of the ideogrammic
method in the criticism of the arts; and upon the need, in criticism and
elsewhere, to make dissociations.

The apposite passages from Pound's prose are as follows:

It is mainly for the sake of the melopoeia that one investigates
troubadour poetry.
One might almost say that the whole culture of the age, at any
rate the mass of the purely literary culture of the age, from 1050 to
1250 and on till 1300, was concentrated on one aesthetic problem,
which, as Dante put it, 'includes the whole art.'
That 'whole art' consisted in putting together about six strophes
of poesy so that the words and the tune should be welded together
without joint and without wem.
The best smith, as Dante called Arnaut Daniel, made the birds sing
IN HIS WORDS; I don't mean that he merely referred to birds
singing—

In the canzone beginning
L'aura amara
Fals bruoills brancutz
Clarzir
Quel doutz espeissa ab fuoills.
Els letz
Becs
Dels auzels ramencz
Ten balps e mutz
                              etc.

And having done it in that one strophe he kept them at it, repeating
the tune, and finding five rhymes for each of seventeen rhyme sounds
in the same order.

Having done that he constructed another perfect strophe, where
the bird call interrupts the verse.

Cadahus
  En son us
    Mas pel us
      Estauc clus.

That again for six strophes WITH the words making sense.

The music of these songs has been lost, but the tradition comes up again, over three centuries later.

Clement Janequin wrote a chorus, with sounds for the singers of the different parts of the chorus. These sounds would have no literary or poetic value if you took the music away, but when Francesco da Milano reduced it for the lute, the birds were still in the music. And when Munch transcribed it for modern instruments the birds were still there. They ARE still there in the violin part.

That is why the monument outlasts the bronze casting. . . .
          (ABC of Reading, pp. 52-54.)

HEAR Janequin's intervals, his melodic conjunctions from the violin solo.

"I made it out of a mouthful of air"
wrote Bill Yeats in his heyday. The *forma,* the immortal *concetto,* the concept, the dynamic form which is like the rose pattern driven into the dead iron-filings by the magnet, not by material contact with the magnet itself, but separate from the magnet. Cut off by the layer of glass, the dust and filings rise and spring into order. Thus the *forma,* the concept rises from death

    The bust outlasts the throne
    The coin Tiberius.
          (Guide, p. 152)

Here, that is, in Janequin we find ground for one of the basic dissociations of music. If I have said it ten times in one way or another, nothing wd. excuse me for omitting restatement. . . .

In music there is representation of the sole matter wherein music can be "literally" representative, namely sound. Thus the violinist reading Janequin's music transposed said: a lot of birds, not one bird alone.

Down on through Vivaldi and Couperin there is this kind of music, music of representative outline.

And in distinction to it is music of structure, as J. S. Bach in fugue or keyboard toccata, or Hindemith today in his Schwannendreher.

Not contradictory, not hostile one to the other, but two blessed categories, each for a particular excellence. As exclusive, to take a simile on one line only, not as simile of kind or of a like sort of difference, but a simile focussed on mutual exclusivity as indicating its *degree*—as exclusive "as Velasquez and Ambrogio Praedis". . . .
(Ibid., pp. 151-153.)

Canto 76

Canto 76 appears to balance various breaks—or divisions *("break* his political system"; "no more an altar to Mithras"; "they have *broken* my house"; "the huntress in *broken* plaster"; "will the world ever take up its course again?"; "spring of their squeak-doll is *broken*"; "*broken* ant-hill"; etc.) with a break-through out of the quotidian toward an experiencing of the mysteries. It is not quite clear whether Pound's "bust thru" is being made now while Pound is in the concentration camp and is described in terms of events which took place earlier in his career; or whether he is merely recording the memory of the earlier event, a recurrence of which is not now possible for him. The evidence does not clearly support either supposition. But on the assumption that the Pisans do record a gradual movement toward Pound's coming to an inner harmony, I hold the opinion that the former hypothesis obtains. Regardless of which hypothesis one chooses, Pound's continued belief in the existence of the mysteries, of their fecundating properties when rightly approached, of the significance of the magic moment of mètamorphosis, of the benevolence-breeding property of the mystical union remains unaltered.

The visual image which opens this canto (of the sun in clouds) and the answer to Pound's question of how the figures of Alcmene and the others appear to him (that the sun "leads in his fleet here") recall the line in Canto 36, "Formed like a diafan from light on shade" and lead to a consideration of Cavalcanti's theory of love; and then beyond Cavalcanti to Plotinus's theory of emanation; and beyond Plotinus to Dante and Kung:

... the divine light so penetrateth through
the universe, in measure of its worthiness,
that nought hath power to oppose it.
    (*Paradiso*, 31, 22-4.)

The celestial and earthly process pervades and is substantial; it is on high and gives light, it comprehends the light and is lucent, it extends without bound, and endures.
    (*Confucius*, p. 183.)

Various references in this canto take us back to Cantos 16, 17, and 20, and it will be necessary to pause over them. In Canto 16, Pound, having with Plotinus's assistance escaped hell, moves on alone through a kind of purgatory in which he is cleansed, then into an earthly paradise where he sees the Malatesta brothers. His forward motion stops, interrupted by a long passage of reveries upon those who had "walked eye-deep in hell," some of them dying "pro patria, / non 'dulce' non 'et decor.' "

In Canto 17 he wakes and moves further into the earthly paradise, down a slope from oak-woods, through vineyards to the shore of an un-named sea. Here he encounters a variety of things, in motion but silent, the scene bathed in pale green light from an unknown source. The background is classical, Elysian; fertility symbols predominate, the human characters are artist-rulers and craftsmen of the Renaissance, recoverers and trans-

mitters of the Greek attitude toward life. Dante went from the earthly
paradise through the sphere of fire, on to the sphere of the moon, and so
on; Aeneas left Elysium, *via* the ivory gate, and sailed for Caieta;
Odysseus returned from the shades to get further instructions from Circe
and then sailed past the coast of the sirens and by the strait of Scylla and
Charybdis, was cast on the Island of Trinacria, where his men killed the
oxen of the Sun, and finally (swimming on a mast after a shipwreck)
arrived on the island of the Phaeocians. Pound, too, makes a journey, in
part by sea, through the Mediterranean area where, as Canto 3 said, the
gods float in the azure air. There are points of resemblance between
Pound's voyage and that of Odysseus: as the latter sailed between Scylla
and Charybdis, Pound passes between "great cliffs of amber." Between
them is the Cave of Nerea, a place similar to one encountered by Odysseus
on Trinacria:

> We haul'd our bark, and moor'd it on the strand,
> Where in a beauteous grotto's cool recess
> Dance the green Nereids of the neighboring seas.

He seems next to have gone into North Africa, as Odysseus did, and he
spies upon the rites of Zothar as Odysseus "spied" upon the sirens.

These points of resemblance suggest that Pound has shifted out of the
Dantesque context of the Hell cantos and that his protagonist (himself)
in this canto assimilates the protagonist (Odysseus) of Canto 1. The concluding "So that" of Canto 1 and the introductory "So that" of the present
canto (17) reinforce this suggestion. Thus there would seem to be double
emergence from Hell: as Odysseus, representing the Greek spirit, came
again into light to fructify (with the assistance of Plotinus) the Italian
Renaissance, so Pound, exponent of 20th century humanism, cleansed of
the 20th century's excrementa of false values, emerges as the knowledge-
able Odysseus of our time to view and participate in a new renaissance.

At the conclusion of Canto 20, the forward movement is resumed, this
time as a processional. Pound says of the canto that its main subject is the
"lotophagoe: lotus eaters, or respectable dope smokers; *and general
paradiso*. You have had a hell in canto XIV, XV; purgatorio in XVI etc."
(Letters, pp. 210-11.) But the whole canto is not paradisal. In it, several
ways of life are juxtaposed. There is, first, the sanity of Provence where
art, love, life, the very "smell of that place" suffered no severance one from
the other until the Albigensian hysteria brought its dichotomies. Second,
one aspect of the Italian Renaissance is revealed in the violence and
madness of Este. But Este's violence does not comprehend the man. He
compares with Borso, who kept the peace, and Sigismondo, who combined
the brutality and violent nature of Este with a tremendous capacity for
love—of Ixotta, of art, of philosophy. We are thus reminded that the

tangled thickets of the jungle are places of birth and re-birth as well as of sudden death and that, conversely, just outside the clearing, the jungle always encroaches. Third are the lotus eaters, who float like smoke or air-borne flames over the jungle or recline on safe shelves above it, neither taking sustenance from it nor bringing order to it. Their dope-dream contrasts and compares with the delirium of Este. (Their escape from the realities of life and death is dissociated, too, from the Franciscan acceptance of poverty which, based on Francis's hatred of avarice and disorder, is less an escape from than a sermon-by-example against a wrong way of life.) Odysseus's crew are the fourth group. They, like the lotus-eaters, live a half-life, in part by compulsion, in part by wrong choice. The compulsion was political and economic, of that sort common to any society in which the workers are considered expendable. Their wrong choices were made because they knew no better; given a minimum of education, they chose in terms of immediate appetite. Fifth is the life of Pound making the most of those days (now gone) when a man could go easily and without danger from one European country to another in search of enlightenment. We see Pound studying Greek, Latin, Provencal, re-creating for himself (and, here, for us) a time when no man feared "to recognize creative skill in his neighbour." (This matter of easy intercourse between nations is of major importance in Pound's opinion. He recalls, in one of his broadcasts, that he was cut off from Germany after the first World War to his own disadvantage. And he looks into the past to a similar situation: ". . . Rothschild, the stinker . . . getting hold of the Austrian postal service and censorship in time of Napoleon. Hundred years after that, Austria is the dumbest . . . country in Europe, and she flopped." (30 April 1942.) Sixth, there is a vision of what could be: the animals of the jungle tamed, made useful; animals, men, and women moving together forward as in a triumph, or as in a religious festival celebrating the bounty of nature well-used by man.

Such a situation hinges upon recognition of the continued existence of the gods and upon coming into contact with them. On p. 30 of Canto 76, Pound either makes that contact or is reminded of a time when he did—when he "Lay in soft grass by the cliff's edge" and saw the "ferae familiares," etc. He questions (pp. 36-7) the way in which the divine and the human come to grips—of how Anchises, laying hold of Aphrodite's "flanks of air," produced Aeneas, of how concept is materialized; he inquires what the figures he sees in his vision are. They are neither souls nor persons; they are intangible but formed—a fluid, moving, weighable crystal. And they are under the aegis of fertility and intelligence.

Forrest Read (Sewanee Review, 65, p. 407) putting emphasis upon the "yet" in "nor is this yet atasal," and defining atasal as "that revelation of and union with reality which he seeks," argues that Pound is saying expli-

citly that he has not yet achieved that sought union and that he will not
until Canto 83. I do not myself know whether the adverb is so definitely
chronological—it may equally well be defined as meaning "moreover."
Granting Read's opinion, however, does not qualify the fundamental consideration: that the break through quotidian is possible and must be
striven for by the active, properly-directed will.

Canto 77

The function of Canto 77 is to show what is required that the active
will be given right direction. To accomplish this teaching, it dissociates
various kinds of actions (particularly initiating actions), emphasizing
that "If the root be in confusion, nothing will be well governed" *(Confucius,* p. 33), and, of course, stressing the absolute necessity of attaining
precise verbal definition. Indeed, it might be called the "Integrity" canto.
The passages in Kung's text which most strictly apply here are these:

> Know the point of rest and then have an orderly mode of proce-
> dure. . . .

> Things have roots and branches; affairs have scopes and beginnings.
> To know what precedes and what follows, is nearly as good as having
> a head and feet. *(Confucius,* p. 29.)

> He said: Center oneself in the invariable: some have managed to do
> this, they have hit the true center, and then?
> Very few have been able to stay there.

> Kung said: People do not move in the process. And I know why.
> Those who know, exceed. (The intelligentzia goes to extremes.) The
> monkey-minds don't get started. . . . *(Confucius,* p. 105.)

1. Pages 42-4—several kinds of action are counter-pointed: Abner knew
well enough the "point of rest"—but he was scarcely "moving in the process"; Von Tirpitz defines precisely; Maukch suggests an irrelevant action;
le beau monde ("society . . . that reads the best books, possesses a certain
ration of good manners and, especially, of sincerity and frankness, modu-
lated by silence. . . .") sometimes "hits the true center"; the bureaucrat
exceeds; Pound, at 19, takes an initial action and, "Sochylism" having
come, ends up watching Arcturus through a smoke-hole; "the bloke"
began something he didn't know how to finish; Frobenius introduces the
New Learning to Germany ("der im Baluba"); the city is four times
rebuilt; Cadmus initiates a culture; the "feller," somewhat, but not quite,
like Abner, does nawthin'; Pound and Eliot in England strive for the
center.

2. Pages 44-6—the question here seems to be: "can they again put one
[*e.g.,* a society] together / as the two halves of a seal, or a tally stick?"

And the answer is affirmative—*if* a man "Missing the bull's eye seek the cause in himself"; if he seek the precise definition; if, having defined, he will put his idea into action; if governments remember, with Jefferson, that "the earth belongs to the living"; if they assume control of money, distribute it equitably, refuse to change its value arbitrarily; and if the Australian bushman ("is the sun that is god's mouth"), the Catholic ("learned what the Mass meant"), the pagan ("With drawn sword as at Nemi") remember that "to sacrifice to a spirit not one's own is sycophancy" (Chinese symbols, p. 45.)

The present war has settled nothing, put nothing together. But the situation was quite as desperate when Rome fell. Nevertheless, in that gloom the Church gathered the light about it. Pound dates *(Spirit of Romance,* p. 11) the Middle Ages from "that year early in the sixth century when Cassiodorus retired to the monastery at Vivaria, taking with him the culture of an age that was over and sealed. . . . To his taste and to Chapter XLVIII of the 'regula' of St. Benedict [Pound quotes: "concerning daily manual labour: Idleness is the enemy of the soul; hence brethren ought at certain seasons to occupy themselves with manual labour, and again at certain hours in holy reading"] we may trace much of the inner culture of the Middle Ages."

The basic things endure or recur. Justinian's Code and his churches have not proved "explodable." A priest may die, now or in Anglo-Saxon times, but the Church goes on. Day comes even to the man on whom the sun's gone down, as priest follows priest at Nemi, as the Odysseus stories go on—though with changed names. Horace says truly *(Car.* III, 30—*Dum scandet.* . .), "I have erected a monument more enduring than bronze." Instances of the proper understanding of money extend to 1766 B.C. As Cadmus's seeds moved in the earth to the end eventually that the city might be built, so the ideas of Kung ("only the total sincerity, the precise definition") move toward that end.

3. Page 47—examples of precise definition: a right attitude toward Freud; an acute observation of Amy Lowell; a Japanese dancer's (Miscio Ito's) nail-hitting question; etc.

4. Page 48—the self-aggrandizing action of Ciano, whose will was not to Mussolini's as King Wan's to Shun's (p. 45); and other short-sighted actions.

5. Pages 48-50—a shift of attention from the sabotage of the Italian revolution to that of the American which led to cultural decline as evidenced by the paucity of the army vocabulary, the aptness of the army's use of Hermes's symbol, the effeteness of those whose motion only "confers an existence upon them."

6. Pages 50-51—in the *Guide*, p. 73, Pound makes a distinction between two kinds of philosophical statement: such a one as Spinoza's "The intellectual love of things consists in the understanding of their perfections"; and Swedenborg's "I saw three angels, they had hats on their heads." And Pound goes on: "Both carry conviction. One may be a bit in the dark as to what constituted Swedenborg's optic impressions but one does not doubt that he had such impressions. The standard of conduct among angels in this third heaven furnishes an excellent model for those of us who do not consider that we have entered that district."

Both statements carry conviction because the men who spoke them had convictions—and the courage of them. Other images of such an attitude occur in these pages: on p. 49, the grandmother carrying the gold; on p. 50, André Spire, the French-Jewish poet, Rousselot, the pioneer in phonetics, and Cocteau; on p. 51, the House of Rohan's motto *(Roi je ne suis. . . .)*; Farinata (see Dante's *Inferno,* Canto 10) ; the statement ("se casco") that "if I fall, I do not fall on my knees." The connection with his earlier "anti-sycophancy" remark is obvious.

7. Page 52—allusion to Basil Bunting, a militant pacifist; the inactivity of the Indians; the action of Adams (speaking through Kabir—see *Letters,* pp. 19, 21).

8. Page 53—Dionysus and Kung brought to focus; foretokened visually on pp. 48-9 by the opposition of Demeter (p. 48) and Apollo (p. 49.)

Canto 78

Prominent in Canto 78 are post-war reflections upon the hypocrisy of the "peace-makers," who are aware that the economic war has only begun. Their intelligence (like that of the Trojan elders) is contrasted with that of Cassandra who, like "the little sister," was a precise definer. Napoleon's precise definition of war as being unlike chess; Napoleon and Mussolini both crushed by the obfuscators. Contrast of the "peacemakers" with Lorenzo Medici, peacemaker and poet (who, however, misused the money in his bank). Contrast with the *sinceritas* of Mussolini ("We are tired of government in which there is no responsible person having a hind-name, a front name and an address"—the raison d'être, Pound says, of fascism).

This last is cited by Pound in *The Exile,* No. 2, p. 117, with three other quotations, the four being headed *Modern Thought.* The other three are:

The banking business is declared a state monopoly. The interests of the small depositors will be safeguarded. Vl. Ulianov (etc).

The duty of a being is to persevere in its being and even to augment the characteristics which specialize it. Remy de Gourmont.

People are not charming *enough*. Le Sieur Robert McAlmon.
These come rather close to summing up in prose terms the meaning of
this canto. For example, the Metastasio allusion, the reference to Goedel,
a German soldier who befriended Pound in 1943, and the conversational
fragments ("if you will stay. . ." *et seq.)* on p. 56; the passage from "So
Salzburg" to "neither published nor followed" (pp. 58-9) ; and that from
"many men's mannirs" to "an antipodes" (pp. 60-61), having to do with
civilization plus amenities, may be classified not illogically under Mc-
Almon's remark. The references to Gaudier-Brzeska, Hulme, Lewis,
Upward, Griffith fall logically under de Gourmont's (as does that, ironically, to Lt. Col. Steele, stockade commander, who augments the characteristics which inhere in his name). The various references to money (pp. 57,
58, 59, and so on) show the need for the "Soviet idea," as Pound charac-
terizes the Russian's declaration. And Mussolini's comment (plus the one
Pound used on his letter-head: "Liberty is not a right but a duty") covers
the allusions to cowardice ("o-hon dit. . . pas de tout") and hypocrisy
(e.g., the socialists' use of red herrings, p. 60; the dressing of frogs, brits,
and dutch pimps, p. 59; the efforts to destroy the monuments, efface the
records, black out the words, p. 57).

Mussolini's inability to put certain monetary advice into efficient action
(p. 60) carries on a theme stated in the preceding canto; the allusion to
the 18th amendment intimates a theme to be stated fully in the following
canto. The canto ends, rather ironically, with the image of the white oxen
opposing the canto's initial image of the 40 geese.

Canto 79

Allusion in the previous canto to the constriction of Bacchus leads to
Canto 79, which may be called the "anti-monist" or "tolerance of variants"
canto. Different men want different gods; "different lice live in different
waters"; "some minds take pleasure in counterpoint"; some like a certain
number of shades in their landscapes (not "all of a whiteness") ; some
like to make comparisons, to differentiate, say, Greek from Japanese from
Roman virtues and follies; some love more than one woman; not all want
to pay obeisance to the same god. But the "snot of pejoracy, sans bonhomie and good humour," wield the Flail of Jehovah against such
tolerance.

Against this monolinear kind of mind Pound writes his contrapuntal
canto. Note how many oppositions occur; dirt pile against white moon,
cloud, tower, p. 62; G. Scott ("stalky and grave, a person beautiful in his
simplicity, he was the bearer of news and refreshment to Pound and the
other caged man"--*Poetry,* 73, 217) against the "bad 'uns"; horse whinny-
ing *against* tubas, p. 63; Greek rascality *against* Hagoromo, p. 63; Kuma-

saka (Noh plays) *vs.* vulgarity, p. 63; banner floating *against* Ugolino, p. 64.

But, of course, the important attack is made positively and lyrically in the "lynx song," which brings together Iacchos, Demeter, and Persephone —the three deities celebrated at Eleusis; alludes to the lynx, sacred to Dionysus; Silenus, his companion; the Bassarids, his votaries; Priapus, his and Aphrodite's son; Aphrodite herself; and so on. In short, the lynx song is to be taken as an invocation of the gods and goddesses of fertility. It must therefore be read in connection with Canto 39.

Canto 39 opens with Pound's evocation of the thick, heavy, sexual atmosphere of Circe's court as paraphrased from Book 10 of the *Odyssey*. But following Odysseus's firm stand against her charms, his demand that she show him the way to Hell and the prophetic assistance of Tiresias, the tone changes; in place of drugged dormancy is the sharp eagerness of spring's rebirth expressed in a description of a fertility rite.

> From half-dark to half-dark
>   Unceasing the measure
> Flank by flank on the headland
>   with the Goddess' eyes to seaward
> By Circeo, by Terracina, with the stone eyes
>   white toward the sea
> With one measure, unceasing:
>   "Fac deum!" "Est factus."
> Ver novum!
>   ver novum!
> Thus made the spring,

It is not by chance that the Latin phrase in this passage parallels the final clause of the sentence in the Nicene Creed: "Et incarnatus est de Spiritu Sancto ex Maria Virgine: et homo factus est." Pound has already alluded to an Egyptian fertility myth: thus in this section of Canto 39 he has indicated an unbroken tradition of fertility ritualism extending from pre-historic Egypt, through Eleusis, into Roman Catholicism. He has said it very clearly in *The Spirit of Romance* (p. 95).

> There are, as we see, only two kinds of religion. There is the Mosaic or Roman or British Empire type, where someone, having to keep a troublesome rabble in order, invents and scares them with a disagreeable bogie, which he calls god.
> Christianity and all other forms of ecstatic religion, on the other hand, are not in inception dogma or propaganda of something called the *one truth* or the *universal truth*; they *seem* little concerned with ethics; their general object appears to be to stimulate a sort of confidence in the life-force.

The lynx song of Canto 79 is clearly an image of the Eleusinian rituals. And it is significantly introduced by the words *Kyrie eleison* (Lord, have mercy upon us) from the Mass. Again the conservation of the tradition of the yea-saying religious spirit is being celebrated—celebrated by a man for whom there would seem to be no communication but Nay, Nay. But it is not Pound who says Nay, but those who strive to break the tradition, to constrict Bacchus, to make the monolinear approach to religion and ethics, to supplant ecstasy with asceticism.

Canto 80

Mr. Little's reflections on our rising justice form the bridge between 79 and 80, the latter, by implication, carrying on the former's theme. It is the record of one whose eyes "have seen a good deal" and who wishes to give instruction in the matter of undertaking a *Wanderjahr* with limited means. "Our husky young undergraduates," he says in Chapter 16 of the *Guide* (a gloss for part of this canto), "may start their quest of Osiris in a search for what was the PRADO. . . ." But he recognizes a couple of difficulties: "In 1911 there was an international currency (20 franc pieces) . . . and no god-damned passports. (Hell ROT wilson AND the emperor, I think it was Decius.)" In this "bitch your progress" mood he is reminded that that was an era not only of unobstructed communication but of good bread, in that time "before the world was given over to wars."

Other themes already developed are touched upon here: the "faith in a possible collaboration / To raise up the ivory wall," p. 72; the need for unity—"this is from heaven / the warp and woof," pp. 72-3; the need to see cities and many men's manners—"It is said also that Homer was a medic," p. 81; the assurance of renovation—"there is according to some authors a partial resurrection," p. 75; and the need for intelligence to ensure that renovation not fail—"the problem after any revolution is what to do with / your gunmen," p. 74; the basic unity between East and West —"and we note that dog precedes man in the occident / as of course in the orient," p. 77; the distinction between the indiscriminate sentimentality of Dumas and the compassion, when fitting, and strict justice, when required, of Artemis, pp. 78-9; the revolution of the word—"He stood . . . / the door behind" "and now they complain of cummings," p. 85; the right of the individual to live his own life—"meum est propositum," p. 85 (from the *Confessio Archipoetae*); and so on.

But the basic theme underlying the canto is "Amo ergo sum," and the canto is a record of the things and people (chiefly in London) that throng Pound's memory—locus of that love. This love, it must be recognized, has a new quality, for Pound has drunk the bitterness of the centuries; the tears he has created flood over him. If he has not descended to the sentimentality of Dumas, he has moved (being at the end of his tether)

toward humility and compassion from the justice and egoism of Artemis
and Cythera (pp. 78-9).

The canto ends with three images revealing this: (1) a carefully
wrought lyric in three quatrains suggesting that the natural world is
oblivious of the schismatic upheavals of human history and goes calmly
about its business; (2) this lyric bracketed on the one side by a statement
of a quite changed attitude toward England, "now that Winston's out,"
from that expressed in Cantos 14-15 regarding post-World-War-I England;
and (3) on the other side by Pound's rescue of a midge from a hungry
lizard, and by a continuing sympathetic description of England.

The *Letters*, the *Guide to Kulchur*, *Polite Essays*, and earlier cantos
will illuminate most of the references in this canto which are not self-
explanatory.

Canto 81

Canto 81 in effect makes a distinction between the sabre-chop that
kills and the scalpel-incision that cures. The lyrical evocation in Canto 80
of England's past (pp. 92-4) is carried on into 81 (pp. 97-8) to make the
point. On a visit to Maurice Hewlett's house (p. 92) Pound had been
strongly affected by a vision of England's long history. He expressed it
in an early version of Canto 1:

. . . procession on procession by Salisbury,
Ancient in various days, long years between them;
Ply over ply of life still wraps the earth here.

In Canto 80, the concept remains, but darkened by the recollection of the
bloody divisions that have brought England to its present state of "rust,
ruin death duties and mortgages": the War of the Roses; the long
enmity between England and France; England's increased insularity
after Henry's break with the Church; the Reformation and Counter-
reformation; etc.

Canto 81 shifts from political to literary history and draws a relation.
In the time of Chaucer ("Your eyen two. . .", p. 98) there had been a
European unity of culture in which men of all nations could participate.
There had been a unity of word and music to produce singable song. But
as nation divided from nation and the Church underwent schism, word
parted from music--"and for 180 years almost nothing." Then again the
temporary impact of the continent upon England, and again word and
music in cooperation; but once more the division, the economic wars, the
destruction of France, the attritional decline of England--and the cultural
level now at perigee.

All of this comes under the heading "sabre-chop"—the division of flesh from flesh through hate ("Such hatred, I had never conceived such," as Bowers said of the Spanish war, p. 95;—"Te cavero le budelle" / "La corate a te," p. 96), a mortal wounding of a Spain of good humor and good bread—though of much Catholicism and little religion. It stands in contradistinction to the surgeon's separation, humanely motivated, of morbid growth from healthy flesh. Mussolini's march on Rome, Pound's attacks upon rhetoric (involving, for example, breaking the pentameter) are types of scalpel-strokes upon the body social.

And beyond the division, however humanely motivated, is the process of uniting. In his "Lawes and Jenkyns" lyric, Pound himself writes singable song of the sort that Lawes and Jenkyns set to music and that in our century Arnold Dolmetsch restored to a limited popular favor. He thus gathers "from the air a live tradition," but he is able to do so because he has approached that tradition with an active, positive love so that it became his "true heritage." Another uniting process is involved in this passage. One reason why words get divorced from music is that man becomes self-consciously and arrogantly man, sets himself qualitatively apart from the other members of the scale of created beings to exist out of harmony with natural process. Pound, considering the ant, gets a new perspective, an enhanced humility, an increased accord with the process.

Canto 82

The metaphor of the scalpel-stroke, with its connotation of swift cut and the job done, is quite inaccurate, as Canto 82 suggests. "To have gathered from the air a live tradition . . . this is not vanity," Pound says in closing 81. It is also not an easy thing to do. On p. 103, Pound quotes Landor's "With Dirce in one bark convey'd"; in the *ABC of Reading* (p. 185) he had quoted it with this admonition: ". . . a man wanting to conserve a tradition would always do well to find out, first, what it is." There are many and exceedingly vocal conservers of tradition who do not know what it is—wherefore the *ABC of Reading*. To revert to metaphor, before the surgeon can get to work, he must counteract his patient's faith in the witch-doctors.

Page 101 of Canto 82, with its allusions to Swinburne, Browning ("On the Alcides' [*sic*] roof"; see *Make It New*, p. 150), Elkin Matthews, etc. expands the idea. The following quotations are illuminating:

It ought sometime to be said . . . that the serious Victorians, from Hardy to Swinburne, did NOT accept the current code of morality and that they had a great contempt for that church which . . . interfered "neither with a man's politics or his religion." (*Guide*, p. 290.)

... out of the lot of them only Browning (and Swinburne?) had a revivalist spirit. Whether as an artistic device to rouse pity and terror, or as defence mechanism, flaunted in writing because it did not work in their private lives, the others wrote as non-interveners.

Whether from truly deep instinct, whether because intuition showed them the hopelessness of staving off a great and unguessed war ... (*Guide*, p. 290.)

... they say he [Blunt in 1914] has barred his front door and put up a sign "Belligerents will please go round to the kitchen."

Ricketts has made the one mot of the war. the last flare of the '90's: "What depresses me most is the horrible fact that they can't *all* of them be beaten." ... This war is possibly a conflict between two forces almost equally detestable. Atavism and the loathsome spirit of mediocrity cloaked in graft. (*Letters*, p. 46.)

Beddoes' editor omits Landor from the list of poets writing english after the death of Shelley. My god what an England! (*Guide*, p. 286.)

Conserving the tradition, breaking through an impenetrable crystalline provincialism to get it recognized as the true heritage are of a part with the difficulty of initiating monetary reform. As Mencken said (p. 96): "... I believe that all schemes of monetary reform collide inevitably with the nature of man in the mass. He can't be convinced in anything less than a geological epoch."

In Canto 82, Pound takes a further step in his movement toward union with the process. In the "pull down thy vanity" lyric of the preceding canto, he had utilized an opportunity to draw a comparison between man and ant; in the "Tudor rose" song, between man and flower. A wisdom emerged from these comparisons. But now (p. 104) drawn to earth the mother and embracing her, he comes to a wisdom unalloyed by metaphor —the wisdom of the grave. And he gives up all pretensions, completely pulls down his vanity, fatalistically willing to be no more than *connubium terrae*. In the "lynx song" he had made demands upon the earth; now he expects nothing. It is not, however, a willing submission: terror, loneliness, tears, despair are attributes of the momentary state. Nevertheless out of that moment he derives an understanding not heretofore permitted him.

Canto 83

Canto 82 has commented upon the necessity of knowing what the components of civilization are. Canto 83 lists some of those for which Pound's love is "Still wie die Nacht, tief wie das Meer" and which therefore cannot be reft from him. (And the closer he is to fate, the better it suits an old man to take pleasure in such love.)

In Chapter 9 of the *Guide to Kulchur*, Pound defines "civilization" ideogrammically, "contrasting the fine flower of a civilization with a species of rot and corruption." Against parties in London gardens and other examples of "good society" he sets "a few evenings in Brancusi's old studio, wherein quiet was established," and he quotes Allan Upward's "The quality of the sage is like water." On p. 224 he speaks of Gemisto ("more known by his sarcophagus in Rimini than by his writings") and the effect of his conversation:

> And they say Gemisto found no one to talk to, or more generally he did the talking. He was not a proper polytheist, in this sense: His gods come from Neptune, so that there is a single source of being, aquatic (Udor, Thales etc. as you like, or what is the difference). And Gemisto had distinct aims, regeneration of greek people so they wd. keep out the new wave of Barbarism. . . .
> At any rate he had a nailed boot for Aristotle, and his conversation must have been lively. Hence (at a guess) Ficino's sinecure, at old Cosimo's expense . . . . Porphyry, Psellus, Iamblichus, Hermes Trismegistus . . . .

Plethon was one man against the grouped dignitaries of the Church meeting at Ferrara, "yet he is supposed to have set off a renaissance." And Erigena was one man, but the Church dug up his bones, a hint that his continuing influence worried officialdom. Briefly, the defeatist "Nothing that you can do" (which may very well come from the "fatigue deep as the grave") is refuted by the knowledge that the conspiracy of intelligence, always a minority movement, can sink roots to ensure that the hidden city may move upward. For civilization starts with the individual, who, with a clear purpose examining his motivations, finds that examination to be "a root, the centre of steadily out-circling causations from immediate order to a whole series of harmonies and good conducts" (Guide, p. 79) which have their effect not only upon the self-examiner but upon his milieu. This can occur in the worst of times as well as the best, as witness Yeats's perdurable peacock, and the novecento Madonna as perfect as a quattrocento.

The insistence upon water in this canto stands in sharp relief against the earth-motif of its predecessor. It is almost as though an "Earth Sermon" were being followed by a "Life by Water." Where earth in Canto 82 was only a grave, it is now the life-enduing stuff from which mint springs, of which "a very neat house" can be built, through the conduits of which an emissary may go "and have speech with Tiresias, Thebae." From the wisdom of the grave Pound has won through to the wisdom of Jacob's well and of the empty sepulchre.

Canto 84

Canto 83 ends with a note upon the citizenry's present tendency not to heed what goes on in the senate or parliament. Canto 84 (after a brief memorial of J. P. Angold's death) suggests results:

Representative ("democratic") government cannot survive unless the jaw-house is put on the air. If people "elect" weasels and speechless apes who cannot stand the test of radio-diffusion, naturally they (the people) will continue to be bled, starved and kept in rotten houses by A . . . s, B . . . s, C . . . s, D . . . s, and the dither of bank-pimps now reigning. *(Guide,* p. 241.)

The best govt. is (naturally?) that which draws the best of the nation's intelligence into use. Roosevelt's alleged aim was O.K. But the small town professor and other objects professionally labelled "brain," "intelligence," do not necessarily fill the bill. *(Loc. cit.)*

Roosevelt's cabinet, with the exception of Ickes, has not the necessary acumen to consider these questions [the nature of money and the infamy of starving the people] with the seriousness you wd. find in any european seminar outside of England. *(Guide,* p. 250.)

This being the case we deviate from our norm of spirit, the Brothers Adams, and pay our homage to a "sputtering tank of nicotine and stale whiskey" (Mr. Churchill) or a Vandenberg who has not read Stalin. We allow a lower state of civilization to continue than that of Chun-Tchi who "found the Odes to be so full of virtue; deemed them so valuable as an instrument of government, that he ordered a tartar version," or that of Mussolini, who "told his people that poetry is a necessity *to the state,*" and Carlo Delcroix, who was "convinced that poets ought to 'occupy themselves with these matters,' namely, credit, the nature of money, monetary issue, etc." *(Guide,* p. 249.)

This being the case, we will continue to destroy whole towns "for hiding a woman," and no man (nor any girl swineherd, p. 118) will sit in safety under his vine and under his fig tree *(Micah,* Chap. 4). And those who speak out against this case will be defined as traitors by the patriots who do not fail to receive their dividends from Imperial Chemicals in time of war.

Still, bad as the case may be (for him personally, for society at large), Pound maintains his hope. Carson the desert rat lost his shirt (forgetting the time-element in his consideration of ends and beginnings), but he learned something; Pound's great-aunt "had a run for her money"; "out of all this beauty something must come": if the princes abhor judgment and pervert all equity, still the opportunity for all people to walk every one in the name of his god remains open. Wagadu is not dead, but only sleeping.

And if nightfall brings frost, dawn will bring

morning moon against sunrise
like a bit of the best antient greek coinage.

*   *   *

Assuming that in the Pisan cantos, we have made an ascent into the paradisal area of Pound's poem, in the newly issued group, published under the title *Section: Rock-Drill*, the ascent continues. Even here, attention continues to be directed to the anti-paradisal; nevertheless, significant lyrical passages show that we have risen, or are rising, to super-Everest heights.

Canto 85, Pound footnotes, "is a somewhat detailed confirmation of Kung's view that the basic principles of government are found in the Shu, the History Classic." As it stands, unexplicated, with page after page of Chinese ideograms, it will probably seem to most readers the least rewarding of the cantos to date. But there is poetry (visual and otherwise) in those ideograms for the reader willing to shake off his Occidental provincialism, and, for the reader willing to explore Pound's source, there are lessons to be learned in the art of good government. Pound made the study of Chinese history relatively easy and pleasant in the Chinese cantos by doing most of the student's work for him. Here he shifts the responsibility to the student, who must himself read Couvreur's *Chou King*, a book in which the Chinese text is given simultaneously with two translations—the two translations being in French and Latin. In contriving this canto Pound has devised a fool-proof method of separating the sheep from the goats. If you want to make the most of this canto, you have got to read French, Latin, Chinese, and a little Greek. If not, you remain a goat. Space forbids presenting either sheep or goat with a pony. However, the following page references to the 4th edition (1934) of Couvreur's *Chou King* may be useful: p. 108 for Pound's p. 4; pp. 114 and 123 for Pound's p. 5 (the Four Tuan are Love, Duty, Propriety, Wisdom); pp. 121 and 124 for p. 6; pp. 127, 130, and 131 for p. 7; pp. 132 and 150 for p. 8; pp. 153 and 156 for p. 9; pp. 157-60 for p. 10; pp. 160-161, 169, and 171 for p. 11; pp. 172-3, 180, 185-6 for p. 12; pp. 187, 189, 201, 235 for p. 13; pp. 252, 264, 272 for p. 14; pp. 283-5 for p. 15; pp. 285-6, 289-292 for p. 16; pp. 295, 298, 306 for p. 17; pp. 308-9, 328, 336-7, 341-3 for p. 18; pp. 302-3, 305 for p. 19.

The reader, of course, ought not go to the *Chou King* merely to check these references; as a well-tempered Poundian, he will read the book (preferably in French and Latin and Chinese) and thus come to the awareness specified in Canto 89 as being essential: "To know the histories, to know good from evil, and know whom to trust."

Canto 86 continues the study of *Chou King*: pp. 305-6, 310, 313, 317 for p. 20; pp. 318, 320, 361, 366-9 for p. 21; pp. 369-370, 375, 384 for p. 22; pp. 388-9 for p. 26; pp. 390-94 for p. 27; pp. 393-4 for p. 28. But set against the good-government situation described in the *Chou King* are images of those who lied, who falsified history, who were illiterate or hysterical or venal. And these in turn counterpoint with Brancusi, Alexander, Theresa, and others, each of whom acted in some way with propriety.

Canto 87 offers a mixture of positive and negative images, most of them already introduced in the Pisan or earlier cantos. Among the former are such persons as Mussolini, early American presidents, Antoninus, Salmasius, Richard St. Victor, Dante, Y Yin, Ocellus, and Erigena; prominent among the latter are Roosevelt, Churchill, and an unnamed mathematician. Included as new images are Jacques de Molay, who may have been martyred for making loans without interest; the Orestes-Athena situation; and the rather ambiguous figure of John Heydon. Important to the canto is the chapter in the works of Mencius in which the Chinese sage discusses agriculture and education. A sample:

1. The duke Wan of T'ang asked *Mencius* about *the proper way of* governing a kingdom.

2. Mencius said, "The business of the people may not be remissly attended to. It is said in the Book of Poetry,
   'In the day-light go and gather the grass,
   And at night twist your ropes;
   Then get up quickly on the roofs;—
   Soon must we begin sowing *again* the grain.'

3. "The way of the people is this.—If they have a certain livelihood, they will have a fixed heart. If they have not a certain livelihood, they have not a fixed heart. And if they have not a fixed heart, there is nothing which they will not do in the way of self-abandonment, of moral deflection, of depravity, and of wild license. When they have thus been involved in crime, to follow them up and punish them:— this is to entrap the people. How can such a thing as entrapping the people be done under the rule of a benevolent man?

4. "Therefore, a ruler who is endowed with talents and virtue will be gravely complaisant and economical, showing a respectful politeness to his ministers, and taking from the people only in accordance with regulated limits.

5. "Yang Hoo said, 'He who seeks to be rich will not be benevolent. He who wishes to be benevolent will not be rich.'

6. "The sovereign of the Hea dynasty enacted the fifty *mow* allotment, and the payment of a tax. The founder of the Yin enacted the seventy *mow* allotment, and the system of mutual aid. The founder of the Chow enacted the hundred *mow* allotment, and the share system. In reality, *what was paid* in all these was a tithe. The share system means mutual division. The aid system means mutual dependence.

7. "Lung said, 'For regulating the lands, there is no better system than that of mutual aid, and none which is not better than that of taxing. By the tax system, the regular amount was fixed by taking the average of several years. In good years, when the grain lies about

in abundance, much might be taken without its being oppressive, and the actual exaction would be small. But in bad years, the produce being not sufficient to repay the manuring of the fields, this system still requires the taking of the full amount. When the parent of the people causes the people to wear looks of distress, and, after the whole year's toil, yet not to be able to nourish their parents, so that they proceed to borrowing to increase their means, till the old people and children are found lying in the ditches and water-channels:— where, *in such a case*, is his parental relation to the people?'

8. "As to the system of hereditary salaries, that is already observed in T'ang.'

9. "It is said in the Book of Poetry,
      'May the rain come down on our public field,
      And then upon our private fields!'
It is only in the system of mutual aid that there is a public field, and from this passage we perceive that even in the Chow dynasty this system has been recognized . . . ." (Bk. III, Pt. 1, Chap. III, 1-9.)

Canto 88 breaks into four sections: (1) the story of the duel between John Randolph and Henry Clay, abbreviated by Pound from T. H. Benton's account in his *Thirty Years' View*; (2) a continuation of Pound's perennial war against the perennial war of the usurers upon mankind; (3) some images of the hard, the definite, the precise; and (4) a return to the subject of money, through Adams, C. H. Douglas, and Anatole France, but concentrating, this time, upon the common sense and rugged honesty of Thomas Hart Benton. Pound's source is again Benton's account of his career in the United States Senate (1820-1850) in the *Thirty Years' View*. He teasingly gives a few page references, but far from enough for complete annotation. To get the whole picture, the reader will need to consult Benton's prose. The labor involved is not particularly arduous since Benton's book makes very good reading.

Canto 89, which goes on with the Benton story, seems to be a kind of mid-term examination by means of which Pound can determine how well his students have followed his lectures to this point. The requirement of his course in civilization is, as has been said, that we know the histories, know good from evil, and know whom to trust. If the reader going through this canto can dissociate the majority of the heroes from the villains, the right economic practice from the wrong, the sensible comment from the stupid, he may consider that he has been properly receptive to Pound's practice of "Drilling it into their heads." And his state of mind will be such as is imagized in the succeeding cantos. A new character, General John C. Fremont (with his guide Kit Carson) is introduced here. Like Odysseus and Hanno, he made an exploratory journey (a kind of periplum); like Agassiz, he was an exact observer of plants and minerals; like Malatesta, he encountered difficulties from his fellow army officers, business men, and politicians. He ties with Benton in that he married the latter's daughter. An irony occurs in his having encountered Sutter some years before gold was discovered at Sutter's Mill; when Fremont's account of his expedition was published, several appendices were included offering advice to prospective gold-miners.

In Canto 90, Paradise is regained—by the reader who has followed on the heels of the poet, and by the poet himself, who has been elevated "from under the rubble heap." There are here nothing but paradisal images: the grove has its altar; the stone takes form in the air; the great cats materialize out of nothing; beatific spirits come together; there is an ascending procession; and the freed shades of Tyro and Alemene (seen by Odysseus in hell in Canto 1) are no longer shadows but lights. The Cavalcantian relation between Love and the Intellectual Light is clarified: neither is static, neither is self-contained or self-concerned; each is an emanation, and in its outward flow it creates.

Canto 91 continues the ascent, from the circle of light to the circle of crystal. In this canto, images not used before in the *Cantos*, or, if used, only in abbreviated hint, make their appearance: (1) Apollonius, who said intelligent things, despised blood-sacrifice and was thus a civilizer, who made a journey similar to those of Odysseus, Hanno, Fremont, and Pound himself; (2) the Princess Ra-Set, daughter of the Egyptian solar deity (the Egyptian religion Rā, primarily concerned with cosmological ordering, seems to have stood in relation to Osiris worship, concerned with life, death, and resurrection, as Kung stands toward Eleusis; (3) Sir Francis Drake, who made his famous periplum, who originated modern naval tactics (made it new), who was for every statesman and historian in Europe the real protagonist, at whose hands the Armada, and with it, Catholicism, suffered grievous loss; (4) Brute, who, having sought aid of Diana (as Odysseus did of Tiresias), having sacrificed without blooding the altar, sailed west to find his fixed abode in Britain; (4) Merlin, fathered by one of "certain spirits there be betwixt the moon and earth" (see Geoffrey of Monmouth's *Histories of the Kings of Britain)*, who relates with Frobenius in having found water by "practical" divination, and with Ra-Set in having had a glass boat (as did Arthur, who like Odysseus visited the shades, and who has been connected with Osiris—by Louis Spence in *The Mysteries of Ancient Britain).* The ascent is halted (on p. 73) for a return to "filth under filth," but is resumed in a paradisal passage out of which not all the quotidian elements have been distilled.

Canto 92, opening on a high level, describes dramatically the agonizing nature of attempted mystical union; drops suddenly to the infernal; and ends with a mixture of positive and negative elements, and with Pound's comments on his unceasing fight against usury, the degradation of the sacraments, and de-sensitization.

Canto 93 introduces an important Egyptian newcomer, Kati or Nebkeure Akhtoi (11th dynasty, 2252-2228 B.C.). He is famous for having written a letter of advice to his son that became a classic. In the letter he discusses the defense of the realm, the management of the kingdom, and so on. And he is quoted (by Arthur Weigall, *A History of the Pharaohs*, I, 272-4) as having written as follows:

Copy your fathers who have gone before you, and whose words are. recorded in writing. Open and read them, and imitate one who knows. Make a lasting monument for yourself in your subjects' love of you; but . . . strengthen your boundaries and your frontiers . . . . Respect a life of energy, for self-complacence will make a wretched man of you; . . . yet a fool is he who is greedy of what others possess. This life upon earth passes: it is not long, and fortunate is he who is remembered. The possession of a million men will not avail a king (in that regard), but the memory of the good man shall live forever . . . . Speak truth in your palace that the nobles . . . may fear you. Uprightness of heart befits a king, and it is the interior of the palace that inspires the outside world with fear. Do justice that your name may endure forever . . . . Do not (lightly) degrade magistrates from their posts; and take care that you do not punish wrongfully . . . .
O, that you may reach me (in the underworld) without an accuser! Slay not any that is near to you, for God, in whose care he is, commends him to you . . . . Instil the love of yourself in all the land. A good character is that which is remembered. . . .

The similarity in point of view between Kati's counsel and that of Kung needs no comment. What bemuses Pound, of course, is that any liberal historian can speak seriously of Progress four thousand years after Kati; more than that, he implies that a species of academic treason has diverted our attention from the study of a continuing tradition of practical morality, citing as examples of such diversion the ignoring of certain illuminative passages in Dante's *Convivio* and Shakespeare's *King John* and *King Richard II* (1st scene, 2nd act, in each instance).

Forrest Read *(op. cit.,* p. 417) has remarked that:

Pound's epic movement issues . . . in his creation of a new self out of materials of the past and present, out of achieved harmony with the process, and out of union with the rhythms of the process. The entire movement beginning with Canto LXXVI, after exit from the shut-in world of Canto LXXIV and the restful pause of Canto LXXV, lives as formation of the plant whose growth has moved from the seeds to the ultimate flower.

He has already summarized Cantos 80-83 as follows:

Canto LXXX: Integral creative movement which reconciles sensibility and nature, affirms purification of will and preparation for resolution and revelation.

Canto LXXXI: Revelation as recreated self is articulated in the consciousness.

Canto LXXXII: Impact of revelation and fundamental basis of existence expressed "past metaphor"; "man, earth: two halves of the tally"; immersion in "fluid ΧΘΟΝΟΣ"; end of periplum.

Canto LXXXIII: Articulation of wisdom, union with the process, of which Pound has become consciously a part. (P. 416.)

This analysis suggests that the movement within the Pisans has brought the "plant" to its "ultimate flower." That this must not be quite the case may be argued merely from the continuation of the poem in *Rock-Drill*. But there are the further bits of evidence within the present canto: that Pound still recognizes in himself a deficiency and is required to pray for compassion; that still "where shall come leaf on bough / naught is but air"; and, indeed, that the time is "not yet. . . ! Not yet! / do not awaken. / The trees sleep, and the stags, and the grass; / the boughs sleep unmoving." There is still a journey to go.

It would seem apt to refer to Canto 94 as the "Justice Canto." Having placed "l'AMOR" beyond civic order, Pound apparently puts "above them: Justice." References to Coke and Aristides, and a passage referring to the development of law from Gaius to Justinian (who, by the way, had erected two of Pound's architectural touchstones—Sant' Apollinare in Classe and San Vitale) give credence to the idea. Another ordering of experience is described in "Above prana, the light, / past light, the crystal. / Above crystal, the jade!" An important distinction is made between the durability of consciousness and that of stone: "The clover enduring, / basalt crumbled with time." *(Cf.* "We are the plant . . . not merely set stone"; in Canto 12 and elsewhere, this theme is imagized in "And we sit here / under the wall, / Arena romana, Diocletian's, les gradins / quarante-trois rangées en calcaire.") A distinction is made between compassion and sentimentality: in Canto 93, Pound had said, "J'ai en pitié des autres / Pas assez! Pas assez!"; now he steels his heart a bit— "pity, yes, for the infected, / but maintain antisepsis, / let the light pour." As an aid toward making such distinctions, toward achieving a proper balance between Justice and Mercy, Pound here offers a list of suggested readings: Kung, the Confucian Odes, Mencius, Dante, and Agassiz.

The leading character of this canto, however, is Apollonius, who, in the battle for supremacy between Christianity and Paganism, was set up as a man of wisdom and miraculous powers, comparable to Christ. Ironically, in his efforts to reform the various religious cults (he was particularly opposed to animal-sacrifice), Conybeare says, "he prepared the ground for Christianity." He was also, Pound is gratified to note, sound on the subject of money, as is witnessed by his comparison of the Ethiopian-Egyptian system of bartering "what they have got for what

they have not" with the Greek pretense that "they cannot live unless one
penny begets another, and unless they can force up the price of their goods
by chaffering or holding them back. . . ."

The reviewer of *Rock-Drill* for the London *Times Literary Supplement*
has commented that Pound's two themes are "the rebel-hero in exile and
the emergence of order from chaos," the former imagized by the various
Odysseus-like figures to be found throughout the *Cantos*, the latter by the
story of Aphrodite born of the sea foam. It ought to be clear that his
version of the poem as a whole is so simplified as to bear only a remote
resemblance to its original. Nevertheless it applies nicely to the 95th
canto. The rebel-hero has been a main character, of course, all through
the poem. And in Canto 95, after all the variations—into Malatesta,
Hanno, Napoleon, Mussolini, Jefferson, Jackson, Fremont, Drake, Brute,
Apollonius, and the others—he re-appears in his own form as Odysseus
ship-wrecked, near to destruction, but, in the nick of time, saved by
Leucothoe. So Canto 95, the latest canto to be published, ends on a note
of hope, a note struck earlier in the canto by such phrases as "there is
something decent in the universe," and "damn it there were men even in
my time," and "the crystal wave mount to flood surge," to specify a few.
And in this canto appears an image, not so much of order emerging from
chaos, as of fruitfulness attended but not nullified by order (or justice),
in Pound's bracketing of Dionysus and Zeus Eleutherios, "the brace of
'em / that Calvin never blacked out. . . ."

Of the *Rock-Drill* cantos, this, with its personal recollections, seems
most like a throw-back to the Pisan group. Why this should be, it is quite
impossible to say. And what sort of cantos, with what new images, will
appear next on the scene, who but Mr. Pound knows?* What one does
know is that, like those just reviewed, they will be loaded with information and wisdom from the most varied sources and will contain lyric
passages beyond the scope of any other poet now writing in English,
passages invoking "the radiant world where one thought cuts through
another with clean edge, a world of moving energies . . . magnetisms
that take form or that border the visible. . . ."

---

*Cantos 96 and 97 have been published (in *Hudson Review*, vol. 9). One directs attention to Byzantium and to Justinian—temple-builder and codifier of laws; the other to
Alexander Del Mar's historical survey of monetary crimes. I have not included them in
this study, since they may undergo alteration before appearing, with their successors,
in book form.

Chapter 7

A rather large claim was made for the poetry of the *Cantos* at the close of the foregoing chapter. And it must be justified. For, assuming that the reader has learned how to hack his way through this forest of images, he may yet ask the question: Why bother? Or, less succinctly: Is there enough poetry here to merit the expenditure of time and study which is entailed? Late in the 18th century, Erasmus Darwin wrote a long and learned poem *(The Botanic Garden)* with the laudable purpose of making the study of botany easy and pleasant. The purpose was worthy, the information was compendious, but the poetry was abominable. And no one, save the eccentric scholar, now reads the poem. Is the *Cantos* another *Botanic Garden*, or, to name others equally forgotten, a *Creation*, a *Universal Beauty*, or a *Pleasures of the Imagination?*

That my answer will be negative is attested by the fact of this book. However, an unsupported statement of opinion is valueless. Evidence must be adduced.

What I propose to do is this: to select passages from the *Cantos* which seem to me to have poetic worth and set them beside well-thought-of passages (from poems late or old) which possess a resemblance of one kind or another. It will be my opinion that, in each instance, the Pound passage will readily survive the comparison. I shall not hesitate to use Pound's translations: a translation on occasion is as much the translator's as is his most personal utterance. Indeed, it should prove instructive to open my list of parallels with two translations, one from Ovid's *Metamorphoses*, the other (not in the *Cantos* but characteristically Poundian) from Sophocles' *The Women of Trachis*, comparing them with translations by Rolfe Humphries and E. F. Watling respectively. The basis of comparison between the translations and that between the "parallel passages" that follow them will, of course, be quite different.

160

I

God-sleight then, god-sleight:
    Ship stock fast in sea-swirl,
Ivy upon the oars, King Pentheus,
    grapes with no seed but sea-foam,
Ivy in scupper-hole.
Aye, I, Acoetes, stood there,
    and the god stood by me,
Water cutting under the keel,
Sea-break from stern forrards,
    wake running off from the bow,
And where was gunwale, there now was vine-trunk,
And tenthril where cordage had been,
    grape-leaves on the rowlocks,
Heavy vine on the oarshafts,
And, out of nothing, a breathing,
    hot breath on my ankles,
Beasts like shadows in glass,
    a furred tail upon nothingness.
Lynx-purr, and heathery smell of beasts,
    where tar smell had been,
Sniff and pad-foot of beasts,
    eye-glitter out of black air.
          (Canto 2, pp. 7-8.)

The ship stood motionless as if in dry-dock.
The men pulled oars with more than double effort,
They spread all sail and tried to get her running,
As ivy wound around the oars, and clung there,
And spread above the freeboard, and caught the sails
With heavy, drooping clusters. And the god,
His forehead berry-garlanded, was waving
A wand with ivy tendrils. All around him
Lay tigers, phantom lynxes, spotted panthers . . .
(Ovid, *Metamorphoses*, tr. by Rolfe Humphries, Bk. 3, ll. 661-8.)

II

```
Khoros:  APOLLO
                and Artemis, analolu
                        Artemis
            Analolu
            Sun-bright Apollo, Saviour Apollo
                        analolu
            Artemis,
            Sylvan Artemis,
            Swift-arrowed Artemis, analolu
            By the hearth-stone
                        brides to be
            Shout in male company:
                        APOLLO EUPHARETRON.
            Sylvan Artemis,
                torch-lit Artemis
            With thy Ortygian girls,
                        Analolu
            Artemis,
                    Io Zagreus,
            Join now, join with us
                            when the great stag is slain,
            Lord of hearts, Artemis,
            Ivied Zagreus,
                        Analolu
            Dancing maid and man,
            Lady or Bacchanal
                        dancing toe to toe
            By night,
            By light shall show
                        analolu
                        Paian.
```

(Sophocles, "Women of Trachis, a version by Ezra Pound," *Hudson Review*, v. 6 no. 4 (Winter, 1954), pp. 492-3.)

Now let the house be filled
With maiden voices singing at the hearth
For joy; and let the shouts of men together
Praise the bright arrow-armed
Apollo, our defender!
Sing, women, sing to Artemis,
Apollo's sister, huntress of the deer,
The fire-encircled; praise
Her neighbour-nymphs!
O master of my soul,
I float on air, the sweet
Music of flutes would win me now,
And twining ivy-tendrils whirl me round
In Bacchanalian dance.
Paean! Paean!
(Sophocles, "Women of Trachis," in *Electra and Other Plays,* tr. by
E. F. Watling, p. 126.)

III

The ant's a centaur in his dragon world.
Pull down thy vanity, it is not man
Made courage, or made order, or made grace,
    Pull down thy vanity, I say pull down.
Learn of the green world what can be thy place
In scaled invention or true artistry,
Pull down thy vanity,
          Paquin pull down!
The green casque has outdone your elegance.
"Master thyself, then others shall thee beare"
    Pull down thy vanity
Thou art a beaten dog beneath the hail,
A swollen magpie in a fitful sun,
Half black half white
Nor knowst'ou wing from tail
Pull down thy vanity
       How mean thy hates
Fostered in falsity,
       Pull down thy vanity,
Rathe to destroy, niggard in charity,
Pull down thy vanity,
       I say pull down.
          (Canto 81, p. 99.)

I met a traveler from an antique land,
Who said: Two vast and trunkless legs of stone
Stand in the desert. Near them, on the sand,
Half sunk, a shattered visage lies, whose frown,
And wrinkled lip, and sneer of cold command,
Tell that its sculptor well those passions read,
Which yet survive, stamped on these lifeless things,
The hand that mocked them, and the heart that fed:
And on the pedestal these words appear:
"My name is Ozymandias, King of Kings:
Look on my works, ye Mighty, and despair!"
Nothing beside remains. Round the decay
Of that colossal wreck, boundless and bare
The lone and level sands stretch far away.

(P. B. Shelley, *Ozymandias.*)

IV

Autumn moon; hills rise about lakes
against sunset
Evening is like a curtain of cloud,
a blurr above ripples; and through it
sharp long spikes of the cinnamon,
a cold tune amid reeds.
Behind hill the monk's bell
borne on the wind.
Sail passed here in April; may return in October
Boat fades in silver; slowly;
Sun blaze alone on the river.

Where wine flag catches the sunset
Sparse chimneys smoke in the cross light

(Canto 49, p. 38.)

Season of mists and mellow fruitfulness,
    Close bosom-friend of the maturing sun;
Conspiring with him how to load and bless
    With fruit the vines that round the thatch-eaves run;
To bend with apples the mossed cottage-trees,
    And fill all fruit with ripeness to the core;
        To swell the gourd, and plump the hazel shells
    With a sweet kernel; to set budding more,
And still more later flowers for the bees,
Until they think warm days will never cease,
        For Summer has o'er-brimmed their clammy cells.
                (John Keats, *Ode to Autumn.*)

V

Lithe turning of water,
      sinews of Poseidon,
Black azure and hyaline,
      glass wave over Tyro,
Close cover, unstillness,
      bright welter of wave-cords,
Then quiet water,
      quiet in the buff sands,
Sea-fowl stretching wing-joints,
      splashing in rock-hollows and sand-hollows
In the wave-runs by the half-dune;
Glass-glint of wave in the tide-rips against sunlight,
      pallor of Hesperus,
Grey peak of the wave,
      wave, colour of grape's pulp, . . .
      (Canto 2, pp. 9-10.)

Children dear, was it yesterday
We heard the sweet bells over the bay?
In the caverns where we lay,
Through the surf and through the swell,
The far-off sound of a silver bell?
Sand-strewn caverns, cool and deep,
 Where the winds are all asleep;
 Where the spent lights quiver and gleam,
 Where the salt weed sways in the stream,
 Where the sea-beasts, ranged all round,
 Feed in the ooze of their pasture-ground;
 Where the sea-snakes coil and twine,
 Dry their mail and bask in the brine;
 Where great whales come sailing by,
 Sail and sail, with unshut eye,
 Round the world for ever and aye?
When did music come this way?
Children dear, was it yesterday?
      (Matthew Arnold, *The Forsaken Merman.*)

VI

And from the plain whence the water-shoot,
Across, back, to the right, the roads, a way in the grass,
The Khan's hunting leopard, and young Salustio
And Ixotta; the suave turf
Ac ferae familiares, and the cars slowly,
And the panthers, soft-footed.
Plain, as the plain of Somnus,
          the heavy cars, as a triumph,
Gilded, heavy on wheel,
          and the panthers chained to the cars,
Over suave turf, the form wrapped,
Rose, crimson, deep crimson,
And, in the blue dusk, a colour as of rust in the sunlight,
Out of white cloud, moving over the plain,
Head in arm's curve, reclining;
The road, back and away, till cut along the face of the rock,
And the cliff folds in like a curtain,
The road cut in under the rock
Square groove in the cliff's face, as chiostri,
The columns crystal, with peacocks cut in the capitals,
The soft pad of beasts dragging the cars;
Cars, slow, without creak, . . .

(Canto 20, pp. 94-5.)

Coffin that passes through lanes and streets
Through day and night with the great cloud darkening
          the land,
With the pomp of the inlooped flags with the cities draped
          in black,
With the show of the States themselves as of crepe-veiled
          women standing,
With processions long and winding and the flambeaus of
          the night,
With the countless torches lit, with the silent sea of faces
          and the unbared heads,
With the waiting depot, the arriving coffin, and the sombre
          faces,
With dirges through the night, with the shout and voices
          rising strong and solemn,
With all the mournful voices of the dirges poured around
          the coffin,
The dim-lit churches and the shuddering organs—where
          amid these you journey,
With the tolling, tolling bells' perpetual clang,
Here, coffin that slowly passes,
I give you my sprig of lilac.

(Walt Whitman, *When Lilacs Last in the Dooryard Bloomed.*)

VII

The slough of unamiable liars,
        bog of stupidities,
malevolent stupidities, and stupidities,
the soil living pus, full of vermin,
dead maggots begetting live maggots,
        slum owners,
usurers squeezing crab-lice, pandars to authority,
pets-de-loup, sitting on piles of stone books,
obscuring the texts with philology,
        hiding them under their persons,
the air without refuge of silence,
    , the drift of lice, teething,
and above it the mouthing of orators,
        the arse-belching of preachers.

(Canto 14, p. 63.)

Therewith she spewd out of her filthie maw
A floud of poyson horrible and blacke,
Full of great lumps of flesh and gobbets raw,
Which stunck so vildly, that it forst him slacke
His grasping hold, and from her turne him backe:
Her vomit full of bookes and papers was,
With loathly frogs and toades, which eyes did lacke,
And creeping sought way in the weedy gras:
Her filthie parbreake all the place defiled has.

(Edmund Spenser, *The Faerie Queene*, Canto 1, 20.)

Now, *I* say that in each of the above bracketed excerptings, the Pound passage shows to advantage—or, at least, does not appear to disadvantage. Among the things to be noted here are these:

1. Pound's dramatization of the Dionysus incident into a truly "magical moment" as opposed to Humphries' re-telling of a charming but un-believed-in fairy tale.

2. Pound's transmutation of a command to sing for joy to the joyful song itself.

3. The contrast between Pound's didacticism based upon eye-on-the-object observation, poignantly felt, and delivered in down-to-earth ima-gery—the whole clearly fixed in the here and now—and Shelley's didacti-cism based upon an imaginary incident, phrased in a language no man ever spoke, and thus only a fable artificially contrived to point a moral which must take to itself some of the artificiality of its context.

4. Pound's ability to evoke the thinness of his Autumn as surely as Keats evokes the fatness of his.

5. Pound's avoidance of any tincture of sentimentality or of the obvious "poeticizing" of Arnold's parallel "where" clauses.

6. Pound's variations in rhythm and syntax as opposed to Whitman's rather heavy-handed, cataloguing parallelism.

7. Pound's play of wit, relieving yet enhancing a horror; his choice of details, somewhat more interesting, because connected with real life, than Spenser's.

If I am right, and the reader confirms my finding, I have made progress —but I am not in a position to rest my case. For I have quite consciously chosen passages which are generally admired, which, save that they (most of them) are imagistic rather than rhetorical, paragraphed rather than stanzaic and, so to speak, un-sentenced, and in general unrelated to the conventional *genres* of English poetry, are still at a far remove from the puzzlingly eccentric.

But what of, say, the Chinese cantos, which purport to narrate the history of China? Does poetry inhere in them? That they are essential to Pound's plan and not to be considered a digression from the main business of the poem or an exploitation of a personal idiosyncrasy has already been made manifest. They are at least as integral to the over-all plan as the European cantos, and they must be read with even greater sympathy and attention if only to correct our insularity and our delusion of Occidental superiority. And Pound is under the obligation of engaging our attention and enlisting our sympathy by bringing all his poetic powers to bear upon his subject.

Such sympathy Carne-Ross has been unable to muster. He objects to these ten cantos on the ground that here (as in the American cantos) "the poetic vitality of the writing has markedly diminished." *(Examination,* pp. 142 ff.) And he gives two examples "to suggest the right and wrong way of turning history into poetry." The first is from Milton:

> Not *Babilon*
> Nor great *Alcairo* such magnificence
> Equal'd in all their glories, to inshrine
> *Belus* or *Serapis* thir Gods, or seat
> Thir Kings, when *AEgypt* with *Assyria* strove
> In wealth and luxurie.

The second is from Canto 54:

> For three hundred years, four hundred, nothing quiet,
> WALL rose in the time of TSIN CHI
> TCHEOU lasted eight centuries and then TSIN came
> and of TSIN was CHI HOANG TI that united all China ....

Comparing the two, Carne-Ross says, "Milton has realized his subject so completely that further information . . . would only add distracting detail to an already completed picture; Pound, on the other hand, simply informs us that a wall was built—presumably it is the famous one, but in spite of the capital letters his reference leaves the image of the wall which we have in our minds quite unqualified." And he concludes: "It is not unfair to say that the difference between the two passages quoted above is that Milton's *animates* history while Pound's merely *includes* it."

Exception may be taken to Carne-Ross's liking for the Milton passage. Some readers will find that Milton has not animated but killed history dead. The devices of negative simile and inversion produce an effect of pomposity and ponderousness which distracts attention from the meaning; the abstractions—magnificence, glories, wealth, luxury—are blob-words; the separation of subjects from infinitives confuses the sense; perhaps too great dependence is placed upon the connotative effects of the proper nouns. It seems to me a tenable position that more dramatic action and more significance show in the simplicity and forward drive from "For three hundred years, four hundred, nothing quiet" through "WALL rose ...." to "united all China" than in the trombone sonorities and the rocking-horse motion of the Milton passage. Exception may also be taken to the choice of passage from Pound. Is there no animation of history in the lines which immediately precede those chosen?

> So that Tien-tan chose bulls, a thousand
>   and covered them with great leather masks, making
>   dragons
>   and bound poignards to their horns
>   and tied torches, pitch-smeared, to their tails

and loosed them by night from ten points
on the camp of Ki-kié the besieger
          lighting the torches
So died Ki-kié and that town (Tsié-mé) was delivered.
          (Canto 54, p. 21)

Or is history not animated in the thumbnail sketch immediately preceding that?

Thus of Kung or Confucius, and of 'Hillock' his father
when he was attacking a city
his men had passed under the drop gate
And the warders then dropped it, so Hillock caught
the whole weight on his shoulder, and held till his
last man had got out.
          Of such stock was Kungfutseu . . . .
          (Canto 53, p. 20.)

Carne-Ross says that about "the various personages mentioned, we are
told nothing, so their effect on our minds and imagination is nil." But
reference to the succeeding lines (which he has not quoted) reveals that
Pound has told a good deal more than nothing about CHI HOANG TI:

and of TSIN was CHI HOANG TI that united all China
who referred to himself as the surplus
or needless bit of the Empire
      and jacked up astronomy
and after 33 years burnt the books
          because of fool litterati
by counsel of Li-ssé
          save medicine and on field works . . . .
          (Canto 54, p. 21.)

Indeed, there is not a page in the Chinese cantos which does not make
quick the dead or shed light on an era:

Said Chao-kong: Talk of the people
          is like the hills and the streams
          Thence comes our abundance.
To be Lord to the four seas of China
          a man must let men make verses
          he must let people play comedies
          and historians write down the facts
          he must let the poor speak evil of taxes . . . .
          (Canto 53, p. 16.)
          RITE is:
Nine days before the first moon of spring time,
that he fast. And with gold cup of wheat-wine
     that he go afield to spring ploughing
that he plough one and three quarters furrows
     and eat beef when this rite is finished,
          so did not Siuen
that after famine, called back the people . . . .
          (Canto 53, p. 17.)

And Lou-kia was envoy to Nan-hai, with nobility,
and wished that the *king* (the books Chu king and Chi king)
     be restored
to whom KAO: I conquered the empire on horseback.
to whom Lou: Can you govern it in that manner?
whereon Lou-kia wrote 'The New Discourse' (Sin-yu)
   in 12 chapters, and the books were restored . . . .
        (Canto 54, p. 22.)

TçIN OU dismissed too many troops
    and was complimented on dragons
      (two found in the soldiers' well, green ones)
and the country was run by Yang Siun
while the emperor amused himself in his park
    had a light car made, harnessed to sheep
The sheep chose which picnic he went to,
ended his days as a gourmet . . . .
        (Canto 54, p. 28.)

    Came the XIIth dynasty: SOUI
YANG-KIEN, rough able, wrathy
    flogged a few every day
      and sacrificed on Mt Tai Chan
Built Gin Cheou the palace
    pardoned those who stood up to him.
Touli-Kahn, tartar, was given a princess
    now was contempt of scholars
OUEN kept up mulberry trees
    and failed with his family
YANG (kouang) TI ordered more buildings
    jobs for two millyum men
    and filled his zoological gardens . . . .
      (Canto 54, pp. 30-31.)

And the Emperor TAÏ TSONG left his son 'Notes on Conduct'
whereof the 3rd treats of selecting men for a cabinet
whereof the 5th says that they shd/ tell him his faults
the 7th: maintain abundance
The 10th a charter of labour
and the last on keepin' up kulchur
   Saying 'I have spent money on palaces
    too much on 'osses, dogs, falcons
but I have united the Hempire (and you 'aven't)
Nothing harder than to conquer a country
   and damn'd easy to lose one, in fact there
ain't anything heasier.
   Died TAÏ TSONG in the 23rd of his reign.
And left not more than fifty men in all jails of the empire
none of 'em complaining of judgement.
   And the tartars wanted to die at his funeral
   and wd/ have, if TAÏ hadn't foreseen it
     and writ expressly that they should not. . . .
       (Canto 54, p. 33.)

Carne-Ross to the contrary, it is in these cantos particularly that Pound has given proof that the imagistic process can be successfully used in sequential narrative, and can bring to life and invest with élan what might otherwise have been drab, if not dead. In this function exists a distinction between prose and verse; in the degree of success achieved in acting upon this function exists a difference between verse and poetry.

Does such success attend Pound's efforts to revitalize American history? Carne-Ross again, finding these cantos "extremely dull," thinks not. And he explains:

> The trouble with these Cantos is that for page after page Pound is content simply to versify "images" or fragmentary pieces of information from the period he is seeking to present. Whether or not they are important in themselves (and it is often very hard to believe that they are) need not for the present concern us, what matters is that they shall be felt into poetry, and again and again Pound has simply not done this. The method of writing which appears to such advantage in the Sigismundo Cantos here signally fails, and we are led to reflect that what counts is not the method, or the theory, but the quality of the writing itself. *(Examination,* p. 142.)

And he says again:

> Has Pound forgotten his injunction "Do not re-tell in mediocre verse what has already been done in good prose"? Possibly American historians are poor historians.

More readers, I think, will agree with Carne-Ross than will disagree with him. Yet, since there are readers who find no diminution of poetical vitality here, it is worthwhile to consider reasons for the discrepancy of opinions. I think, in the first place, that Carne-Ross does not feel at home in American history as he does in European. His not recognizing the importance of many of Pound's images is indicative. This being the case, he fails to educe from the fragments the whole pictures of the American heroes as an American is (or ought to be) able to do. (Pound notes that "Jackson is regarded as a tobacco-chewing half-wit . . . . Van Buren either vilified or forgotten. Only abnormal Englishmen have ever heard of such presidents." *(Social Credit,* p. 12.) One detects in Carne-Ross's remarks, too, a hint of that European snobbery which perpetuates the belief that what happened in the "colonies" lacked real significance in the history of the world. He appears to approach these cantos with an initial, if unconscious, antipathy which his lack of understanding can only fortify. Third, as Pound says, the American conflict from 1800 to 1850 was "not a showy theatrical shindy." Where the Italian cantos are in fancy dress, with sword-fighting and all, the American cantos deal with men in conservative business dress who argued, discussed, wrote letters and speeches, bought votes, and cornered markets. We have moved from

Sabatini to the *Correspondence of Thomas Jefferson*. And finally, since the heroes of these cantos spoke and wrote in English, thus affording Pound the opportunity not to translate but merely to select and compress, these cantos are less in Pound's style than are those in which he had to supply the translation or paraphrase. Pound spoke for Sigismondo; Adams speaks for himself.

Only in terms of this last consideration, it seems to me, does Carne-Ross have a defensible position. The question must be asked: does the prose of Adams (and others) approach to poetry? Here opinions may validly differ. Pound's is that poetry evidences itself in the best utterances of the American statesmen. In the *Guide to Kulchur* (p. 181), Pound makes a valiant effort to approve Samuel Johnson's *Vanity of Human Wishes* and *London* but he comes to this conclusion:

> Johnson's verse is not as good prose as that often found in Tom Jefferson's letters. There is probably no couplet in the two reprinted poems that has the quality of Jefferson's.
> "No man has a natural right to be a money-lender save him who has money to lend." Or any other of the citations on p. 116 and following of my Jefferson and/or Mussolini.

One of the latter is a favorite of Pound's:

> . . . and if the national bills issued be bottomed (as is indispensable) on pledges of specific taxes for their redemption within certain and moderate epochs, and be of proper denominations for circulation, no interest on them would be necessary or just, because they would answer to every one of the purposes of the metallic money withdrawn and replaced by them.

It is not clear that Pound considers this poetry, but he does consider it literature ("language charged with meaning to the utmost possible degree"). And if it lacks the emotional potential required of poetry, it also lacks the "obligatory comparisons, the mythology the poet don't believe in, his so-called dignity of style, *à la Louis XIV,* and all that trail of what they call poetic ornament" that characterized the "poesie" which Stendhal and Flaubert forced to give way to the new prose so superior to it. If Pound has made poetry of Jefferson's (or Adams's) prose, it has been by applying the axiom of Dichten = Condensare. If he has not, it will still remain, in his estimation, on a higher level than the "poesie" of an earlier day. And the reader who disbelieves this, as Carne-Ross does, will be charged by Pound with having failed to recognize the revolution of the word which took place in 19th century prose and which made poetry the inferior art "until it caught up with the prose" of Stendhal and Flaubert. (Quotes in this paragraph from pp. 28 and 96-7 of the *ABC of Reading.*)

A word, however, on Pound's theory and method before coming to the question of the quality of the writing. In the American cantos, Pound's business is to portray a man observing a scene, meditating upon what he observes, formulating in written form those meditations, and reflecting, later, upon those observations, meditations, and formulations. He is not depicted, as Malatesta was, from the omniscient point of view, author standing outside. Pound does not, on the other hand, create Adams's stream of thought and emotion, as Joyce created Bloom's, though fragmentations, ellipses, unexpected juxtapositions, abrupt temporal shifts, and the like are common to both. The Joyce portrayal is a triumph of imagination; Pound's is (if it succeeds) a triumph of selection and disposition. Among the conditions necessary to success here are these: (1) that the character be of a stature and intrinsic interest sufficient to warrant treatment in detail; (2) that the method of "abbreviated quotes" satisfactorily reveal the character; (3) that the result, the revelation of a character of heroic stature, be in language sufficiently "charged" as to merit the designation "poetry." Briefly, the question is this: is there as much reason to read Pound on Adams rather than Adams's letters as to read Shakespeare on Caesar rather than Plutarch?

A part of the first condition is satisfactorily met: Adams is a great man—far greater than the Malatesta whom Pound has (in Carne-Ross's opinion) so satisfactorily portrayed. But is he interesting? Certainly he lacks theatricality. He never "stood in the water up to his neck / to keep the hounds off him," as Malatesta did, nor set out for Rome to assassinate the pope; he was not, as Mussolini was, captured by Partisans, rescued by Nazis, re-captured and dramatically hanged; his trips to Europe were without incident compared to the journeys of Odysseus or Hanno or Fremont; he did not marshall great armies, as Napoleon did. The drama of Adams consists in what he thought and felt (as he read or observed), what he said, what he wrote, what he willed. If a man thinking thoughts which are to assist in producing so miraculous an experiment in government as is embodied in the Constitution of the United States is interesting, Adams is interesting.

But question arises as to whether Pound has met the second condition. What virtue is to be derived from an exposure to an arrangement of broken quotations instead of to a generalization educed by a historian from a reading of Adams's writings and expressed with due obeisance to rhetorical propriety? The question answers itself. In the first instance you are meeting Adams face to face, hearing him speak in his own peculiar idiom and intonation; in the second, you come to him through two glasses darkly—that of the historian's rhetoric, and that of the historian's mind. Pound's method does have its advantages, then: it comes nearer giving a true picture; it produces the dramatic illusion of immediacy, and (since the reader is not being spooned pre-digested pap) it coerces thought.

Is it poetry? Certainly not the poetry we are familiar with. But is it poetry at all?

So far as I can see, it is poetry of a kind. It is not of that kind which the following excerpts exemplify:

> Or if the secret ministry of frost
> Shall hang them up in silent icicles
> Quietly shining to the quiet moon.

> Bring me my bow of burning gold!
>   Bring me my arrows of desire!
> Bring me my spear: O clouds unfold!
>   Bring me my chariot of fire.

> Batter my heart, three-personed God; for you
> As yet but knock, breathe, shine, and seek to mend.

But then, neither are the following:

> There are in our existence spots of time,
> That with distinct pre-eminence retain
> A renovating virtue, whence—depressed
> By false opinion and contentious thought,
> Or aught of heavier or more deadly weight,
> In trivial occupations, and the round
> Of ordinary intercourse—our minds
> Are nourished and invisibly repaired;
> (Wordsworth, *The Prelude,* Bk. 12, ll. 208-215.)

> These head the troops that rocky Aulis yields,
> And Eteon's hills, and Hyrie's watery fields,
> And Schoenos, Scholos, Graea near the main,
> And Mycalessia's ample piny plain;
> Those who in Peteon or Ilesion dwell,
> Or Harma where Apollo's prophet fell;
> (Pope's *Iliad,* Bk. 2.)

> To the blanc Moon
> Her office they prescribed; to the other five
> Their planetary motions and aspects,
> In *sextile, square,* and *trine,* and *opposite,*
> Of noxious efficacy, and when to join
> In synod unbenign; and taught the fixed
> Their influence malignant when to shower—
> Which of them, rising with the Sun or falling,
> Should prove tempestuous.
> (Milton, *Paradise Lost,* Bk. 10, ll. 656-664.)

> 'Tis not unknown to you, Antonio,
> How much I have disabled mine estate,
> By something showing a more swelling port

Than my faint means would grant continuance:
Nor do I now make moan to be abridged
From such a noble rate; but my chief care
Is to come fairly off from the great debts
Wherein my time something too prodigal
Hath left me gaged.
       (Shakespeare, *The Merchant of Venice*, Act 1, Scene 1, 11.
       122-130.)

Each of these is written in meter: each is, then, if not poetry, at least
verse. And since each would seem, compared to the passages cited above,
to lack some quality which, though undefinable, all agree to call "poetical," *verse* would appear to be the apt word. Written in varying meters,
and in varying degrees of pomposity, all agree in having, primarily, a prose
purpose; in all, the words are clearly the vehicle for the meaning and
not vice versa, and the cerebral dominates over the imaginative almost to
the latter's exclusion.

But didactic poetry must serve a prose purpose. Dante must engage in
theological exposition; Pope must clarify the Great Chain of Being
theory; and Pound must deal with Adams's political thought and
activity. The question remains: are the lines in which he proffers his
exposition of Adams as constructive governor "charged with meaning" to
the degree that the expository lines quoted above are charged? The only
test is comparison. Following are excerpts selected at random from the
Adams cantos:

I told Hartley their policy with Holland was wrong all wrong
if they backed the Stadtholder the Emperor and French wd/
back the republicans and all Europe enkindle
    England
now had stronger reason to cultivate Holland
and not push up the Bourbon
    expedient that an intercourse
and commerce be opened, laws of Gt Britain on
plantation trade contrived solely to benefit Britain
    said Dutch vessels had gone to America
    loaded with linens, duck, sailcloth etc
    copper corrodes ships' iron
most agreeable day I ever spent at Versailles
    (17 May '83)
        (Canto 65, p. 125.)

By this course, said one member, free election is taken away
common rights our ancestors have left us
By this course, said another, the Chancellor
could call a parliament of only such as he please
    After repeal of American Stamp Act
we have mortification to see one Act of Parliament after another,
money collecting from us continually without our consent
by an authority

> in the constitution of which we have no share
> and see the little coin that remained among us
> transmitted to distance
> > with no hope of return
> > (Canto 66, p. 129.)

> The philosophers say: one, the few, the many.
> > Regis   optimatium   populique
> > as Lycurgus in Spartha, reges, seniores et populus
> > > both greeks and italians
> archons, suffestes or consuls
> Athenians, Spartans, Thebans, Achaians
> using the people as its mere dupe, as an underworker
> > a purchaser in trust for some tyrant
> dexterous in pulling down, not in maintaining. Turgot
> takes a definition of the commonwealth
> > for a definition of liberty.
> Where ambition is every man's trade is no ploughing
> How shall the plow be kept in hands of owners not hirelings?
> > (Canto 68, p. 141.)

> that there were Americans indifferent to fisheries
> > and even some inclined to give them away
> > this was my strongest motive
> > for twice going to Europe.
> fish boxes were rec'd in my absence.
> 'Their constitution, experiment, I KNOW
> that France can not be long governed by it.'
> > To Price, 19 April 1790
> aim of my life has been to be useful, how small in
> any nation the number who comprehend ANY
> system of constitution or administration
> > and these few do not unite.
> > (Canto 70, p. 158.)

They do not suffer from the "heavier or more deadly weight" of the Wordsworth and Milton passages, nor from the artificiality of the reiterated epithet-noun combinations (each epithet with its enfeebling "-y") of the Pope; they do not generate the feeling of a necessity imposed upon the poet (Well, I've got to get some exposition in here) that the Shakespeare passage does.

Poetry? Perhaps not; but surely not "mediocre verse." My objection, contrary to that of Carne-Ross, is not to the quality of the lines but to the method by which the Adams cantos are developed. They are altogether too crowded with fragments; they require too much shifting between the poem and Pound's source to become as meaningful as one would like; they lack continuity, do not flow; and there is too little variety and relief from focus upon Adams. Pound seems to have over-run limits here as (or so it seems to me) Joyce did in the question-answer sequence (pp. 650 *et seq.)* of *Ulysses*.

178

Pound apparently does not think so, since he has used much the same technique in the *Rock-Drill* cantos—I have in mind particularly the passages in Cantos 88-9, in which he arranges fragments from Benton's account of his career as a senator. Consider the following lines:

> Mr Jefferson lining up for Louis Philippe,
>   a fact which shd have been known to
>   M. de Tocqueville.
> Privilege to serve with King and Macon
>   & John Taylor of Caroline.
> Entangling alliance with none,
>   would be from their cultivation,
> That is to say: revenue from the waste lands would be.

From these, and the following unquoted lines, a portrait of an American is supposed to emerge; I do not think it does. It will when the reader refers to the chapters from which Pound drew his material. But that reader may with reason wonder whether Pound's series of fragments was necessary and whether a note directing attention to the Senator's book would not have sufficed. Hugh Kenner has spoken to this point:

> All paraphrase blunts, and a statement about Senator Thomas Hart Benton's ideas has less force than his words as he arranged them. To tesselate his words, as Pound does in Cantos 88-89, poses difficulties arising from our ignorance of their context; not to use them would pose the anomaly of that to which the poem refers outside itself evincing more ultimate interest and durability than that which it places on record. Pound should be credited with having weighed the perils of the method he has elected. *(Poetry, 9, p. 240.)*

But for Pound merely to have weighed the perils of his method does not satisfy the requirements. His business is either to win through them or, failing that, to elect another method. My own opinion is that Benton on Benton is to be preferred to Pound on Benton: from him the reader gets the whole figure; from Pound he does not because the images do not exert a sufficiently powerful catalytic effect upon his imagination.

Which is to say, in sum, that, as there are aridities in *Paradise Lost* or the *Prelude*—some intentional and necessary, some not—there are aridities in the *Cantos*.

But a good answer may be made to such a comment: namely, that, granting the prosy flats in Milton and Wordsworth, there are always to be anticipated the plateaus and the peaks. The rebuttal to this argument can only consist in directing the reader's attention to such passages in the *Cantos* as the following: canto 2; canto 3, pp. 13-15; canto 16, pp. 68-70; canto 17; canto 20, pp. 91-95; canto 21, pp. 98-100; canto 25, pp. 117-119; canto 27, pp. 130-132; canto 30; canto 36; canto 39; canto 40, pp. 49-51; canto 43, pp. 10-11; canto 44, pp. 17-18; canto 45; canto 47; canto 49;

canto 52, pp. 4-7; the Chinese cantos *passim*; canto 65, pp. 114-117; canto 74 *passim*; conto 76 *passim*; canto 79, pp. 66-70; canto 80, pp. 92-94; canto 81, pp. 97-100; canto 83; canto 90; canto 91, pp. 70-73; canto 92, pp. 78-80; canto 93, pp. 88-91. If these passages stimulate no affirmative response, the argument is over.

One critic left cold by Pound's poetry is Sona Raiziss, and she has used against Pound the very method I have been using in his favor. Her thesis is that Pound, because his poetry does not produce the metaphysical *frisson*, because he does not succeed "by a line or a phrase in disturbing the spirit as well as the ear and the brain," must be considered a poet inferior to Eliot. She quotes Eliot (p. 168) as saying of Pound: "His eye is indeed remarkable, it is careful, comprehensive, and exact; but it is rare that he has an image of the maximum concentration, an image which combines the precise and concrete with a kind of almost infinite suggestion." And F. R. Leavis is produced to support her argument that in Pound's experiences are "none of Mr. Eliot's complex intensities of concern about soul and body: the moral, religious and anthropological preoccupations are absent."

The trouble with this sort of argument is that it aggrandizes a taste, and a set of values founded upon that taste, which has developed during the past forty-odd years and which was relative to that time, into an absolute. What has been valid during the period 1920-1960, it is implied, is valid *sub specie aeternitatis*. The underlying unstated assumption is quite false. One poet is not greater than another because he can be stipulated as being Metaphysical as opposed to, say, Classical. The best that one can say is that, at this particular instant because of the intellectual stresses of our time, an articulate segment of that minority preoccupied with poetry finds a greater affinity with the kind of poetry written by Donne than with that written by Spenser. Its taste inclines toward Herbert rather than Herrick, toward Blake rather than Jonson. Perhaps Pound would say that it inclines toward the Hebraic rather than the Hellenic, and quote Santayana:

> The Jews . . . like other Orientals, had a figurative way of speaking and thinking; their poetry and religion were full of the most violent metaphors. Now to the classic mind violent and improper metaphors were abhorrent. Uniting, as it did, clear reason with lively fancy, it could not conceive one thing to *be* another, nor relish the figure of speech that so described it, hoping by that unthinkable phrase to suggest its affinities. But the classic mind could well conceive transformation, of which indeed nature is full; and in Greek fables anything might change its form, become something else, and display its plasticity, not by imperfectly being many things at once, but by being the perfection of many things in succession. While metaphor was thus unintelligible and confusing to the Greek, metamorphosis was perfectly familiar to him. (*The Life of Reason*, p. 220.)

The above pairing of Jonson and Blake recalls Eliot's statement that Pound fails in combining "the precise and concrete with a kind of almost infinite suggestion."

It is not clear where Eliot thinks Pound's images fail—in their lack of concreteness or lack of almost infinite suggestiveness. Probably the latter. At least, it is not difficult to find concrete images in the *Cantos*, as, for example:

> When the mind swings by a grass-blade
>   an ant's forefoot shall save you.

> Petain defended Verdun while Blum
>   was defending a bidet.

> Light and the flowing crystal
>   never gin in cut glass had such clarity

> For me nothing. But that the child
>   walk in peace in her basilica . . . .

> Languor has cried unto languor
>   about the marshmallow roast

> As a lone ant from a broken ant-hill
> from the wreckage of Europe, ego scriptor.

> If the hoar-frost grip thy tent
> Thou wilt give thanks when night is spent.

> Lotophagoi of the suave nails, quiet, scornful

> That llovely unconscious world
>   slop over slop, and blue ribbons

There is no taint of imprecision or of abstraction in these excerpts; this is plain language from truthful James. In each a clear visual image; in most a dramatic action implicit or explicit; in some, the material for an effective motion-picture sequence.

I do not know whether by quantitative analysis an accurate reckoning of the number of suggestions in any of these images can be made. Perhaps Eliot would not himself make such a count but would rest satisfied in an illusion of infinite suggestion. In any case, that number would be governed by the reader's capability of response. And this capability is not merely a matter of sensitivity; it is a matter involving the reader's total character, his unique total history. Which is to say that Eliot has uttered as God's truth Mr. Eliot's opinion.

Nevertheless an important question is raised. Do Pound's images fail in suggestiveness? Consider the "broken ant-hill" simile. What does it suggest? the infinite labors of an infinite number of ants smashed in an instant by a boot (worn, perhaps, by the sluggard?); the battlefield and

the lone survivor; the Coliseum; Waterloo, Gettysburg, Verdun; men as
ants, in the army, on the assembly line, in city streets, under Communism
—but as super-ants rushing on the populous business of constructing the
means of their destruction. Not suggestive? One need only compare it
with so widely esteemed a line as "The paths of glory lead but to the
grave" to recognize its imagination-stirring potential.

The images I have cited are more or less self-sufficient. Others lose their
virtù when removed from the poem. Of one such Sona Raiziss says that
"Pound's Canto IV offers a fine classic reminiscence in these lines:

> Dew-haze blurs, in the grass, pale ankles moving.
> Beat, beat, whirr, thud, in the soft turf
>   under the apple trees,
> Choros nympharum, goat-foot, with the pale foot alternate"

and goes on to say, "But Eliot adds a slight metaphysical *frisson* in the
comparable—

> I heard the beat of centaur's hoofs over the hard turf
> As his dry and passionate talk devoured the afternoon."

Out of its context and for the uninformed reader of Pound, the passage
may seem no more than "classic reminiscence." In context (introducing
an Ovidian metamorphosis and a Provençal recurrent, an image of the
neo-Platonic theory of emanation, a recognition of the unity of fundamental beliefs in Asia and Europe, and variant images of fertility) and
read aright, it becomes apparent that what Leavis calls "the moral, religious, and anthropological preoccupations" are anything but absent. And
when Pound concludes the canto with "The Centaur's heel plants in the
earth loam" (after describing a Catholic procession), he would seem to
have added somewhat more than "a slight metaphysical *frisson*." Perhaps
the difference is this: that to respond to the Eliot requires only sensibility; to respond to the Pound requires an educated sensibility—that is
to say, in Eliot's own term, an undissociated sensibility.

* * *

I have intended in the foregoing pages no more than to suggest that the
opinions expressed by critics of Pound's poetry are only opinions, not
Truths, and are therefore subject to revision. It was not my intention to
deny them utterly. Nor have I wished to convey the impression (which
one sometimes gets from the Pound-idolators) that his poem is written
throughout on the level attained by Dante at his best. It is, however, my
conviction that what happened to the long poems of Darwin. Blackmore,
Akenside, and Brooke will not happen to Pound's epic. It will not happen
because, regardless of its difficulties, regardless of its deficiencies, the

poem has so many pages crackling with vitality, so many descriptive passages of extraordinary beauty, so many memorable single lines that it will rise above the ruck of 20th century poems, as Pope's did above the laborious productions of the Brookes, Akensides, *et al.* It is a poem of which it may be said that familiarity breeds respect. Because of its bulk and unconventional form and technique, and because of the human tendency that permits political bias to dictate literary taste, too few readers have become its familiars. But as more learn to distinguish its quotidian from its durable and its durable from its permanent attributes, the number will increase; the poem will come into its own.

LITERATURE CITED

Adams, Brooks. *The Law of Civilization and Decay.* New York, Macmillan, 1896.

Benton, Thomas Hart. *Thirty Years' View, or, A History of the Working of the American Government for Thirty Years, from 1820-1850.* New York, Appleton, 1854-56. 2 vols.

Blast; Review of the Great English Vortex, no. 1, June 20, 1914. London, J. Lane, 1914.
British Union Quarterly, 120 (4 June '38) p. 13.

Charlesworth, Barbara Anne. *The Tensile Light, a Study of Ezra Pound's Religion.* Thesis (M.A.) Coral Gables, Fla., University of Miami, 1957.

Chou King; texte chinois avec une double traduction en français et en latin, des annotations et un vocabulaire par S. Couvreur. 4e. ed. Sien Hsien, Imprimerie de la Mission Catholique, 1934.

Conybeare, F. C., translator. Philostratus, *The Life of Apollonius of Tyana, the Epistles of Apollonius and the Treatise of Eusebius.* Cambridge, Harvard University Press, 1948-50. 2 vols.

Del Mar, Alexander. *Barbara Villiers, or A History of Monetary Crimes.* Washington, The Cleaners Press, n.d.

De Schloezer, Boris. "Stravinsky: his Technique," translated by Ezra Pound, *Dial,* 86 (1929) pp. 9-26, 105-15, 464-74.

Douglas, C. H. *The Control and Distribution of Production.* 2nd rev. and enl. ed. London, S. Nott, 1934.

_____*Credit-Power and Democracy, with a Draft Scheme for the Mining Industry,* with a commentary on the included scheme by A. R. Orage. London, C. Palmer, 1920.

Edwards, John. *Annotated Index to the Cantos of Ezra Pound.* Berkeley, University of California Press, 1957.

------*The Pound Newsletter,* nos. 1-10, publ. Dept. of English, University of California, 1954-6.

------*A Preliminary Checklist of the Writings of Ezra Pound.* New Haven, Kirgo-Books, 1953.

Eliot, T. S. *After Strange Gods, a Primer of Modern Heresy.* New York, Harcourt, Brace, 1934.

------"Isolated Superiority," *Dial,* 84 (Jan., 1928), p. 7.

------*The Use of Poetry and the Use of Criticism; Studies in the Relation of Criticism to Poetry in England.* London, Faber and Faber, 1933.

Fenollosa, Ernest. *The Chinese Written Character as a Medium for Poetry,* with offset of the Calcutta edition of *Pivot.* Washington, D. C., Square Dollar Series, n. d.

------*Epochs of Chinese and Japanese Art, an Outline History of East Asiatic Design.* London, W. Heinemann, 1912. 2 vols.

Gerhardt, Rainer M. *Die Pisaner Gesänge, eine Sendung.* Eigentum, Hessischer Rundfunk, "Abendstudio," Frankfurt, 1952.

Grandgent, Charles H. *Dante.* New York, Duffield, 1921.

Holter, Elizabeth Sage. *ABC of Social Credit,* with an appendix by Allan R. Brown. New York, Coward, McCann, 1934.

Hubbell, Albert. Review of *Guide to Kulchur. New Yorker,* (4 Oct. 1952), p. 121.

Humphries, Rolfe, translator. Ovid, *The Metamorphoses.* Bloomington, Indiana University Press, 1955.

Kasper, John, ed. *Gists from Agassiz.* New York, Square Dollar Series, Kasper & Horton, 1953.

Kenner, Hugh. "Homage to Musonius," *Poetry,* 90 (July, 1957), pp. 237-43.

------*The Poetry of Ezra Pound.* Norfolk, Conn., New Directions, 1951.

Leary, Louis, ed. *Motive and Methods in the Cantos of Ezra Pound.* New York, Columbia University Press, 1954.

M., H. M. *An Outline of Social Credit*. n.p., n.d.

Mayo, Robert, ed. *The Analyst*, nos. I-XIV, publ. Dept. of English, Northwestern University.

Mencius. *Works*. In *Ssu Shu, The Four Books: Confucian Analects, The Great Learning, The Doctrine of the Mean, and The Works of Mencius*. Shanghai, Chinese Book Co., 1933. Bk. III, Pt. 1, Chap. III, 1-9.

Mailla, Moyriac de. *Histoire générale de la Chine, ou Annales de cet empire traduites du Tong-Kien-Kang-Mou*. Paris, 1777-85. 12 vols.

The New Age, a weekly Review of Politics, Literature and Art, vols. 16-26 (1915-1919).

New English Weekly, VIII (1935) pp. 85 and 105.

Pauthier, Guillaume. *China ou Description historique, géographique et littéraire de ce vaste empire, d'après des documents chinoise. 1e. partie, comprenant un résumé de l'histoire et de la civilisation chinoises depuis les temps les plus anciennes jusqu'à nos jours*. Paris, F. Didot, 1837.

Pound, Ezra. *ABC of Economics*. London, Faber and Faber, 1933.

_____*ABC of Reading*. Norfolk, Conn., New Directions, 1951.

_____*America, Roosevelt, and the Causes of the Present War*, translated by John Drummond. (Money Pamphlets, no. 6) London, P. Russell, 1951.

_____*Antheil and the Treatise on Harmony*. Paris, Three Mountains Press, 1924.

_____"Cantos 96 and 97," *Hudson Review*, 9 (Spring, 1956; Autumn, 1956), pp. 7-19; 387-98.

_____*The Cantos of Ezra Pound*. New York, New Directions, 1948.

_____*Confucian Analects*. New York, Square Dollar Series, 1950.

_____*Confucius: the Great Digest & Unwobbling Pivot*; translation and commentary by Ezra Pound. New York, New Directions, 1951.

_____*The Exile*; ed. by Ezra Pound. Nos. 1-4, Spring, 1927—Autumn, 1928. No. 1 pub. Dijon, M. Darantiére: no. 2-3, Chicago, P. Covici; no. 4, New York, Covici-Friede.

_____*Gold and Work*. 1st English ed. (Money Pamphlets, no. 2.) London, P. Russell, 1951.

_____*Guide to Kulchur*. Norfolk, Conn., New Directions, 1952.

_____*Introduction to the Economic History of the United States*. (Money Pamphlets, no. 1.) London, P. Russell, 1950.

_____*Jefferson and/or Mussolini, l'Idea Statale, Fascism as I Have Seen It*. New York, Liveright, 1936.

_____*Letters*, 1907-1941, ed. by D. D. Paige. New York, Harcourt, Brace, 1950.

_____*Make It New; Essays*. New Haven, Yale University Press, 1935.

_____*Patria Mia*. Chicago, R. F. Seymour, 1950.

_____*Pavannes and Divisions*. New York, Knopf, 1918.

_____*Personae, the Collected Poems of Ezra Pound*. New York, New Directions, 1950.

_____*Polite Essays*. London, Faber and Faber, 1937.

_____*Section: Rock-Drill, 85-95 de los Cantares*. New York, New Directions, 1956.

_____*Social Credit: an Impact* (1935) 2nd ed. (Money Pamphlets, no. 5.) London, P. Russell, 1951.

_____*The Spirit of Romance*. Norfolk, Conn., New Directions, 1952.

_____*A Visiting Card*. (Money Pamphlets, no. 4.) London, P. Russell, 1952.

_____*What Is Money For?* (2nd ed.) and *Introductory Text Book* (2nd ed.) (Money Pamphlets, no. 3.) London, P. Russell, 1951.

_____Sophocles, *The Women of Trachis*, a version by Ezra Pound. *Hudson Review*, VI, 4 (Winter, 1954) pp. 487-523.

Raiziss, Sona. *The Metaphysical Passion; Seven Modern American Poets and the Seventeenth Century Tradition*. Philadelphia, University of Pennsylvania Press, 1952.

Rattray, David, "Weekend with Ezra Pound," *The Nation*, 185 (16 Nov. 1957), pp. 343-5.

Read, Forrest, "The Pattern of the Pisan Cantos," *Sewanee Review*, 65 (Summer, 1957) pp. 400-419.

Russell, Peter, ed. *An Examination of Ezra Pound, a collection of essays.* Norfolk, Conn., New Directions, 1950.

Sachar, Abram, *A History of the Jews.* New York, Alfred A. Knopf, 1955.

Santayana, George. *The Life of Reason, or The Phases of Human Progress.* New York, Scribner, 1954.

Steffens, Lincoln. *The Autobiography of Lincoln Steffens*, complete in 1 vol. New York, Harcourt, Brace, 1931.

Watling, E. F., translator. Sophocles, *Electra and Other Plays (Ajax, Electra, Women of Trachis, Philoctetes).* (Penguin Classics.) London, Penguin Books, 1953.

Watts, Harold H. *Ezra Pound and the Cantos.* Chicago, H. Regnery, 1952.

Weigall, Arthur. *A History of the Pharoahs.* New York, E. P. Dutton, 1925. 2 vols.

Whitehead, Alfred North. *Dialogues, as Recorded by Lucien Price.* Boston, Little, Brown, 1954.

Williams, Charles. *The Figure of Beatrice; a Study in Dante.* London, Faber and Faber, 1953.

Zielinski, Thaddeus. *La Sibylle*, 1925 (translated in *Edge*, No. 2 (Nov., 1956).

Index